A. K. J.

G000146327

Microsoft® Access 97 Quick Reference

Microsoft® Access 97 Quick Reference

Written by Rick Winter

Microsoft Access 97 Quick Reference

Copyright© 1997 by Que® Corporation.

All rights reserved. Printed in the United States of America. No part of this book may be used or reproduced in any form or by any means, or stored in a database or retrieval system, without prior written permission of the publisher except in the case of brief quotations embodied in critical articles and reviews. Making copies of any part of this book for any purpose other than your own personal use is a violation of United States copyright laws. For information, address Que Corporation, 201 W. 103rd Street, Indianapolis, IN, 46290. You may reach Que's direct sales line by calling 1-800-428-5331.

Library of Congress Catalog No.: 97-66486

ISBN: 0-7897-1212-1

This book is sold *as is*, without warranty of any kind, either express or implied, respecting the contents of this book, including but not limited to implied warranties for the book's quality, performance, merchantability, or fitness for any particular purpose. Neither Que Corporation nor its dealers or distributors shall be liable to the purchaser or any other person or entity with respect to any liability, loss, or damage caused or alleged to have been caused directly or indirectly by this book.

99 98 97 6 5 4 3 2 1

Interpretation of the printing code: the rightmost double-digit number is the year of the book's printing; the rightmost single-digit number, the number of the book's printing. For example, a printing code of 97-1 shows that the first printing of the book occurred in 1997.

All terms mentioned in this book that are known to be trademarks or service marks have been appropriately capitalized. Que cannot attest to the accuracy of this information. Use of a term in this book should not be regarded as affecting the validity of any trademark or service mark.

Screen reproductions in this book were created using Collage Plus from Inner Media, Inc., Hollis, NH.

Credits

PRESIDENT
Roland Elgey

SENIOR VICE PRESIDENT/ PUBLISHING
Don Fowley

PUBLISHER
Joseph B. Wikert

PUBLISHING DIRECTOR
Brad R. Koch

GENERAL MANAGER
Joe Muldoon

EDITORIAL SERVICES DIRECTOR
Elizabeth Keaffaber

MANAGING EDITOR
Thomas F. Hayes

ACQUISITIONS MANAGER
Angela Wethington

SENIOR PRODUCT DIRECTOR
Lisa D. Wagner

PRODUCT DIRECTOR
Dana S. Coe

SERIES DEVELOPMENT COORDINATOR
Carolyn L. Kiefer

PRODUCTION EDITOR
Brian Sweany

EDITOR
Lisa M. Gebken

ASSISTANT PRODUCT MARKETING MANAGERS
Karen Hagen
Christy M. Miller

TECHNICAL EDITOR
Verley and Nelson Associates

MEDIA DEVELOPMENT SPECIALIST
David Garratt

TECHNICAL SUPPORT SPECIALIST
Nadeem Muhammed

ACQUISITIONS COORDINATOR
Tracy M. Williams

SOFTWARE RELATIONS COORDINATOR
Susan Gallagher

EDITORIAL ASSISTANT
Virginia Stoller

BOOK DESIGNER
Ruth Harvey

COVER DESIGNER
Nathan Clement

PRODUCTION TEAM
Bryan Flores
Julie Geeting
Brian Grossman
Donna Wright

INDEXER
Tim Tate

Composed in *Century Old Style* and *Franklin Gothic* by Que Corporation.

To my sons Danny and Jimmy. You give me joy and an incentive to work.

About the Author

Rick Winter is a Senior Partner at PRW Computer Training and Services. Rick is a Microsoft Certified Trainer and Certified Professional for Access and has trained thousands of adults on personal computers. He is lead author of *Special Edition Using Microsoft Office 97* and *Special Edition Using Microsoft Office Professional for Windows 95*; co-author of Que's *Excel for Windows SureSteps, Look Your Best with Excel* and *Q&A QueCards*. He has also contributed to over 20 books for Que. Rick is the revision script writer for *Video Professor Lotus 1-2-3 Version 2.2 and 3.0 Level I* and *Lotus 1-2-3 Version 2.2 and 3.0 Level II*, and script writer for *Video Professor Lotus 1-2-3 Version 2.2 and 3.0 Level III*. Rick is past president and currently involved with Information Systems Trainers, a professional training organization based in Denver, Colorado (**http://www.istrn.org**). Rick has a B.A. from Colorado College and an M.A. from University of Colorado at Denver.

Acknowledgments

Thank you to Joyce Nielsen for providing fast responses to my questions and for surviving one of the other books in this series (the *Excel 97 Quick Reference*). Thank you to my sister and fellow author, Patty Winter, for providing backup when I was swamped with this book and for giving me a head start by creating the Word book in this series.

I would also like to thank the folks at Que and Verly & Nelson Associates. Special thanks especially go to Dana Coe, Angie Wethington, Brian Sweany, Lisa Gebken, Donna Nelson, and Darlin Verly for giving me the opportunity to write this book, for catching my mistakes, and for making the book much better than it would have been without their help.

One last special thanks, to my wife (and our bookkeeper) Karen. She keeps my life organized and is supportive, even when I'm working late nights to meet a deadline and the office/house is dishelveled by another Que book.

We'd Like to Hear from You!

As part of our continuing effort to produce books of the highest possible quality, Que would like to hear your comments. To stay competitive, we *really* want you, as a computer book reader and user, to let us know what you like or dislike most about this book or other Que products.

You can mail comments, ideas, or suggestions for improving future editions to the address below, or send us a fax at (317) 581-4663. For the online inclined, Macmillan Computer Publishing has a forum on CompuServe (type **GO QUEBOOKS** at any prompt) through which our staff and authors are available for questions and comments. The address of our Internet site is **http://www.mcp.com** (World Wide Web).

In addition to exploring our forum, please feel free to contact me personally to discuss your opinions of this book: I'm **73451,1220** on CompuServe, and **dcoe@que.mcp.com** on the Internet.

Thanks in advance—your comments will help us to continue publishing the best books available on computer topics in today's market.

Dana Coe
Product Development Specialist
Que Corporation
201 W. 103rd Street
Indianapolis, Indiana 46290
USA

NOTE Although we cannot provide general technical support, we're happy to help you resolve problems you encounter related to our books, disks, or other products. If you need such assistance, please contact our Tech Support department at 800-545-5914 ext. 3833.

To order other Que or Macmillan Computer Publishing books or products, please call our Customer Service department at 800-428-5331.

Table of Contents

Calculations 135

Forms and Reports 163

Introduction

The *Microsoft Access 97 Quick Reference* is the latest in a series of comprehensive, task-oriented references and details how to use the features and functionality of Access 97. Compiled for the intermediate-to-advanced user who wants a concise, comprehensive reference, the *Microsoft Access 97 Quick Reference* is loaded with detailed instructions outlining important tasks you need to complete.

The *Microsoft Access 97 Quick Reference* presents the tasks and functions most often sought by users of Access 97. The book also includes a comprehensive glossary with many terms and definitions that refer to the newest features in Access 97.

New Ways of Working

Que's Quick References help the reader cover the most ground with the least amount of hassle, and in a minimum of time! Tasks include steps that the reader can complete—usually no more than five steps to any task.

The goal of the author is to help you get your work done in the least amount of time, with a minimum of reading and learning. The author knows that your time is valuable, and that you might not need to use some of the included tasks very often. That's why each task in this book is written with economy in mind. The reader should be able to recognize a need, take this book off the shelf and complete a task within minutes; then put the book back on the shelf for future reference. It just doesn't get any faster or easier.

Expanded Coverage

Unlike other low-cost references, Que's *Microsoft Access 97 Quick Reference* covers every major functional element of Access 97. More importantly, each element is covered separately, in its own dedicated section in this book. You can be confident that this book covers a lot of ground. The *Microsoft Access 97 Quick Reference* even includes the reference to Access functions that are the most useful.

Who Should Read This Book?

The *Microsoft Access 97 Quick Reference* is written for casual to advanced computer users who need a fast reference to Access 97 tasks, functions, and features. It is an ideal companion to Que's *Special Edition Using Microsoft Access 97*. The Quick Reference size makes it ideal for travel.

If you are upgrading from Access 95 or Access 2, you will find this reference useful for finding new features and looking up new ways of getting a job done. If you are converting from other field data types—for example, dBASE, Paradox, or Btrieve—this Quick Reference might be the right amount of instruction you need to transfer your know-how investment to new products.

As a reference, this book is not intended to tutor learners. If you are just starting to use Access software for the first time, or are a very casual user, you might want to consider Que's *User-Friendly Using Microsoft Access 97* or *The Complete Idiot's Guide to Microsoft Access 97* as a book to get you up to speed. For beginner or very casual task reference, check out Que's *Easy Microsoft Access 97*. If you want the most complete reference as well as tutorial and foundation information, then you need Que's *Special Edition Using Microsoft Access 97*. This *Microsoft Access 97 Quick Reference* makes an ideal companion to the comprehensive Special Edition.

Features of the *Access 97 Quick Reference*

If you take a moment to glance over the table of contents, you'll note that each logical part of the Access 97 product has its own dedicated section in this book. Topics are organized into working groups under each logical part of Access, with related tasks sorted under each topic in alphabetical order. In some cases, tasks have been specially sorted by the author when task grouping, sequencing, or relationships indicate the order.

Content Tuned to Your Needs

You can't be expected to know everything; and yet, you don't have to be told everything either. That's why the Quick References author has been given wide latitude in determining what extra information you might find valuable to complete a task. By tuning the presentation to your needs, you can spend less time sifting through background information or cross-referencing related information just to be sure you're using a task appropriately. For example, the author often indicates which *conditions* must exist in order to complete a task. The author explains why one task is best to use over another—all in very succinct text. Where it is obvious to you what conditions must exist or which task is best, you won't be slowed by text telling you what you already know.

Expert Advice

Our expert author knows when a specific task is appropriate and when that task should be avoided. For example, there is no point in making a bulleted list if only one list item exists. This book tells you when a task is in order, and when you should avoid using a task when it's out of context or is not appropriate at a specific location in your document, database, or presentation. This expertise of the author transfers directly to your work through this approach.

Navigation and Steps

Author expertise can also help keep tasks simple by including or eliminating steps that guide you to where you enter information or perform an action. Tasks in this book that do detail how to get where you're going do so because the author believes that getting there is confusing for the reader.

In other cases, where your starting point is not relevant or where you are likely to know where a menu or dialog box is located, the author keeps it simple by not adding the navigational detail. The same assumptions apply where individual actions can be compounded into a step. Beginners often need "baby steps" to avoid confusion. The need for such care soon passes for most, and the user is better able to work with a step that is a logical group of actions. The result is a more readable set of steps.

The author has limited the length of commands and steps to just the words you need to read to complete each task in a minimum of time. Intermediate users of Windows-based applications rarely need to be told when to click the OK button!

Expert Mentoring

You also get background information, when appropriate, to the topic or task. Tasks are often introduced so that your understanding of the real purpose of the task is clarified. Although mentoring is best done through the full *Special Edition Using* series, there are times when a little mentoring before a task greatly enhances the understanding of that task or function. The author keeps this in mind while using his extensive user experience to determine when to provide that reinforcing conceptual information.

A Comprehensive Glossary

With the Internet awareness of the Microsoft Access 97 product comes a lot of jargon that will be new to you. This book has a glossary of terms specific to who you are and what you're doing. These terms are contained in various sections of the book as italicized words. Look them up as you go along or scan for any terms that might not be familiar. Ever wonder what *concatenation* is? You don't have to complete a task to find out. You can check out such terms or definitions in the glossary.

Task Reference

This Quick Reference is divided into sections, all dedicated to Access 97 functional areas. In each section, you will find an alphabetical listing of topics that are detailed with tasks.

To find all tasks that Access' online Help system, for example, go to the "Database Essentials" section, find the task topic "Help," and then turn to the tasks that cover activities in that topic area. Tasks follow one another and are sorted in alphabetical order, unless there is special value in completing multiple tasks in order.

When a prerequisite task must be read to understand the task you are reading, a cross reference will let you know: (See "Help: Help Contents and Index," "Help: Searching for Topics," or "Help: Office Assistant" before you complete this task). When other tasks might be more useful, or might be used instead of the task you are viewing, a cross reference will let you know where to find it: (See also "Width of Column" in the Database Essentials part of this book). And when other related tasks might be useful after completing a task, a cross reference at the end of the task will direct you to their location: (For formatting numbers, see also "Query: Format Field" in the Queries and Filters part of this book, and "Format: Numbers and Dates" in the Forms and Reports part of the book).

Conventions Used in This Book

This book uses certain conventions in order to guide you through the various tasks. Special typefaces in this Quick Reference include the following:

Type	**Meaning**
italic	Terms or phrases that might be found in the Glossary; required function variables that must be entered.
underline	Menu and dialog box options that appear underlined on-screen.

continues

Type	Meaning
boldface	Information you are asked to type.
italic boldface	Optional function variables that can be entered.
`special type`	Direct quotations of words that appear on-screen or in a figure.

Elements printed in uppercase include functions, such as SUM(), and file names.

When a direction is given to "click," this means click the left side of the mouse control for those mice with alternate keys. When it is necessary for the right or alternate side of the mouse to be used, the direction "right-click" will be given.

In most cases, keys are represented as they appear on the keyboard. The arrow keys usually are represented by name (for example, the up-arrow key). The Print Screen key is abbreviated PrtSc; Page Up is PgUp; Insert is Ins; and so on. On your keyboard, these key names might be spelled out or abbreviated differently.

When two keys appear together with a plus sign, such as Shift+Ins, press and hold the first key as you press the second key. When two keys appear together without a plus sign, such as End Home, press and release the first key before you press the second key.

Various toolbar buttons, such as the one next to this paragraph, are used throughout the steps and are identified with a visual icon next to the appropriate step. These icons resemble the on-screen toolbar button and make it easier for you to find them quickly.

Many tasks include warnings, cautions, notes, and tips. These are described in-depth in this section.

The author has gone to great lengths to protect you from disaster, often warning you of impending, often irreversible danger before you get in over your head. Warnings are just one way this Quick Reference will inform you when you need to know.

WARNING AutoRecover does not save your documents—only certain recovery information! Be sure to save all documents you are working on at frequent intervals.

The completion of some tasks might change several aspects of a document or the way your MS Access package works in the future. Cautions inform the reader about unforeseen events that might not occur as expected. Cautions are not as severe as warnings, but you will want to read cautionary information.

CAUTION Do not turn the power off before exiting Access. You could damage your database. If you need to repair a damaged database, there is a repair procedure that might (or might not) work.

Notes often advise and direct you while you complete a task. Expect to find pieces of great wisdom while you complete tasks.

NOTE Only controls that have Control Source properties can take an expression with a calculated result. Expressions can be any valid Access function or operator, values, fields, or identifiers, and must start with an equal sign.

Tips offer expert input from those who really know the software. Tips often include time-saving solutions and ways to shortcut your way to success. If you're looking for a shortcut key, tips are where you'll find them!

TIP To change additional options for a specific pivot table field, double-click the field button. Choose the options you want in the PivotTable Field dialog box; then choose OK.

All tasks in this book are not for everyone. In some tasks, if you are not already familiar with the instances of use of a task, we might direct you to a *Special Edition Using* book. A *Special Edition Using* is the most complete core tutorial reference on the topic and can provide you with both background information and tutorial style learning that will help you to understand the topic more thoroughly.

NOTE This feature's task requires understanding of a complex subject. If you are not familiar with this feature, you will probably want to become acquainted with it by reading *Special Edition Using Microsoft Access 97* for a complete tutorial coverage. ■

Related Books

No one book can cover all of the needs of every user. Que offers a complete line of Office 97-related titles. Look for Quick References on each of the Office 97 components as well as Windows 95. *Special Edition Using Microsoft Access 97* is the most complete tutorial and reference volume available for Access 97, and answers end-user questions with clear, concise, and comprehensive authority. *Special Edition Using Microsoft Office 97 Professional* is the most complete tutorial and reference volume available for Office 97, and Que's *Net Savvy Office 97* concentrates its content on getting the most of Office 97's extensive Internet and intranet features. Ask your bookseller for the availability of other Que titles.

Database Essentials

There are several fundamental tasks in Access 97 that you will use frequently. In this section, you can quickly reference essential Access operations for entering text, numbers, and dates and times; as well as special features that speed data entry, such as AutoCorrect. You'll discover how to quickly obtain the Help you need while using Access. For example, you can explore tasks for using the new Office Assistant to provide detailed assistance as you complete a task.

This section also explains how to find data, navigate in the Access objects and in dialog boxes, and select data. In addition, you'll find tasks that explain how to use Undo and Spell Check, and start and exit Access.

Correct Mistakes: AutoCorrect

Access 97 has a feature called AutoCorrect that can automatically correct your mistakes and reduce your typing time. Use AutoCorrect to correct typing errors, correct two capital letters in a row, correct the accidental use of Caps Lock, capitalize names of days, capitalize the first letters following a period and a space character (defined as a sentence), and correct text you type (such as replacing misspelled words). If you have used Word 97 or other Office 97 products, AutoCorrect might be familiar to you.

AutoCorrect only works when you are adding data to a table, query, or form. It does not work in Design View of any object, nor while you are programming.

Steps

1. Choose Tools, AutoCorrect.

2. To correct that nagging word you always spell wrong or to expand an abbreviation of text you continuously type, enter the incorrect word or abbreviation in the Replace text box and the correction in the With text box.
3. Check other options such as Correct Two Initial Caps, Capitalize First Letter of Sentence, Capitalize Names of Days, and Correct Accidental Use of Caps Lock Key.
4. If you have any exceptions to the first letter and two initial caps, choose the Exceptions button and enter them on the correct tabs. Choose OK to return to the AutoCorrect dialog box and then OK again to finish.

When you type an AutoText, Access will automatically convert the entry to whatever you added in the With text box in Step 2.

NOTE Access shares the AutoCorrect entries with the other applications in Microsoft Office. If you add entries in Access, the same entries will be available in Word, Excel, and PowerPoint. If you do not want a form's text field to use AutoCorrect, go to *Design View*, double click the text control, and change the Allow AutoCorrect property to No.

Correct Mistakes: Undo

You can use the Undo command (Ctrl+Z) on the Edit menu or the Undo button on the toolbar to remove your most recent change.

Steps

1. To remove edits to a record you have saved, click the Undo button on the toolbar.

If you begin editing another record or use a filter, Undo Saved Record or the Undo command will not be available to you.

Data: Copy

Access can cut, copy, and paste data from a *datasheet* or a form through the Windows Clipboard. Only one selection can be manipulated at a time, but a selection can include one piece of data or several pieces of data. All data types are supported.

When you copy a selection, the data is copied to the Clipboard and the original data is left intact. If you want to copy entire records, see "Records: Copy."

NOTE This procedure works in all views of Access. If you are unable to use the toolbar for some reason (for example, if you are in a dialog box), press Ctrl+C to copy and Ctrl+V to paste.

Steps

1. Highlight the data you want to copy.

2. Click the Copy button on the toolbar.

3. Move to the desired location and click the Paste button on the toolbar.

TIP If you want to copy the value from the same field in the previous record, press Ctrl+' (apostrophe). You can be in Form or Datasheet View.

Data: Edit

Access offers you several different methods for editing data: one *field* at a time, several fields at a time, one *record*, or many records at a time. The simplest method for editing data is to edit the data in a field of a datasheet, or a form in *Form View*. To edit multiple records at one time, see "Action Query: Update Query" in the *Query* and *Filters* part of this book.

Steps

1. Open a datasheet or a *form* in Form View.
2. Position the insertion point in the field you want to modify or, if desired, select the portion of text you want to replace.
3. Enter the new or replacement text.

TIP Some field types will display a plus pointer when you move the cursor to the leftmost part of the field. If you click at that point, you select the entire field.

You will see a triangle in the record selector when a record is current (in a datasheet) or a pencil icon when you are editing the record.

When you enter or edit data in a multiuser situation, Access might lock the record that is being edited by another user. Other users can view the data, but cannot edit that data. A locked record displays a circle with a slash (lock symbol) in the record selector. A locked record cannot be edited until the lock is released. Locks are released when the data is saved or when the user with the lock moves off that record. (See also "Record Locks" in the Special Features and Programming part of this book.)

Data: Enter

Entering data in datasheets or forms is similar to entering data in an Excel worksheet or Word *table*.

Steps

1. Open the *form* or datasheet and go to the desired *record*. If you want a new record, click the New Record button on the toolbar.

2. Type your entry. If the entry is an OLE object, either paste the data from another source or choose Insert, Object and choose the *object* type and object from the dialog boxes. If the entry is a lookup, select from the drop-down arrow. If the entry is a hyperlink, you can type or use the Insert Hyperlink button on the toolbar.
3. Tab to go to the next field. Repeat Step 2, tabbing to each field. If you need to go to the previous field, press Shift+Tab.

   When you reach the last field on the record, Tab will place you on the first field of the next record.

For entering specific data types, see also "Dates and Times: Enter," "Hyperlinks: Enter," and "OLE Objects: Enter."

NOTE When you work on a form, the Tab Order settings will determine the sequence of fields you move to when you press Tab or Enter. The Tab Order does not have to be the same order as the fields appear on the form. (See "Forms: Tab Order" in the Forms and Reports part of the book.)

Data: Find

There are several ways of locating data in Microsoft Access. If you are interested in locating data in groups of records, then you should apply a filter or a query to your data set. (See "Filter Data" and "Query: Run" in the Queries and Filters part of the book.) For locating a particular value one occurrence at a time, you can use the Find dialog box. If you need to find and replace data, see "Data: Replace."

Steps

1. Open a *table*, *query*, or *form*, and position the insertion point in the field you want to search (optional).

2. Click the Find button on the toolbar.
3. Enter the *string* or value you want to search for in the Find What text box. If you want to enter only a portion of the string, use asterisks such as **jon*** for entries beginning with jon or ***jon*** for jon anywhere in the field.
4. Choose Find First to go to the first match; then Find Next to go to the next match. Choose Close when you are finished with your search.

NOTE While you are in the Find dialog box, you have options such as the search direction, whether you want to search for a portion of text or the whole field, match case, search dates as you type them (as formatted), and whether to search all fields or the current field.

Data: Replace

You can use the Replace command to find and replace all or some of the occurrences of a particular value for an entire field or a portion of a field. You can use the *Datasheet* or *Form View* for this purpose. You can also use an update query to replace an entire field with alternative values. (See "Action Query: Update Query" in the Queries and Filters part of the book.")

In the Replace dialog box, you specify the value or string that will replace your match. You can use the Replace All button to perform a single replacement for all matches or you can replace values one at a time using the Find Next and then the Replace buttons in sequence.

NOTE If you want to find and replace *Nulls* or zero length strings, you have to manually enter the replacement values directly in the *records* rather then use the Replace dialog box.

Steps

1. Open a *table*, *query*, or *form* in Datasheet or Form View and click in the field you want to work with.
2. Choose Edit, Replace.
3. Enter the value to find in the Find What text box and the value used to replace it in the Replace With text box.
4. Choose the Find Next button followed by the Replace button to replace the next occurrence.
5. Or, choose the Replace All button to replace all matches. Choose Close when you are done.

Data: Select

You can select fields in a datasheet in many different ways, using your mouse, menu commands, or the keyboard.

Steps

1. Open a table, query, or form in Datasheet View.
2. Click and drag on the data of interest, or click in a field and press F2 to select an entire field's value. See the following table for additional selection techniques.

3. Click a column header to select all field data, or click a row selector to select all the data in a record. Extend your selection by pressing the Shift key and clicking at the end of your new selection range.
4. Click the All Records selector to the left of the leftmost column header to select all the data in your datasheet.

Datasheet Selection Techniques

To Select this	Do this
Field data	Click and drag a selection, then release the mouse.
To extend a field selection	Hold the Shift key and click at the end of the new selection range.
An entire field	Move the pointer to the left edge of the field. When you see a plus sign cursor, click there.
An entire field	With the insertion point in that field, press F2.
Adjacent fields	Drag the left edge of the current field to extend range of selection.
Adjacent fields	With a field selected, hold down the Shift key and press the appropriate arrow key.
A column	Click the column header.
The current column	Press Ctrl+Spacebar.
Adjacent columns	Click the column header and drag over additional column headers to extend the range of selection.
A record	Click the record selector to the left of the row.
Multiple records	Click a record selector then drag down over additional record selectors.

continues

Continued

To Select this	Do this
Multiple records	Press Shift+Spacebar, and then Shift+Up arrow or Shift+Down arrow.
All records	Choose Edit, All Records, or click the All Records selector to the left of the leftmost column header.

Data: Sort

You can sort by the values in a *field* or by the values in two or more fields. If you use more than one sort field, the primary sort key is always fully sorted. Sorts can be either ascending or descending, and can be performed at any time. When you use the sort buttons, a temporary *filter* is created. For more control over sorts, you can use one of the filter procedures in the Queries and Filters part of this book or you can create your own query. (See "Filter Data" and "Query: Create with Design View.")

Steps

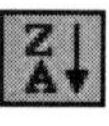

1. Click the Sort Ascending or Sort Descending button on the toolbar to sort by the current field, or on a group of selected fields (columns).
2. To change the sort order, click and drag the first sort field (column) to the left, select multiple columns, and again click one of the sort buttons.

   The leftmost selected sorted column is the primary sort key.

Choose Records, Remove Filter/Sort to remove a filter and sort and return your records to their natural order (as well as view your entire set).

Database Open

Access enables you to open one *database* at a time. If you have a database open in view and you open another database, Access closes the first one and opens a new one (in other words, you do not have to close one database to open another).

Steps

1. Choose File, Open. If you are in the *Database window*, click the Open Database button on the Database toolbar.
2. Locate the database file in the Open dialog box and choose the Open button.

Like other applications within Microsoft Office, Access also enables you to choose from one of the last few files open on the bottom of the File menu.

NOTE If you want to bypass your startup options (such as opening a form or disabling toolbars), hold down Shift when you choose the Open button. If you are in a multiuser environment and need to open the database so no one else has access while you are developing or editing, check Exclusive on the Open dialog box.

Database Window: View Objects

The *Database Window* is the control center and container for all tables, queries, forms, reports, macros, and modules. Unlike other database applications, all objects (tables, reports, forms) are in one file rather than separate files on a hard disk.

Steps

1. To bring up the Database window while another window is displayed, press F11.

2. To see descriptions and dates modified and created in addition to object names, click the Details button on the toolbar.
3. To open an *object* (*table, query, form, report*), click the tab of the object type and then double-click the name in the Database window.

While you are in the Database window you can copy, delete, or rename the objects. (See the tasks "Database Object: Copy," "Database Object: Delete," and "Database Object: Rename" within the File Management part of the book.)

Dates and Times: Enter

Entering dates and times is generally like entering any other data (see "Data: Enter") with a couple of shortcuts. When the field is formatted (see "Data: Format" in the Table and Database Design part of this book) you might enter data one way (for example, **10-5-97**) but it appears in the field as a different format (for example, **10/5/97**).

Steps

1. Open the *table*, *form*, or *query* and move to the *field* in which you want to enter the data.
2. To enter today's date, press Ctrl+; (semicolon). To enter the time, press Ctrl+: (colon). If you want to enter a date in this year you can leave off the year and enter the month and day (for example, **3/17**). After you leave the field, the date or time will format according to the format property for the field.
3. If you want new records to default to the current date or time, choose the Design button. Go to the field's Default value in a table or right-click the control in a form, choose Properties and go to Default value. Type in **Date()** for current date or **Now()** for either current date or time (depending on format). Return to the *Datasheet* or *Form View*.

NOTE Entering the current date and time depends on your system clock being set correctly. If you need to reset your clock, right-click the time on the far right of your taskbar and choose Adjust Date/Time.

There are special considerations while working with dates in queries and filters. (See "Criteria: Dates" in the Queries and Filters part of this book.)

Exit Access

Unlike other programs such as Word or Excel, you do not need to save changes after you edit a record. You save changes automatically by moving to a different record on a datasheet or a form. However, when you are editing or creating a design of an object, you will be prompted to save changes when you close Access.

Steps

1. Click the Close (X) button on the top right of the Access window.
2. If you are in design mode for any object, choose whether you want to save changes to the object.

> **CAUTION** Do not turn the power off before exiting Access. You could damage your database. If you need to repair a damaged database, there is a repair procedure that might (or might not) work. (See "Database Repair" tasks in the File Management part of this book.)

Freeze Display of a Table Field

If you have a wide table that is wider than your screen, it might be difficult to identify which record you are in when you scroll to the right. You can freeze one or more identifying fields so they stay on the left side of your screen.

Steps

1. Open a *table*, *query*, or *form* in *Datasheet View*.
2. Use the black down arrow mouse pointer on the column headers to select one or more adjacent columns.
3. Choose Format, Freeze Columns.

To undo the frozen columns, choose Format, Unfreeze All Columns.

Help: Context Sensitive

Microsoft Access contains several different types of help, with different amounts of information. You will find access to various help methods on the Help menu or you can use the What's This? button on the right of a window's title bar.

Steps

1. Press F1.

   Access opens Office Assistant or displays help on the topic it most closely associates with your current condition or position in the program. If Access goes directly to the topic, when you finish reading the help, go directly to Step 4.
2. If the Assistant opens, type a question and then press Enter.
3. The Assistant gives you a list of possible options that it thinks you might want help on. Click one of the topics.
4. When finished with the help window, click the Close (X) button. If you want to close the Assistant, click its Close (X) button as well.

The Microsoft on the Web command lists a variety of resources on the Internet related to Microsoft Access. If you select one of the commands on this submenu, Windows opens your browser and attempts to locate this Web page. In order for the Web page to be loaded, you must have an active connection to the Internet; otherwise, the page won't be found.

Help: Dialog Boxes

Dialog boxes include a question mark in the title bar (beside the Close button) that enables you to obtain Help information on the options and buttons displayed in the dialog box.

Steps

1. To get more information on a button or option in a dialog box, click the Question Mark (?) button in the dialog box title bar. (If the ? button is not visible, press Shift+F1.)

2. Click the area of the dialog box for which you need Help. A pop-up box appears to explain how to use the button.
3. Click the pop-up box to remove it from the screen.

Help: Help Contents and Index

Access provides an extensive online Help system to get you up to speed on database tasks. At any point, you can access Help to provide assistance, display definitions of common features, and access tips you can use to perform a task more quickly. The Help Contents and Index feature enables you to find detailed Help information on a specific topic.

Steps

1. Choose Help, Contents and Index; then click the Contents tab.
2. Double-click the desired category.
3. Click the topic you want; then choose Display.
4. View the Help information; then click the Close button when you are done.

TIP Use the Index tab in the Help Topics dialog box if you want to look up specific words that are listed in an index format. Click the Index tab and begin typing the word you are searching for. Then, click the desired index entry in the list box and choose Display.

Help: Office Assistant

The *Office Assistant*, a new feature included with Access and other Microsoft Office applications, provides tips, Help information, and interprets what Help you might need based on your current actions. The Office Assistant is an on-screen, interactive program that can be customized to provide help as you work in Access.

If you are experienced in Access and find the Office Assistant to be somewhat bothersome, you can temporarily close the

Office Assistant to remove it from the screen. You also can customize options that specify when the Office Assistant should appear.

Steps

1. Click the Office Assistant. (If the Office Assistant doesn't already appear on-screen, click the Office Assistant button on the toolbar.)
2. In the text box, type the question or topic for which you want Help; then choose the Search button.
3. If a list of subtopics appears, click the topic that most closely matches the procedure for which you want Help. A Help window appears.
4. View the Help information; then click the Close button when you are done.

You might decide that you want to hide the Office Assistant and display it only when you need it. To hide the Office Assistant, click the Close (X) button on the Office Assistant. Click the Office Assistant button in the toolbar to redisplay the Office Assistant.

To customize how the Office Assistant works, right-click the Office Assistant and choose Options. Select the options you want to use; then choose OK.

TIP When a light bulb appears in the Office Assistant, click it to display a tip related to what you are doing.

TIP To change the look of your assistant, right-click the Office Assistant and select Choose Assistant. In the Gallery tab, use the Next and Back buttons to scroll through the different assistants. When you see the assistant you want to use, choose OK.

Help: Print Help Information

You can print most of Access's online Help information for easy reference when you are working with Access. (See "Help: Help

Contents and Index," "Help: Searching for Topics," or "Help: Office Assistant" before you complete this task.)

Steps

1. Choose Help, Contents and Index; then click either the Contents, Index, or Find tab. Or, click the Office Assistant and type your question.
2. Navigate to the Help window you want to see.
3. In the Help window, choose the Options button; then click Print Topic.
4. Make any desired changes in the Print dialog box; then choose OK to begin printing.
5. Click the Close button in the Help window when you are done.

Help: Search for Topics

When you're not sure where to find a Help screen on a certain topic, you can use the Find tab to search for Help using specific keywords and then choose from a list of selections. You can also use the Office Assistant to search for help topics. (See "Help: Office Assistant.")

Steps

1. Choose Help, Contents and Index; then click the Find tab.
2. In the text box, type a word that you want to find.
3. In the middle list box, select a word or phrase to narrow your search.
4. In the bottom list box, select the topic you want; then choose Display.
5. View the Help information; then click the Close button when you are finished.

NOTE The first time you use Find, Access builds a word list of Access terms. This might take a few minutes.

Help: Tip of the Day

The Tip of the Day feature provides an easy way to familiarize yourself with some of Access's capabilities. When this feature is enabled, a tip on using Access appears each time you start Access. To see additional tips while you are using Access, you can access the Office Assistant and click the Tips option. (See also "Help: Office Assistant.")

Steps

1. Click the Office Assistant. (If the Office Assistant doesn't already appear on-screen, click the Office Assistant button in the toolbar.)
2. Choose Options.
3. In the Options tab, click the Show the Tip of the Day at Startup check box; then choose OK.

If you don't want the tip of the day to show, repeat Steps 1-3 and uncheck the Show the Tip of the Day at Startup check box.

TIP If you see a light bulb displayed in the Office Assistant, click it to see a helpful tip on your current actions.

Help: Toolbar Buttons

Access provides ScreenTips to help you remember the names and functions of the toolbar buttons. ScreenTips are the small pop-up labels that appear next to a toolbar button when you move the mouse pointer onto the button and pause.

Steps

1. To find more information on a toolbar button (in addition to the ScreenTip), press Shift+F1.
2. Click the toolbar button for which you need Help. A pop-up box appears to explain what you use the button for.
3. Click the pop-up box to remove it from the screen.

TIP To turn ScreenTips on or off, choose View, Toolbars, Customize; then click the Options tab, and clear or check the Show ScreenTips on Toolbars check box. Click Close. You can also have ScreenTips show shortcut keys by choosing Show Shortcut Keys in ScreenTips.

Hyperlinks: Copy

A *hyperlink* field stores a description of an address as either an URL (Uniform Resource Locator) for a Web address or UNC (Universal Naming Convention) for an intranet address of a document. The actual address is stored internally, with a description that is browsed by others. The procedure describes how to copy a hyperlink from any Office application to your database.

Steps

1. Right-click a hyperlink.
2. Choose Hyperlink, Copy Hyperlink command on the shortcut menu to copy it to the Clipboard.

3. Move to another hyperlink field on a table, query, or form and click the Paste button.

Hyperlinks: Enter

You can enter hyperlinks to Web sites or to documents on your computer or your network. Your table contains the hyperlink description as underlined text. When you click that link, you open your browser or the appropriate application and bring that document into view. You must first create a hyperlink field before you can enter a hyperlink. (See "Hyperlinks: Create Field" in the Table and Database Design part of this book.)

Steps

1. Open a *table, query,* or *form* in *Datasheet* or *Form View.*
2. Move the insertion point into the Hyperlink field.
3. Enter the text you want to display for the hyperlink if you want to provide an explanation of the underlying address.

4. Click the Insert Hyperlink button on the toolbar. Enter the UNC path (path and filename) or URL address (web address) into the Link To File or URL text box.
5. If desired, enter the location in the Named Location in File (Optional) text box; then choose OK.

NOTE To enter a hyperlink based on the location of the current file, and not on an absolute path, check the Use Relative Path for Hyperlink check box. If you do not know the location of your document, choose the browse button on the Insert Hyperlink dialog box.

Hyperlinks: Modify

If you want to edit a *hyperlink*, you will run into a problem when you click the hyperlink because that activates the hyperlink. Instead you need to use the right mouse button or press Tab to enter the field for editing.

Steps

1. Click the *field* before the hyperlink and press Tab to enter the hyperlinked field.
2. If desired, type the new description for the hyperlink.
3. Right-click the hyperlink field and choose Hyperlink, Edit Hyperlink command on the shortcut menu to enter the Edit Hyperlink dialog box. Enter the UNC path or URL address into the Link To File or URL text box.
4. Optionally, enter the location in the Named Location in File text box; then choose OK.

Navigate in a Datasheet

Navigating a datasheet uses techniques that are very similar to navigating most spreadsheets. You can move through columns (fields) and rows (*records*) using standard keystrokes. If you need to find data you can also use the Find button. (See "Data: Find.")

Steps

1. Double-click a table name in the Tables tab of the Database window to open its datasheet.
2. Press the Tab key to move to the right; the Shift+Tab key to move to the left; or use the arrow cursor keys to move in any direction.

   When you move past the furthest right *field* you move to the next record; and when you move before the first field you move to the previous record. See the following table for additional navigation information.

Datasheet View Navigation

To Navigate in Datasheet View	Do the Following
To advance a field to the right	Press Tab.
To move a field to the left	Press Shift+Tab.
To advance to the next record	Press the Tab key on the last field in a record.
To go back to the rightmost field in the previous record	Press Shift+Tab in the leftmost field of the current record.
To move to the first record in the Navigation selector	Click First Record button
To move to the previous record	Click Previous Record.
To move to the next record	Click Next Record.
To move to the last record	Click Last Record.
▶* To move to the first blank record	Click New Record button on toolbar.
To move to a particular record Number text box, enter a press	Double-click the Record record number, then Enter.

If all else fails, you can always navigate by clicking an insertion point on any *record* or field in view. Move the scroll bars to view other records and click in any record or field of interest.

TIP You might want to set some of the options on the Keyboard tab of the Options dialog box to change the behavior of the arrow and Enter keys during record navigation. Select Tools, Options and click the Keyboard tab to change options. The options include: whether Enter moves to the next field or record; whether the arrow key moves to the next field or character; whether a field is selected when you enter; and whether you can press Tab or Enter to go to the next record, or if you will cycle back to the first field.

Navigate in a Dialog Box

Navigating in a dialog box is the same for any windows application. You can use the keyboard or mouse to make choices. Any time a dialog box is open, you must answer the questions or at least choose Cancel or Close before you can do other tasks.

Steps

1. In many dialog boxes (such as Save As) when you first enter, text in a text box is already selected. Just start typing to replace the text, you do not need to click first.
2. To move to different areas of the dialog box, press Tab to go forward, Shift+Tab to go backward. If the option is a few Tabs away, click the option.
3. Click check boxes and option buttons to activate or deactivate them. For drop-down buttons, click the arrow and make a choice.
4. When you make choices with the mouse, the OK button or its equivalent remains the default choice and accepts all choices when you press Enter.

TIP You can choose any option with an underlined letter in a dialog box by pressing the Alt key and that letter. For example, to select the Next button, press Alt+N.

Navigate with the IntelliMouse

The Microsoft IntelliMouse pointing device includes a small wheel between the left and right mouse buttons. The wheel rolls forward and backward and depresses. The IntelliMouse makes navigating in Access 97 easier.

Steps

1. To scroll the datasheet a few rows at a time using the IntelliMouse, roll the wheel up to scroll up, and down to scroll down.
2. To move to the next records in *Form View*, roll the wheel down. To move to the previous records, roll the wheel up.
3. To pan in the datasheet, form, or print preview window using the IntelliMouse, hold down the wheel as you drag in any direction to move the window in that direction.

NOTE The wheel button on the IntelliMouse will function only if you install IntelliPoint 2.0 (or later) software and are using applications that take advantage of the IntelliMouse.

OLE Objects: Enter

One of the strengths of Access is its capability to accept non-textual data. This includes graphics, sounds, videos, and Windows application files. For example, in an employee *database*, you could include an employee's resume created in Word. In a Real Estate database, you could include a video tour of a house. Entering text and numbers is more straightforward. (See "Data: Enter.") To accept graphics and other similar data, you must first create a field with an OLE Object data type. (See: " Data Types: Changing" in the Table and Database Design part of this book.)

Steps

1. Open a *table*, *query*, or *form* in *Datasheet* or Form View and move to an OLE data type field.

2. Choose Insert, Object to bring up the Insert Object dialog box.
3. If you need to create the data, choose the Create New option button and in the Object Type list box, double-click the type of application you want to create. Create and save the data.

   If the file is already on disk, choose the Create From File option button and enter the location and name of the file in the File text box

If you need to edit an OLE object, double-click the object in a field. Access will launch the application that created the file or change toolbar buttons and the menu to allow you to edit the data.

NOTE With some objects you can also first go to the application and copy the object. Then, go into an OLE object field on a datasheet or form and paste.

Records: Add New

You add new *records* to *tables* in either the *Datasheet* or *Form View* in Access.

Steps

1. Open the table or related tables in either the Datasheet or Form View.

2. Click the New Record button on the toolbar.
3. Enter the data you want in the first field, then press the Tab key to advance to the next field.
4. At the end of the record (the last field), press the Tab key to advance to the next record.

Access does not create a new record until you actually enter data into the first field of a new record.

Records: Copy

You can select one or more *records* in a datasheet and copy them to another datasheet. You can also copy data from a *form*; however, this is not practical because of the tab order. If you are copying data from a datasheet to a different part of the same datasheet, you probably need to redesign your *database*. You should not have information repeated often in your *table*. (See "Optimization: Split Database" in the Special Features and Programming part of this book.)

Steps

1. Open the table, *query*, or form in *Datasheet View*, then select the record(s) you want to copy.

2. Click the Copy button on the toolbar.
3. Open the datasheet that is the target for these records and set up the datasheet by moving fields so that the fields match up to the records on the Clipboard. You can click and drag column headers to change the order of fields in a datasheet.
4. To add the records at the end of the datasheet, choose Edit, Paste Append.

NOTE If your primary key is an AutoNumber data type, the records will be renumbered using the sequence starting with the last number. If you have any indexed fields with no duplicates allowed (including a primary key that is not an AutoNumber field), Access will not allow you to copy data within the same table and you will get an error message.

Alternatively, you can cut records from one part of the datasheet and paste them in a different location in the current or other datasheet. You can also replace records by first copying records and then selecting the records to replace before you paste. However, because the primary key (which you should have in most cases) maintains sort order, moving records within the same table will not make a difference in the display order.

Records: Delete

You can manually delete *records* one at a time, or delete groups of records simultaneously through the use of delete queries. Delete *queries* enable you to delete groups of records in a single operation. (See "Delete Query" in the Queries and Filters part of this book.)

Steps

1. In *Datasheet* or *Form View*, click or drag along the record selectors to select the record(s) to be deleted.

2. Click the Delete Record button on the toolbar.

CAUTION When you delete a record in the Datasheet View from a *table* involved in a relationship with another table, make sure that either you are enforcing *referential integrity* or that you take care of cascade deletions in the Relationship window. (See "Relationships Between Tables" in the Table and Database Design part of this book.) Do not delete a parent record and leave orphaned child records behind.

NOTE You can set a *property* in the Design View called Allow Deletions that controls whether users can delete records in a form. You can also set a property called Allow Additions that controls whether records can be added.

TIP If one of your fields is an AutoNumber field and you delete many records at the end of your table, the next AutoNumber will follow all the deleted records. If you want to reset your AutoNumber to be the last existing record's number, compact your database. (See " Database: Compact" in the File Management part of this book.)

Records: Go To

If you know the record number of the record you want, you can go to the record. Alternatively, use Find to go to the record you need. (See also "Data: Find.")

Steps

1. In *Datasheet* or *Form View*, select the current *record* number at the bottom of the window.
2. Enter the new record number.

Spell Check

You can check the spelling of your data in Datasheet or Form View; and check data in a *table, query,* or *form* in the *Database window.*

Steps

1. Select a single word or any area on a datasheet or form.

2. Click the Spelling button on the toolbar. If a word cannot be found in the dictionary, the Spelling dialog box appears.
3. Accept or edit the word in the Change To text box; and then choose the Change button. Or, choose the Change All button if you want to change this word throughout the document.

   Alternatively, select one of the words from the Suggestions list, and then choose the Change or Change All.
4. If prompted, choose Yes to continue from the top of the document.
5. When an alert box tells you that the entire worksheet has been checked, choose OK.

NOTE You can also choose to ignore fields when you get into the Spelling dialog box.

Width of Column

You may want to change the width of a column when you cannot see all of its contents. To change the width of a text box on a form, see "Controls: Size" in the Forms and Reports part of this book.

TIP If you do not want to change column width, you can also press Shift+F2 to enter a dialog box to see multiple lines of an entry.

Steps

1. In *Datasheet View* of a *table*, *query*, or *form*, move the mouse pointer between two column headings until it is a double-headed arrow.
2. Drag to change the column width. To make the column as wide as the widest entry, double-click.

NOTE Sometimes when you double-click, the column is wider than the screen and you cannot see the border of the column header to drag the column width back. In this case, use Format, Column Width to reset the column.

Window: Arrange

If you want to work on more than one portion of your *database* at a time, you can use the Window commands to display two different windows simultaneously.

Steps

1. Click the Minimize button to minimize any windows that you don't want to arrange.
2. Choose Window; then Tile Horizontally or Tile Vertically, depending on how you want to arrange your windows.

Window: Hide and Unhide

In some cases you might need to keep a window open to have the values available but you also need to have the window out of the way. This could be the case when you need values off a form that will feed criteria in a query or for values on a report.

Steps

1. From the Database window, double-click the object you want to hide.

2. Choose Window, Hide.

To redisplay the window, choose Window, Unhide, and double-click the name of the object from the Unhide Window dialog box.

NOTE To hide the Database window at startup, choose Tools, Startup and uncheck the Display Database Window check box. To display the hidden Database window, press F11. Use the `Object.Hide` method to hide an open object through *VBA*.

Table and Database Design

Before you enter any information in Access, you have to create a *table* somewhere. A table is the foundation for all queries, forms, and reports. The container for all these objects is the *database*.

In this part, you find tasks showing how to create your database file and the tables that belong to the database. You follow steps for creating the basic building blocks of a table—fields. In addition, you find reference information for setting the *data type*, format, default value, size, and other properties of fields. To speed up data retrieval and link to other tables, you can also *index* the fields, set their *primary keys*, and create relationships between tables.

Data: Blanks, Nulls, and Zero-Length Strings

When entering information into your database records, you can leave data out of a *field* if it is not available. However, a blank field can mean more than one thing. It might signify that you don't know what the field's value is or that a value for the field doesn't exist. You can leave a field blank if you don't know what the value is (the value in this field is actually called a *Null* value). If you set the Zero-length property, you can enter "" (two quotes) in the field to indicate there is no value.

Steps

1. To set the Zero-Length property, open the *table* in *Design View* and go to the field. Change the Allow Zero Length property to Yes.
2. If you want to display text to inform you which fields have null versus zero-length strings, click in the Format property. For text *data types*, enter *Text Format;Null*

Format; *Zero-length Format*. Where *Text Format* is any formatting characters you would use for text, *Null Format* is what you want nulls to look like, and *Zero-length format* is what you want zero-length formats to look like. An example is **@;"Unknown";"None"**.

For number data types, there are four options in the Format property: Number Format; Negative Format; Null Format; Zero-Length Format.

3. When finished, close and save the table design.

Data: Format

In addition to decimal places (see "Decimal Places"), you can change the format of a number so that all numbers look consistent in your *table*. Numeric formats include dollar signs, percent signs, and commas. Date formats include spelling the months or using numbers for the month, and how many digits to use for the day and year. Text formats include capitalization.

Queries, *forms*, and *reports* also enable you to change the format places. On these objects you can change Format by right-clicking the *field* or *control* in *Design View* and making the change on the *Property* sheet in the forms and Reports part of this book. (See "Controls: Properties Change " in the Forms and Reports part of this book.)

Steps

1. Click a table name in the Tables tab of the *Database window*, then choose the Design button.
2. Choose the *field* and click in the Format property on the bottom half of the Table Design window.
3. Choose one of the choices from the drop-down list.
4. Click the Close (X) button on the Table Design window and choose Yes to save the changes to the table design.

TIP Text format types do not appear in a drop-down list. Type **>** to convert your entry to all uppercase. You can also press F1 while you are in the Format property box for more detailed codes on all *data types*.

Data Types: Changing

When you create a *table*, you specify the *data type* for each *field* in the Table *Design View*. Text, Number, Date/Time, Currency, and Yes/No data types are self-explanatory. *AutoNumber*, formerly called Counter in previous versions of Access, increments each *record* by one. While Text fields can only contain up to 255 characters, *Memo* can include over 65,000 characters. *OLE Objects* enable you to insert graphics, sounds, and other data types. The Lookup data type will enable you to choose from a list of options. (See "Lookup Columns: Create with Wizard.") The *Hyperlink* data type enables you to launch an Access object (a table, form, query, and so on), another file in another application, or go to a Web site. (See "Hyperlinks: Create Field.")

> **CAUTION** You can change a field's data type but, depending on the particular conversion, this process can lead to data loss.

Steps

1. Click the Tables tab of the *Database window*, click the table name and choose the Design button.
2. Move to the field and click the Data Type column, then choose the data type.
3. Close the Table Design window and choose Yes when prompted to save your change.

Data Types: Setting Defaults

When you first create a field in Table Design View, the field is automatically set to text and the default text field size is 50. If most of your fields are not text or are a different size, you can change these defaults.

Steps

1. Choose Tools, Options and click the Tables/Queries tab.
2. In the Default Data Type drop-down box, choose the data type you use most.

3. Type your most used size for text in the Text box.
4. In the Number drop-down box, choose the most used size for numbers.
5. Choose OK when finished.

NOTE When you import data from another source, you can type which names of fields will automatically be *indexed* in the AutoIndex on Import/Create text box.

Database: Create Blank

A blank *database* is a database file that contains no *objects* or data. It is an empty shell that you will use to add new *tables*, *queries*, *forms*, and *reports*. If you want Access to create some of your tables, forms, and other objects, see "Database: Create New with a Wizard."

Steps

1. In a blank Access window or while the *Database window* from another database is showing, choose the New Database button on the toolbar.
2. Double-click the Blank Database template in the General tab of the New *dialog box*.
3. Enter a name in the File New Database File Name *text box*, specify the storage location of the file in the Save In drop-down *list box*, then choose the Create button.

NOTE You can also press Ctrl+N to start a new database from anywhere in Access. After you give the database a name, Access closes the database that you were working on and opens a blank Database window.

Database: Create New with Wizard

You can create a new database that is blank or let the Database Wizard create one for you that contains the objects you specify for it. The task, "Database: Create Blank" describes the former process. This task describes the use of the Database Wizard. Both procedures begin the same way.

When you use a wizard, Access enables you to choose from sample fields and then create the *tables*, *queries*, *forms*, *reports*, and switchboards for you. A switchboard is a *form* with buttons that help a user navigate through the *database*. You can even have Access populate your database with sample data to help you learn how different features work in the sample database.

Steps

1. When you start Access the Introductory screen is displayed. Click Database Wizard to open the Wizard.

   If you already have Access opened, click the New Database button on the toolbar.

2. Select the database from the Databases tab of the New Database *dialog box*; then choose OK.
3. Specify a location for the database file in your file system using the Save In drop-down *list box*; enter a new name for the database in the File Name *text box* of the File New Database dialog box; then choose the Create button. Access launches the Database Wizard.
4. Choose Next to view the screen that lets you select additional fields and sample data. Click the *check boxes* next to include optional fields (in italics) or uncheck any other fields. Click the check box next to the Yes, Include Sample Data if you want that feature, then choose Next.
5. On the next four wizard screens, select the styles you want for your forms and reports, give the database a name that will appear on the switchboard, and choose to open the database. On the last step, choose Finish.

NOTE To see which sample database wizards are available, look on the Database tab of the New dialog box. These wizards are installed during the default setup. However, if you do not have the wizards, return to setup (through your Office or Access CD), choose the Change Option button while Microsoft Access is selected, and check the Wizards box.

NOTE On the second to last step of the new Database Wizard, you can include a picture on your reports by clicking the Yes, I'd Like to Include a Picture check box, then choose the Picture button to specify a picture file in the Insert Picture dialog box. Several graphic formats such as bitmaps, icons, the Windows Metafile, TIFF, PCX, PICT, JPEG, GIF, and EPS are supported.

Database: Documentor

Data documentation can help you get organized, especially for large *databases*. Database dictionaries describe the database as a whole, each *table*, and each *field*. Access has a Database Documentor that describes these and other parts of your database for you.

Steps

1. From your open database, choose Tools, Analyze, Documentor.
2. When the Documentor *dialog box* opens, select which objects you want to document by choosing the *Object* Type drop down and clicking the *check boxes* next to each item in the Objects list.

   If you want to document everything (which can take a while), click the All Object Types tab and choose the Select All *command button*.
3. When you are finished choosing the objects, choose OK. A preview of your documentation *report* appears onscreen. Print your report if desired.
4. If you want to save the documentation information into a table, choose File, Save As Table.

Database: Examples

One of the best ways to learn Access and find ideas for your own databases is to look at the samples that come with the program. These sample databases might have been installed when you set up Microsoft Office. If not, you will need to go through setup. The files are Northwind, Orders, and Solutions. The first *database* you should look at is Northwind. Orders and Solutions provide examples for application development and programming.

Steps

1. To open a sample database, click the Open Database button on the toolbar.
2. Change the Look In drop-down box to the Samples subfolder of the folder where the Office directory is installed.
3. Double-click Northwind, Orders, or Solutions.

NOTE The Northwind database includes a Show Me menu that explains features of the application. Orders and Solutions have a Show Me button on their toolbars.

Datasheet: Appearance Change

There are numerous ways you can alter the appearance of your datasheet. You must have the datasheet for that *table* in view; these settings apply universally to the table, and not to individual cells. You can modify a table datasheet, *query* datasheet, or the *Form View* of a form.

Steps

1. Double-click the table or query name in the *Database window* to open its datasheet; or click the View button drop-down arrow and choose *Datasheet View* when a form is in view.
2. Choose Format, Font to select a new font, font style, font size, or color.
3. Choose Format, Cells and change the gridline, gridline color, cell appearance, and cell background color in the Cells Effects *dialog box.*
4. Click the Close box to close the datasheet.

   Access remembers your settings the next time you open a datasheet for this *table*, *query*, or *form*.

Additionally, you can change the width of a column or the height of all rows in the datasheet using the Format, Column Width (see "Width of Column" in the Database Essentials part of this book) or Format, Row Height commands. Each column can have its own width, but all rows must be the same size. You can also hide (see "Hide Columns") or freeze (see "Freeze Display of a Table Field" in the Database Essentials part of this book) columns to help see the more of the datasheet.

Datasheet: Appearance Defaults

When you use the Format menu to change the datasheet appearance, only the viewable datasheet changes. (See "Datasheet: Appearance Change.") You can also change the appearance for all datasheets you have not individually changed.

Steps

1. Choose Tools, Options, and click the Datasheet tab.
2. Change any of the options for font, background, and *gridlines*; choose OK.

Decimal Places

Decimal places are basically the numbers after the decimal point (for example, 25 becomes 25.00 when you add two decimal places). When you work with numbers, having all related numbers with the same number of decimal places adds to the professional appearance of your output. Changing the number of decimal places only adds to the visual appearance of a number, not to its value. Another option is to use the Rnd (Round) *function*, which will change the value of a number. If you want to add commas or other symbols with numbers, change the format *property*. (See "Data: Format.")

Forms and *reports* also enable you to change decimal places. On forms and reports, you can change decimal places by right-clicking the *control* in *Design View* and making the change on the Property sheet. (See "Controls: Properties Change" in the Forms and Reports part of this book.)

Steps

1. Click a *table* name in the Tables tab of the *Database window*, then choose the Design button.
2. Choose the number or currency *field* and click in the Decimal Places property on the bottom half of the Table Design window.
3. Choose Auto to let Access determine the number of decimal places (usually two), or type in your own number of decimal places.
4. Click the Close (X) button on the Table Design window and choose Yes to save the changes to the table design.

Field: Caption as Alternate Name

Captions enable you to uniquely name the column header in *Datasheet View* (as opposed to calling it by the *field* name). After you add a *caption* to a field, any new *queries*, *forms*, or *reports* will use the caption as the default for column headers or labels for the field. Queries also have a caption property for each field.

NOTE Labels and column headers for existing queries, forms, and reports do not change when you change the field's caption in Table *Design View*.

Steps

1. Choose the table in the *Database window* and choose the Design button.
2. Move to the field to which you want to add the caption. In the lower half of the Table Design window, click the General tab and click in the Caption box.
3. Type text for the caption. When finished, close the table and choose Yes when prompted to save changes to the design of the table.

Field: Create

You must create a *field* in a *table* to use it in a *query, form*, or *report*. A field holds one specific piece of information in a *record*. Examples include a company name or a salary. It is better to condense the information that goes into a field into the smallest unit you can use. For example, instead of having an entire name in a field, use at least two fields—one for first name and one for last name. You will then be able to sort, find, and *group* information on the last name and use both name fields for mailing labels and letters.

Steps

1. Open a new table or choose an existing table in the *Database window* and choose the Design button.
2. In the top half of the Table Design window, move to a blank row and type a field name.
3. Press Tab and click the down arrow to choose a *data type*.
4. Press Tab again and type a description (which will appear on the *status bar* in Datasheet or *Form View*). If desired, click in the lower half of the window and set any additional field properties.
5. When finished, close the Table Design window and choose Yes when prompted to save the table design.

NOTE The description and other field properties become the defaults for many of the control properties in forms. However, if you change the table's field properties after you create a form, most of the properties do not change on the form.

Field: Default Value

You can set a *default value* for a field in the Table *Design View* on the General tab. When you enter a value or *expression* in that *property*, that default value is entered into each new record when you create the record. You are free to overwrite the default value if you have write privileges for that field. The default value does not affect any *records* you enter before you create the default value. You can have a different default value for the *field* on a *form* than the one you create for the table. (See "Forms: Default Value" in the Forms and Reports part of this book.)

A common default value would be a state or country (entered as **CO** or **USA**). Another common default would be today's date, which you enter as **Date()**.

Steps

1. Click the *table* name in the Tables tab of the *Database window*, then choose the Design button.
2. Move to the field and click in the Default Value *text box*, then enter your value. Or, enter an expression that evaluates to a value.
3. Click the Save button on the toolbar to save your new database rule.

Because this default value is applied at the table level, the mechanism for entering the default value operates in a datasheet or form. During an append operation, default values are not added to the new records that are appended to the table.

TIP Creating default values is a great time saver and speeds up data entry. When you have a field that usually has the same value entered into it, consider setting this property.

Field: Delete

If you no longer need a field, you can delete it. For instance, after you import a table from another source you can change the table design to add fields for first name and last name. After you enter these data for these fields for all your records, you then want to delete the original name field that contained both names.

> **CAUTION** Be sure that you won't be using the field again when you delete. All the information in the field is lost for every *record*. It will be a large task to find and enter the information for a mistakenly deleted field. You can use Undo if you immediately notice you deleted the wrong field or if you choose, when prompted, to not save changes to the database design. However, this task is so potentially dangerous that you should probably back up your database first. (See "Backup Data" in the File Management part of this book.)

Steps

1. Click the *table* name in the Tables tab of the *Database window*, then choose the Design button.

2. Click in the field you want to remove and click the Delete Rows button on the toolbar.
3. When prompted if you want to permanently delete the information, choose Yes (but only if you really want to).

Field: Description

The Description *property* provides information or notes about fields in tables, and queries. Descriptions can be up to 255 characters in length. Descriptions appear in the *status bar* while entering data in a *field* in Datasheet or *Form View*.

This propertyx2 is set in the Table *Design View* for tables, and in the Field Properties Property sheet in the *Query* window for queries. (See "Queries and Filters: Query: Properties" in the Queries and Filters part of this book.)

When you create a control by dragging a field from a Field List, Access copies the Description property to the control's Status Bar Text property. It then displays that description in the status bar whenever the *insertion point* is entered into that field.

Steps

1. Click a table name in the Tables tab of the *Database window*, then choose the Design button.
2. Click in the Description column of the field.

3. Enter a value for the description. You do not need to surround the description with quotation marks.

4. Click the Save button on the toolbar to save your description.

Field: Insert

You can add a *field* at the bottom of the field names section *Table* Design window (see "Field: Create") or you can insert a field in between existing fields.

Steps

1. Click a table name in the Tables tab of the *Database window*, then choose the Design button.

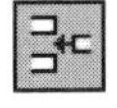

2. Click in the field below where you want your new field to go and click the Insert Rows button on the toolbar.
3. Enter the field name, *data type*, description, and any properties for the field in the field properties section at the bottom of the Table window.
4. Click the Close (X) button on the Table Design window and choose Yes to save the changes to the table design.

Field: Name

You can change the name of a field in your database and your table's data is left unaffected. However, if you have used the field in a *query*, *form*, or *report* created prior to the change, you must manually update that control to reflect the new field name. If you want to see a different name in the column header of *Datasheet View*, you can also change the *caption property*. (See "Fields: Caption as Alternate Name.")

NOTE Field names can be up to 64 characters and include spaces. However, if you are going to upsize your database to a database *server* such as *SQL*, it is better not to include spaces because the table's field name spaces will be converted to underscores. Any queries, forms, or reports based on the tables will produce errors and will need to be modified.

TABLE AND DATABASE DESIGN

Steps

1. Click a table name in the Tables tab of the *Database window*, then choose the Design button.
2. Click the name of the field and edit that name.
3. Click the Close (X) button on the Table Design window and choose Yes to save the changes to the table design.

Field: Rename in Datasheet View

To rename the *field* in a *query*, change the name of the field in the Query Design *grid*. That new name provides the column name for the field in *Datasheet View*, unless the *Caption property* has been set (in which case, the caption is used). The renamed field also provides the name of the Control Source for any *control* in a *form* or *report* that is based on that query.

Steps

1. Open the *table* in Datasheet View.
2. Double-click the column header of the field of interest and enter the new name of the field.

Field: Set Properties

You can set many of the field properties in Table *Design View*. Properties include name, *data type*, description, field length, *validation* rules, default values, and whatever you see on the General or *Lookup* tabs in table design.

Steps

1. Click a table name in the Tables tab of the *Database window*, then choose the Design button.
2. Click the field in the Table Design View.
3. Change the properties on the same row of the field name or press F6 and change the properties in the lower half of the window. The properties include field size, format, decimal places, caption, and default value among others. The actual properties change depending on the data type. For a description of each property, see the blue text on the right or click in the property and press F1.

4. Click the Close (X) button on the Table Design window and choose Yes to save the changes to the table design.

When you click in the text box for some of the *properties*, there is a drop-down arrow representing a list of choices. Click the arrow and then the desired item in the list. Some properties (for example, Input Mask) also have a build button (...) on the right side of the *text box*. You can click this or the Build button on the toolbar to bring up a dialog box with examples. Another option is to begin typing in the text box. Access will automatically complete the entry with the first available option where the first letter matches your entry. For example, in the data type text box, type **n** to select number.

TIP Double-click any property that has multiple choices either in the Data Type or lower section of the design window. This will cycle through the available list of choices. (This is a general feature of Property sheets.)

Field: Size

Field size for text *data type* fields determines the maximum number of characters you can enter for a *field*. You can set the field size for text up to 255 characters and the default is 50 characters unless you change the default. (See "Data Types: Setting Defaults.")

For numbers, field size determines the range of numbers you can enter and whether or not the number can include decimal places. Generally, you want to set the smallest possible field size for text or number but still include all possibilities you might enter. With smaller field sizes, your database file will be smaller and quicker.

Steps

1. Click a *table* name in the Tables tab of the *Database window*, then choose the Design button.
2. Click in the field and then click in the Field Size box.

3. Type in a number from 1 to 255 for text data types. If your data type is numeric, choose one of the field sizes shown in the following table from the drop-down list.
4. Click the Close (X) button on the Table Design window and choose Yes to save the changes to the table design.

You want to choose one of the following numeric field sizes that will accommodate your data using the smallest number of bytes possible.

Numeric Field Sizes

Option	Description	Byte Size
Byte	Numbers 0-255 without decimals	1
Integer	Numbers from about -32,000 to +32,000 with no decimals	2
Long Integer	Very large numbers without decimals (+/- 2 billion)	4
Single	Large numbers with decimals (up to 38 digits before or after the decimal place)	4
Double	Largest possible numbers with decimals	8

NOTE When you create *relationships* between fields from different tables, all data types and field sizes for numbers must match. The exception is an *AutoNumber* field. Because the *foreign key* field will not be an AutoNumber field, the related field in the second table should have Long Integer Field Size.

TIP If you often calculate with a field that has between one and four decimal places, consider using Currency data type instead of Single or Double. Currency uses the faster fixed-point calculation rather than floating point calculations.

Gridlines: Turning On and Off

Access normally prints and displays vertical and horizontal *gridlines* in *Datasheet View*. If you want, you can turn these gridlines off. You can also change the background or font of the cells. (See "Datasheet: Appearance Change.")

Steps

1. Open a *table*, *query*, or *form* in Datasheet View.
2. Choose Format, Cells.
3. Uncheck one or both of the Horizontal and Vertical *check boxes* in the Gridline Shown section of the Format Cells *dialog box*; choose OK.

Hide Column

In some cases you might not want to see all the columns of the datasheet. Perhaps your display is too wide, you don't need to enter all information, or you only want to see relevant information to your task. Another option to help you navigate with many columns is to freeze columns. (See "Freeze Display of a Table Field" in the Database Essentials part of this book.)

Steps

1. Open a table, *query*, or *form* in *Datasheet View*.
2. Right-click the column header and choose Hide Columns.

To return a hidden column to view, use the Format, Unhide Columns command and check the box next to the column you want to see.

CAUTION When hiding columns from view, be careful that you don't inadvertently neglect their data entry.

Hyperlinks: Create Field

You can use hyperlinks in forms and datasheets to jump to the location described in that *hyperlink*. Locations can be other objects in Access *databases*, documents created by Word, Excel, or PowerPoint, and documents on the Internet or an intranet.

Access contains a new *data type* called a hyperlink field. A hyperlink field contains the text and numbers that comprise a hyperlink address, which is the *path* to the object, document, or Web page. A hyperlink address can also be an URL (Uniform Resource Locator) for an Internet or intranet address. Access recognizes a hyperlink address from the entered *syntax*.

Steps

1. Open the table in the *Design View* by selecting it in the *Database window* on the Table tab and clicking the Design button.
2. In the field list, enter the field name for the new hyperlink field.
3. Tab to the Data Type column and select the Hyperlink data type.
4. Click the Close (X) button on the Table Design window and choose Yes to save the changes to the table design.

Index: Create a Composite Index

Access enables you to create indexes based on two or more fields in your table, up to a limit of 10 fields. You can specify that a composite *index* is unique and use it as a *primary key*, or use that composite index to speed up sorting or searching through your data. Access does not allow you to index on expressions. However, in many cases a single field index will be sufficient. (See "Index: Create Based on a Single Field.") A multiple field index can also make up a primary key. (See "Index: Primary Key.")

Steps

1. Click a table name in the Tables tab of the *Database window*, then choose the Design button.

2. Click the Indexes button on the toolbar.
3. Type an index name in the Index Name column of the Indexes window.
4. In the Field Name column, enter the first field in the index.
5. Add additional fields below that line, without naming another index, up to ten fields.

To remove an index, click the Indexes button again, select the rows making up the index and press Delete. When searching or sorting on the non-indexed field, Access now takes longer. If you have no index at all in a table, Access orders the records in the order you enter them in the table.

Index: Create Based on a Single Field

You can *index* a single field to serve as a method for ensuring unique values, to sort your data, or to speed up search and retrieval operations.

When you index a field, you have two options. Yes (No Duplicates) means that you will not have any entries that match in more than one *record*. Yes (Duplicates OK) means that entries can match.

Steps

1. Click a table name in the Tables tab of the *Database window*, then choose the Design button.
2. Click the field in the table *Design View* and set the Indexed *property* in the General tab to one of the Yes options.

Index: Primary Key

A *primary key* is the index used to uniquely identify records in a table. Every table should have one primary index, although other unique indexes can be defined (as so-called candidate indexes). Often, the primary index is used to establish a *relationship* with a *child* table. (See "Relationships Between

Tables.") The field that the primary key is related to in the other table is called a *foreign key*. A primary key can contain one or more *fields*.

Steps

1. Click a table name in the Tables tab of the *Database window*, then choose the Design button.
2. Click the field in the Table *Design View*. If you want more than one field to make up the primary key, hold down Ctrl and click the field selectors of the other fields.
3. Click the Primary Key button on the toolbar to make the selected field(s) the primary key.

To remove a single field primary key, with that field selected in the Table Design View, click the Primary Key button on the toolbar again, or delete the index from the Indexes window.

Index: Set Index Properties

Indexes are listings of values or *expressions* in a *field* or combination of fields. An index in a *database* operates just like the index in a book. Indexes point to where something is located.

Indexes are particularly valuable in a number of database operations. They speed up finding and sorting information when you perform those operations later and also change the sorted view of your table. Indexes are necessary to match the data in a field of one *table* to a field in another, and thus provide the means for relating one table to another.

Steps

1. Click a table name in the Tables tab of the *Database window*, then choose the Design button.

2. Click the Indexes button on the toolbar.

In the Indexes window you can set index *properties*: the Index Name (which by default takes the field name but can be changed), the Sort Order, and whether the index is Primary,

Unique, or Ignores Nulls. The Ignore Nulls option makes the index smaller and speeds up searching records.

Input Mask: Phone Number and Other Entries

As you enter information in Text and Date data type *fields*, you might want certain symbols to appear. For example, a phone number has parentheses and a dash. You can manually type these symbols in each text field or you can create an *input mask* to automatically do the job. An input mask can also verify each character as you type it. To change the display of an entry after you type the entry and move out of the field, you can also format the field. (See "Data: Format.")

TIP The input mask wizard gives examples of the most common input masks you might want. These include phone number, social security number, long zip codes, passwords, and date and time values.

CAUTION Make sure your other field *properties* (such as Format, Default Value, Validation Rule, and Required) do not conflict with your input mask.

Steps

1. Click a *table* name in the Tables tab of the *Database window*, then choose the Design button.
2. Click the field and click in the input mask *property* at the bottom of the Table Design window.

3. If you want to use a predefined input mask, click the Build button to the right of the *text box* and choose one of the samples in the Input Mask Wizard; choose the Next button.
4. On the next two steps of the Input Mask Wizard, choose the placeholder character that you want to appear as the user types each character and whether you want to store the symbols with the table. Choose the Finish button when done.

TIP It is generally better not to include symbols with the table because the entries will be shorter (and thus take up less room in your database). However, if you will be exporting this data to a spreadsheet or other database, you might want to include the input mask symbols.

NOTE You can also type Input Mask characters directly in the property box in Table *Design View*. For a description of the acceptable characters, click in the Input Mask box and press F1.

Lookup Column: Create with Wizard

There are many instances when you might want to look up information to place in a field. This is especially true when you have codes representing values. Instead of trying to remember the codes, you can create a *lookup column* that enables you to choose something like the employee name rather than remember their employee identification number.

Steps

1. Click a table name in the Tables tab of the Database window, then choose the Design button.
2. If necessary, type the name for the field or go to an existing field. Choose Lookup Wizard as the *data type*.
3. If the data is from another table, identify that you want to use an existing table in the first step of the wizard and choose the table in the second step.
4. In the third and fourth step of the Lookup Wizard *dialog box*, double-click the fields that you want to appear in the lookup list and choose whether you want to hide the *key* column (usually an ID column).
5. Give the column a name in the last step of the Wizard and choose Finish. Access will prompt you to save the table.

NOTE The first step of the Lookup Wizard also asks you if you want to type the values rather than use an existing table. It is generally a better idea to use a table because you can use it for more than one combo or list box.

Lookup Column: Properties

After you create a *lookup column* (see "Lookup Column: Create with Wizard"), you might want to change or verify the lookup properties for the field.

The Lookup Column properties identify the source and organization for your drop-down menu. One important lookup *property* is the Row Source, which can be a *query* or *SQL* statement. You can edit the SQL statement by clicking the build button (...) to the right of the Row Source text box and then manipulate the query *builder* just like a normal query. (See "Query: Create with Design View" in the Queries and Filters part of this book.)

Steps

1. Click a table name in the Tables tab of the Database window, then choose the Design button.
2. Choose the lookup field and click the Lookup tab in the Field Properties section of the Table Design window.
3. The first property—Display Control—is usually set to *Combo Box*. This enables you to choose a drop-down arrow or type in the value. If you choose *List Box*, you only choose from the list. If you choose *Text Box*, you remove the lookup portion of the field and only type in the value in the field.
4. If you told the Lookup Wizard to use an existing table or query, the second property—Row Source Type—is Table/Query and the third property will be the name of a query or an SQL statement that you can edit by clicking the build button (...) on the right. If you typed a list of values in the Lookup Wizard, the values that you can edit appear in this area.

5. The *Bound* Column stores in the table the value from the specified column in Row Source. You might need to change the Column Widths property so you can see the entire columns from your Row Source.
6. Click the Close (X) button on the Table Design window and choose Yes to save the changes to the table design.

Relationships Between Tables

When you define a *relationship* between two *tables*, you match the values in one table to values in another table. In order to create a relationship, one or both of the tables requires that the values used in the match be unique. Normally an *index* (usually the *primary key*) in the controlling or parent table is used, and a *field* (called the *foreign key*) in the *child* table is matched.

In addition to defining a relationship, you set *referential integrity* rules in the relationship *dialog box*. When you enforce referential integrity, you say that you do not want any orphan records in the child table. Orphans occur when no records are matched to the parent table. If you choose *Cascade Update* Related *Records*, whenever you change the ID field in the parent table, the field in all corresponding records change in the child table. If you choose *Cascade Delete* Related Records, you will delete any children records when you delete the parent *record*. If you choose neither while enforcing referential integrity, you will be unable to update the ID field or delete the record when child records exist.

Steps

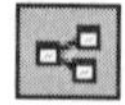

1. With the *Database window* showing, click the Relationships button on the toolbar to open the Relationship window.
2. Click and drag a relationship between a field from the parent table and the field in the child table.
3. The Relationships *dialog box* opens. In the lower half of the window, choose whether you want to enforce referential integrity and how the child table will be updated.

4. Finish creating the relationship by choosing OK and closing the relationship window.

The relationship is represented by a line between the two tables. You can select a relationship and press the Delete key to remove it. You can also right-click the line to view the shortcut menu, and select Edit Relationships to open the Relationships dialog box. A command button on the Relationships dialog box is *join* type. You can choose this to set the default join type for queries. (See "Tables: Combine with Join" in the Queries and Filters part of this book.)

Status Bar: Display User Message

The description *property* of a field appears on the *status bar* when you are in *Datasheet View* or *Form View*. The description becomes the default for the Status Bar property on a form that you can modify. (See "Controls: Properties Change" in the Forms and Reports part of this book.)

Steps

1. Click a table name in the Tables tab of the Database window, then choose the Design button.
2. Choose the field, move to the Description column and type what you want to appear in the status bar.
3. Click the Close (X) button on the Table Design window and choose Yes to save the changes to the table design.

NOTE If the status bar does not appear on your screen, choose Tools, Options, View tab, and check the Status Bar *check box* in the Show section.

Table: Create by Table Wizard

The Table Wizard is a fast way of creating tables. It lets you structure tables based on fields in existing tables, create rudimentary table relationships, and specify a *primary key*.

If you have existing data, you can also import or link the information to create a table. (See "Import Data" in the File

TABLE AND DATABASE DESIGN

Management part of this book.) You can also create a table by going directly to design window (see "Table: Create in Design View") or by working in Datasheet View (see "Table: Create in Datasheet View").

Steps

1. Click the Tables tab in the Database window, then choose New and then select Table Wizard in the New Table *dialog box*, then choose OK.
2. Click the Business or Personal *option button* to view a set of sample *tables*.
3. Select the table(s) you want to view *fields* from in the Sample Tables *list box*; then move the fields of interest from the Sample Fields list box to the Fields in My New Table list box; choose Next.

   Use the Rename Field button to rename any selected field you add. Access uses the same *data type* for your fields when you rename a field.
4. Enter a name for the table in the *text box*; select either Yes for the wizard to set a *primary key*, or No if you will set the primary key; choose Next.
5. Select any desired *relationships* in the My New <Tablename> Table Is list box; then choose the Next button.
6. Select from one of the following: Modify the Table Design; Enter Data Directly in the Table; or Enter Data Into the Table From a *Form* that the Wizard Creates for Me. Choose Finish.

Access creates the new table and saves it to disk. If you select to modify the table design, you view the Design window (see also "Table: Create in Design View"). For the Enter Data Directly selection in the last step, you see a Datasheet window. For the form selection, a form is created for you.

Table: Create in Datasheet View

The datasheet method is a very fast method for creating tables, but is limited in its capabilities. It is best used for small tables where you will add features later to the table design. It does not create table relationships, nor does it provide for data *validation* or other table properties.

Steps

1. Click the Tables tab in the *Database window*, then choose the New button.
2. Select *Datasheet View* in the New Table *dialog box.*

   A datasheet with 20 columns and 30 rows appears with default field names.
3. Rename the column headings by double-clicking them and entering your *field* name(s); press Enter or click another column or value in the datasheet.
4. Enter data into the datasheet; each column is a field, each row is a *record.*

5. Click Save on the Table Datasheet toolbar. Enter the name of the *table* in the Table Name *text box* in the Save As dialog box, then choose OK.

   An alert box is posted asking you if Access can create a *primary key*; click Yes if you haven't created a field with unique values that can identify each row of your datasheet (records in the table); click No if you have created such a field.

NOTE Use a consistent style of data within a column for dates, times, numbers, and so on, so that Access can create a *data type* and display format based on the values it sees you enter.

TIP If you need more than 20 columns, click a column to the right of your new field, then select the Column command from the Insert menu. Access will automatically add rows after the 30th record.

Access creates the new table and saves it to disk. When you have Access create the primary key, it creates an *AutoNumber* field that has sequential numbers entered into it.

Table: Create in Design View

A convenient place to create the structure of your database tables is Table *Design View*. This is where you add and remove fields, and it serves as a convenient venue for getting an overview of the properties associated with your fields and table.

Steps

1. Click the Tables tab in the *Database window*, then choose New. Select Design View in the New Table *dialog box*, then choose OK.
2. Enter a name for a *field* in the Field Name column, then Tab and enter the *data type* in the Data Type column.
3. Enter into the Description column the information you want displayed in the *status bar* when the *insertion point* is in that field in the table. Enter Field Size (number of characters), Format and *Input Mask* (display and allowable characters), *Caption* (for the *Datasheet view*), Default Values, *Validation* rules, and other *properties* in the General *section*.

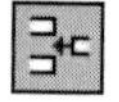

4. Click the next blank line of the field *grid* and create the next field in your database; then repeat Step 5. To insert a field between two other fields, click the Insert Rows button on the Table Design toolbar.

5. To select the field you want to use to create a *primary key*, click the field selector to the right of the field name. Or, select multiple fields for a compound primary key by holding Ctrl and clicking each field selector; then click the *Primary Key* button on the toolbar.

6. Click Save on the Table Design toolbar; enter a name for the table in the Table Name *text box* of the Save Table dialog box and choose OK.

Access creates the new table and saves it to disk.

NOTE You don't have to assign a primary key, but it is recommended. Make sure that the order of a compound primary key is correct. You can change the order by clicking the Indexes button on the toolbar and reordering the field names in the *index* that comprises the Primary Key. However, a compound primary key is used infrequently compared to a single field primary key.

Table: Modify Design

To modify a *table*, you must select that table in the *Database window* and open the table in the Table *Design View*. In this view you can add or remove *fields*; change field names; change a field's *data type*; and add, modify, or delete descriptions, field *properties*, and table rules.

CAUTION Pay particular attention to modifying the data type of an existing field. When you change data types, there is the potential for data loss due to data type mismatch. Your previous field's data may be truncated or discarded completely. Once it is gone, it is gone forever. Therefore, it is a good idea to make a backup of your database or table before you change the design of a table. (See "Backup Data" and "Database Object: Copy" in the File Management part of this book.)

Steps

1. Click a table name in the Tables tab of the Database window, then choose the Design button.
2. Make your changes or additions in the Table Design View.
3. Choose Insert, Rows to add fields, or Edit, Delete Rows to remove fields.
4. Choose View, Indexes to create or modify table indexes, or View, Properties to add or alter table properties.
5. Enter any General field properties like Captions, *Default Values*, Format, *Input Masks*, *Validation* Rule, Validation Text, Allow *Zero Length*, Required (mandatory data entry), and so on, that you want.
6. After you have finished modifying your table, select File, Save. Or, to save the resulting table as a different file, select File, Save As; name and locate your table in the file system using the Save As *dialog box*; then choose OK.

Access saves your table to disk. If you create a new table, that table's name appears in the Table tab of the Database window.

Table: Properties

A number of important *table properties* can be specified that affect how data is stored and accessed. Two different groups of properties can be accessed. The first set of properties are object properties that are the same for *queries*, *forms*, *reports*, *macros*, and modules. They include the object description, whether you want to hide the object in the database window, and whether you want to replicate the object. (See "Replication: Create Replica" in the File Management part of this book.)

The second set of properties you access from inside of Table Design View. You can also set the table description here. Other table properties you can set in Table Design View include a sort order, whether you want to filter out *records*, and a validation rule involving more than one field and the rule's associated error message. (See "Validate Data: Record Validation.")

Steps

1. Right-click the table in the Table tab of the Database window and select the Properties command from the shortcut menu.
2. Enter the description and whether the table is hidden. Or, right-click in the Table *Design View* (to the left of the leftmost column header of the field *grid*), and select the Properties command in the shortcut menu.

   There you can set *validation* rules and validation text, description, the field to sort the table by, and how you want to *filter* the table. An example of a filter would include a name of a field, a comparison sign (equals, greater than, less than), and a value. For example, `Title = "Sales Manager"`.

Of the two different types of Properties sheets, the latter is more useful and used more often. When you open the table from the Database window the Filter and Order By properties are not applied. Click the Apply Filter button to see the results.

Validate Data: Field Validation

You can create rules for a field where the values you enter must fall in a specified range. Otherwise the data is not acceptable. Most likely, the user made a typing error. If you need to use a field name in the *expression*, you will need to change the Table's *Validation* Rule *property*. (See "Validate Data: Table Validation" in the Table and database part of this book.)

Examples of validation rules include `>100` and `between 0 and 50` for number fields, or `>Date()` (greater than today's date). See the *Criteria* sections in the *Queries* and *Filters* part of this book and Expression sections in the Calculations part of this book.

Steps

1. Click the *table* name in the Tables tab of the *Database window*, and then choose the Design button.
2. Move to the *field* and click in the Validation Rule box in the bottom of the Table Design window and enter an expression.
3. If you want an error message to appear if this rule is violated, type the message in the Validation *Text box*.
4. Click the Save button on the toolbar to save your new database rule.

   When you enter a value in that field, the value is allowed if the expression is evaluated as "True."

{Table}

Validate Data: Record Validation

You can create a table *validation* rule to validate the data entered into two or more *fields* in a *record*. When you move off the record, Access checks that the *table* validation rule is not violated. You cannot leave the record without either removing the record's data or fixing a record so that it conforms to record validation.

You enter the record validation rule in the *Properties* sheet for the table. An example of a table validation rule is:

`[ShipDate]>=[OrderDate]`. This means that the shipping date has to be greater than or equal to the order date.

Steps

1. Click the table name in the Tables tab of the *Database window*, then choose the Design button.

2. Click the *Properties* button on the toolbar and click in the Validation Rule box and enter an *expression*.
3. If you want an error message to appear if this rule is violated, type the message in the Validation *Text box*; click the Close (X) button to close the Property sheet.

4. Click the Save button on the toolbar to save your new database rule.

Validate Data: Required Field

Some information in a *table* is so important that the *record* would be useless without the information. This is often the case with name *fields*. You might want to force yourself or another user to enter information in these fields before they can leave the record.

Steps

1. Click a table name in the Tables tab of the *Database window*, and then choose the Design button.
2. Go to the field you want to require.
3. In the field *property* area of the Table Design window, set the Required property to Yes.
4. Click the Close (X) button on the Table Design window and choose Yes to save the changes to the table design.

If you are missing data in this field after you change the Required property to Yes, Access will warn you that the existing data violates the rules you just made. After you save the table, go back and add the missing data.

File Management

Each *table*, *query*, *form*, and *report* is a *database* object that you can copy, rename, create a description of, and set properties for. You can create database objects by importing them from another Access database. You can create tables in Access by importing them from or linking them to another *data source*. You can import as well as export files.

To keep your database in good shape, you need to work with several procedures. Backing up your data is the most important of these operations; however, compacting the database and repairing will be necessary at times. If you are on a network with multiple users, you may want to explore *replication* to decrease network traffic while still updating your databases. With multiple users, you also need to consider security—that is, who should and who should not have access to the database file and the objects inside.

Back Up Data

It is very important to back up your database in order to protect your data. Access automatically saves results to disk, and will overwrite data based on queries and other actions you perform. Often, your backup is the only protection you have from data loss.

You can also copy the database file using any of the following methods: Windows NT Explorer, Microsoft Backup, MS-DOS COPY command, or any other backup software that works with Windows 95.

TIP Compact the database before you back it up to save disk space. (See "Database: Compact.")

Steps

1. From the *Database window*, click the Open button on the toolbar.
2. Navigate to your file's location by using the Look In drop-down *text box* and file list.
3. Right-click the file name and choose Copy.
4. Right-click the file *list box* in the white area (in other words, do not click a file or folder) and choose Paste.

The backup file name is *Copy of <Your Database Name>*.

NOTE If you use the security features of Access, you should also back up the *workgroup* information file occasionally. In Access 1 and 2, the default name for the file is SYSTEM.MDA. In Access 95 and 97, the default name is SYSTEM.MDW.

Access does not create a new *record* until you actually enter data into the first *field* of a new record.

Database Object: Copy

Not only can you back up the entire file, you can also back up individual objects such as a *form* or *report* before you make a major change to the *object*. For example, if you experiment with *action queries*, a good idea would be to copy the underlying *table*.

NOTE When you copy a table with copy and paste, Access asks you if you want to copy just the structure (design), the structure and data, or append the data to an existing table. Copying the structure enables you to modify the table for another use. Copying the structure and data creates a backup copy of the table. Append is an alternative to an Append *Query*. (See "Action Query: Append Query" in the Queries and Filters part of this book.)

Steps

1. Close the *object* you want to copy and any related *form*, *query*, or *report* based on that object.
2. Press F11 to go to the *Database window*.
3. Select the object name from the Database window and click the Copy button on the toolbar.
4. Click the Paste button on the toolbar. In the Paste As *dialog box*, give the object a name.

TIP When you use this copy feature for backup purposes, keep your naming consistent. For example, name the object "Backup of <original name>" or "ZZZ of <original name>." This will put all backups in one spot. When you're done with the backups, delete them (see "Database Object: Delete") and Compact the database (see "Database: Compact").

Database Object: Delete

If you no longer need an *object* (for example, if you have created a backup), it is a good idea to delete the object from the *Database window* to save space and then compact to speed up the database. (See "Database: Compact.")

CAUTION Deleting an object is an irreversible operation. Make sure you truly want to delete the object. Deleting the object will affect any other object that is based on the deleted object. For example, when you delete a *table*, any related table, query, report, or form will not work.

Steps

1. Press F11 to go to the Database window.
2. Select the object name from the Database window and press the Delete key on the keyboard.
3. At the warning prompt, confirm that you want to delete the object.

Database Object: Description

In addition to long names of up to 64 characters for the objects, you can also have descriptions for each *object* in the *Database window.* To see the descriptions, click the Details button on the Database toolbar.

Steps

1. Press F11 to go to the Database window.
2. Right-click the object name from the Database window and choose Properties.
3. Enter text in the Description box; choose OK.

Database Object: Properties

In addition to the description, each *object* has two other properties: Hidden and Replicable. You can hide an object if you want it out of the way or you don't want the user to know about the object. With the Replicable *property*, you choose whether or not you want this object replicated (copied) when you replicate your *database.* (See "Replication: Using Briefcase.")

Steps

1. Press F11 to go to the *Database window.*
2. Right-click the object name from the Database window and choose Properties.
3. Check or uncheck the Hidden or Replicable *check boxes*; choose OK.

To unhide an object you must first be able to see it. Here is an inherent contradiction. However, you can show all hidden objects by choosing Tools, Options, clicking the View tab, and checking the Hidden Object box.

Database Object: Rename

When the current name of the *object* needs to change you can rename the object. After you import a table (see the Import Data tasks in this part), the table name is the same as the old file name. You might want to change the object name in this circumstance and when you copy an object. (See "Database Object: Copy.")

CAUTION If you rename a *table* or *query* that is used in a *form* or *report*, the form or report will no longer work. You can change the Data Source property to re-establish the connection to the table or query (see "Forms and Reports: Data Source" in the Forms and Reports part of this book).

Steps

1. Press F11 to go to the *Database window*.
2. Right-click the object name from the Database window and choose Rename.
3. Enter the new name in the box surrounding the name.

Database Properties

Just as each individual *object* has *properties*, so too does the entire database. The database properties include summary information such as author name, subject, comments, and keywords. If you are using hyperlinks (see "Hyperlinks: Create" in the Table and Database Design part of this book), the *Hyperlink* base enables you to specify the initial folder for all relative links. The Contents tab of the Database Properties *dialog box* provides the names of all the database objects (just like the *Database window*). If you want, you can store additional information about your database through the Custom tab.

Steps

1. Choose File, Database Properties.
2. Click the Summary or Custom tabs and enter any information you want.
3. Click the General, Statistics, or Contents tabs to see more information about your database; choose OK when finished.

NOTE The General tab of the Database Properties dialog box shows file attributes (such as Read-Only, Hidden, or Archive) but the *check boxes* are grayed so you can't make a change. If you want to change these properties, close the database, choose the Open button on the toolbar. Right-click the file name and choose Properties.

Database: Compact

Access stores all of its *objects* and data in a single file. As you delete the information in *tables* and the tables themselves, not all of the space is reclaimed efficiently. Therefore, every so often you should compact your *database* to shrink its size, remove free space, and improve performance. During compacting, Access checks data and validates database structure.

To compact the current database, choose Tools, Database Utilities, Compact Database.

Steps

1. Close your current database and have any connected users close their session to the database you intend to compact.
2. Choose Tools, Database Utilities, Compact Database.
3. Select the name of the database you want to compact in the Database To Compact From *dialog box*; then choose Compact.
4. Enter the name, drive, and folder for the compacted database in the Compact Database Into dialog box; then choose Save.

NOTE If you delete records at the end of a *table* with an *AutoNumber field*, Access normally skips these numbers. When you compact a database, Access resets the AutoNumber field so that the next *record* added is one more than the largest existing AutoNumber. Because compacting improves the efficiency of your database, you might want to programmatically build compacting into your application. The *VBA* statement for compacting is `DBEngine.CompactDatabase` *`olddatabase, newdatabase`*.

Database: Convert

When you try to open a *database* created in a prior version of Access, you will be prompted on whether you want to convert the database or Open the database. When you open the database you can use a prior version to enter data, but you cannot change the design or create a new *object*.

Steps

1. Close any open database.

2. Click the Open Database button on the toolbar. Choose the location and name of the older version file and choose Open.
3. In the Convert/Open Database *dialog box*, choose Convert Database.
4. In the Convert Database Into dialog box, type the name of the file in the File Name *text box*; choose Save.

The database opens and is converted into your new version of Access.

NOTE If you open the old version database (rather than convert it), Access might not bring up the Convert dialog box again. In this case, close any database and choose Tools, Database Utilities, Convert Database; then, choose the database and give it a new name.

Database: Default Folder Set

If you store most of your database files in one folder, you can have Access automatically go to that folder when you first start Access and choose to open a database.

Steps

1. Choose Tools, Options, and click the General tab.
2. In the Default Database Folder text box, type the name of the folder where you store your databases; choose OK.

Database: Repair Closed Database

You can repair a *database* that isn't currently in view. The process is only slightly different than repairing an open database. (See "Database: Repair Open Database.") You might try to open a database and Access informs you that the database needs to be repaired before it is opened. Your database might be corrupted because the power went off while the database was open.

Steps

1. Close your current database.
2. Choose Tools, Database Utilities, Repair Database.
3. Select the database in the Repair Database *dialog box*.
4. Choose the Repair button.

Access will perform data *validation* and other procedures, and repair the database, if possible.

> **CAUTION** Access isn't always capable of repairing badly damaged database files. You should always maintain an active system for backing up your database so that you can revert to your last backup should your current file be unusable.

Database: Repair Open Database

When you open, compact, encrypt, or decrypt a database that is damaged, Access will inform you of the damage and post a *dialog box* that offers to repair it. In instances when you find erratic behavior (maybe tables don't sort correctly or a report takes an unusually long time to run), you might want to initiate the procedure of repairing a database manually before you get an error message.

Steps

1. Click the Open button and check the Exclusive box, select the database file name and choose Open.
2. Select Tools, Database Utilities, Repair Database.

NOTE The VBA statement for repairing a database is `DBEngine.RepairDatabase` *`databasename`*. If you are designing an application for other users, you may want to include a command button for repairs or do automatic repairs somewhere in your code.

Excel: Convert Access Object to Excel Worksheet

You can convert Access *tables*, *queries*, *forms*, and *reports* to Excel worksheets by using the Office Links feature. Excel's strength in this instance is its capability to analyze the data.

Steps

1. Select the *object* (to be converted) in the *Database window*.

2. On the Office Links button, choose Analyze It with MS Excel.

This process Opens Excel, converts the selected object, and saves the name of the object with an XLS extension.

If the object was a *form*, Excel creates one row for each *record* with the *field* names as the first row. Excel ignores any information on a *subform*. If the object was a grouped *report*, the Excel worksheet is in outline format, enabling you to show or hide detail.

Export and Import: Installing Additional Drivers Through Setup

If the file format does not appear on your Files As Type when you are exporting or importing data (see "Export Data: Access to Another File Type"), you might need to install additional data drivers. Access has two sources for these drivers (some of which overlap): the setup program and the ValuPack folder. (See "Export and Import: Installing Additional Drivers Through ValuPack.")

Steps

1. First, close any open applications and insert the Office or Access CD-ROM.
2. On the Windows Desktop, double-click My Computer and double-click the CD-ROM drive. Double-click the Setup icon.
3. On the setup *dialog box*, choose Add/Remove, select the Data Access choice in the Options list, and click the Change *option button*. Choose Database Drivers in the Options list and click the Change Option button.
4. Pick from the list of Options and then choose the OK, Continue, and Yes buttons until you finish the setup.

Export and Import: Installing Additional Drivers Through ValuPack

If you cannot get drivers from the setup program (see "Export and Import: Installing Additional Drivers Through Setup") you can also look at the ValuPack. This is especially necessary for Lotus 1-2-3 and Paradox files.

Steps

1. First, close any open applications and insert the Office or Access CD-ROM.
2. On the Windows Desktop, double-click My Computer and double-click the CD-ROM drive. Double-click the ValuPack folder and then the Dataacc folder.
3. Inside the Dataacc folder is the Dataacc program. Double-click the program icon and choose Yes to install the Microsoft Data Access Pack.
4. After the Data Access Pack is installed, click the Add/ Remove button, choose Data Access Drivers and the Change option button.
5. Pick from the list of Options and then choose the OK, Continue, and Yes buttons until you finish the setup.

Export Data: Access to Access

If you need to export any objects from one Access database to another Access database, you can use the File Save As/Export menu choice. Another option is to import from an Access database. (See "Import Data: Access.")

Steps

1. Click the *object* you want to export in any tab of the *Database window*.
2. Choose File, Save As/Export.
3. Click the To an External File or Database *option button*; then choose OK.
4. Select the Access database you want to export to in the file *dialog box*; then choose Export.
5. If you chose a *table* in Step 1, indicate in the Export dialog box whether you want to export just the table Definition Only, or the Definition and Data by selecting the appropriate option button; then choose OK.

Access copies the object (or table definition) to the database you indicated.

TIP Exporting tables in this manner works for all versions of Access. If you are exporting to Access 95 or 97, you can use the same procedure to copy queries and macros from one Access database to another.

Export Data: Access to Another File Type

Access can export to different *database file* types, or to other data file formats. Single records, multiple records, tables, queries, forms, and reports can all be exported depending on the file type.

Access creates a file in the format you specify. If a file doesn't support long table names, as is the case for FoxPro 2.5 for example, Access truncates the *field* names appropriately in the conversion. In some cases, you may need to install the file driver for the external program. (See "Export and Import: Installing Additional Drivers Through Setup" and "Export and Import: Installing Additional Drivers Through ValuPack.")

Steps

1. Click the table or *query* you want to export in the *Database window*.
2. Choose File, Save As/Export.
3. Choose the To an External File or Database *option button*; choose OK.
4. Select the location of the file in the Save In *list box*. In the Save As Type list box, select the format you want to save the table or query in.
5. Enter a name in the File Name *text box*, then choose Export.

When you export a *table* or query, Access offers you the following file formats as types: Access files; text files (.TXT) in either delimited or fixed width format; Microsoft Excel 3, 4, 5-7, 97; *HTML* files; dBASE III, IV and V; Microsoft FoxPro 2.*x* and 3.0; Microsoft Word Merge; Rich Text Format (.RTF); Microsoft IIS 1 and 2 O (Internet Information Server); Microsoft ActiveX Server; and ODBC Databases. When you purchase the Office 97 ValuPack, included are drivers for conversion to Paradox databases versions 3.*x*, 4.*x*, and 5.0; and Lotus 1-2-3 versions 2 and 3.

NOTE When you select text files as your export type, Access opens the Export Text Wizard, which enables you to set the format of your text to Windows (ANSI), DOS, OS/2 (PC-8); date, time, and number format; and which fields get exported. This wizard also lets you select whether you create a delimited or fixed width text file. (See "Export Data: Text Files.")

Export Data: Access Object to HTML

Access 97 ships with HTML templates that you can use to create Web pages of a particular style. They are stored in the

<path>\Program Files\Microsoft Office\Templates\Access folder by default.

Publishing dynamic *HTML* files to a Web server requires that you determine the format that your particular server requires. For Microsoft IIS, that format is IDC/HTX files; for ActiveX servers, that format is ASP files.

Steps

1. Choose File, Save As HTML. The Publish to the Web Wizard opens; choose the Next button.
2. Choose which objects (on the Tables, Queries, Forms, Reports, or All Objects tabs); choose the Next button.
3. If you have a default template that contains background patterns or other styles for the Web pages, enter it on the third step of the Publish to the Web Wizard; choose the Next button.
4. Choose whether you want to create a Static or Dynamic HTML file; choose the Next button. If you created a dynamic Web page, Access creates the HTML file and links it to the data source you specified. If you created a static Web page, you can copy to file to your intranet/ Internet site.
5. Specify the computer or *data source* used by the Web server, and a username or password if that data source requires it. If you created an ASP file, enter the server URL of the location of the ASP file.

   If you chose Static HTML, identify where you want to store the file.
6. On the last two pages of the Wizard, indicate if you want to create a home page for the objects and if you want to save the settings.

You can create view *forms* that display *records*; data entry forms that add, modify, or delete records; or switchboard forms that navigate to other Web pages. The forms appear similar to the way they look in your *database*.

NOTE When you create a form, you can only output it as an ActiveX Server (.ASP) file. When a form is exported to HTML, most *controls* become *ActiveX controls* and all Visual Basic *code* associated with the controls is ignored. All *data types* are output as unformatted text, and the Format and InputMask properties of the controls are also ignored.

Export Data: Text Files

Exporting to text files is common because most *database*, spreadsheet, and word processing programs will accept this format when another format is not available. There are actually two formats for text files: Fixed Width and Delimited. Fixed Width is the less common of the two. Each *field* in a *record* is a set width (first name goes from positions 1-8, last name is 9-15, and so forth). When you use this option, the Export Wizard enables you to manually change the width between columns. Delimited is the more common of the text file formats and is described in the following steps. Delimited means that there is some character (usually a comma) separating the fields. Text also is usually indicated by quotes.

To begin this procedure, first follow the steps in "Export Data: Access to Another File Type" in the previous task.

Steps

1. Choose Delimited on the Export Text Wizard.
2. Choose which delimiter (Tab, Semicolon, Space, Other) you want between fields, check if you want to Include Field Names on First Row, and define the Text Qualifier (the default is quotes).
3. The last step allows you to change the file name and *path*; choose Finish.

Export Data: Word

You can convert Access *tables*, *queries*, *forms*, and *reports* to Word documents by using the Office Links feature. You might want to use Word for its formatting capabilities and to add additional text describing the data. Access also enables you to create a Word *mail merge.* (See "Mail Merge to Word" in the Outputting part of this book.)

Steps

1. Select the *object* in the *Database window.*

2. On the Office Links button on the toolbar, choose Publish It with MS Word.

This process Opens Word, converts the object, and saves the name of object with a RTF (rich text format) extension.

If the object is a table, query, or form, Word creates a table. Word ignores any information on a *subform.* If the object is a report, Word creates tabbed entries.

Import Data: 1st Steps

When you import data, you store the data in an Access *table.* When you import a text file or spreadsheet, you can append the data directly to a table. When you import from a *database* table the data goes into a new table. Then you can use an Append *query* to add the data to another table in your database. (See "Action Query: Append Query" in the Queries and Filters part of this book.)

You begin importing the same way, regardless of the *data type.* If the data type is not in your Files of Type list, you may need to install a driver. (See "Export and Import: Installing Additional Drivers Through Setup" and "Export and Import: Installing Additional Drivers Through ValuPack.")

Steps

1. Choose File, Get External Data, Import.
2. In the Import *dialog box,* choose folder from Look In drop-down box, and the data type from the Files of Type drop down.
3. Select file name from list and choose the Import command button.

If the file is a database type file from another application (dBASE, FoxPro, or Paradox), these steps are sufficient to import the database to create an Access table.

If the file is text, see "Import Data: Text." If the file is a spreadsheet (Excel or Lotus 1-2-3), see "Import Data: Spreadsheet." If the file is an Access database, see "Import Data: Access."

NOTE After you import the data, Access creates an *object* in the *Database window*. If the import procedure does not prompt you for a new *table* name, Access makes the table name the same name as the file. Access does not overwrite existing objects, but instead avoids duplicate names by adding numbers to each imported table sequentially (such as `Employee1`, `Employee2`). After importing, you might consider renaming the object. (See "Database Object: Rename.")

Import Data: Access

If you want to copy *objects* from another Access *database*, you can use this import procedure or export. (See "Export Data: Access to Access.") You first need to follow the steps in "Import Data:1st Steps" in the previous task and choose an Access database file.

Steps

1. The Import Objects *dialog box* has tabs for *tables, queries, forms, reports, macros,* and *modules.* Click the objects you wish to import from each tab.
2. If desired, choose the Options button and choose whether to import *relationships*, design features (Definition), the data in tables, and whether to import queries as queries or as tables; choose OK.

Access adds each of the objects into their appropriate places in the *Database window.*

Import Data: Checking Data Integrity

When you import data between different sources, you need to make sure the import has a reasonable chance of success. If the data in your original source is not all of the same type, Access will convert the *data type* to text or another data type. If the *field* names are invalid for Access, the import might not work at all.

In some cases, it might be easier to update the data in the original source. In other cases (especially when you no longer have the original program), you have to update the data in Access. It would be unusual if you didn't have to clean up some data. This is notably true when you are importing data into an existing Access *table* versus importing the data into a new table.

Before you even launch Access, check the following in your old program.

Steps

1. Check that field names conform to Access naming rules. For example, Informix allows periods in field names. You will have to remove the periods before importing to Access. Field names also cannot have an exclamation point (!), accent grave (‘), or square brackets ([]).
2. Make all data in a column the same data type. If you have comments in a number field (such as unknown), you need to take them out. Alternatively, import the field as text. If you need to make calculations on the mixed data type field, separate it into two fields. An update *query* might help.
3. If the import does not work, you will get an error message and an additional table, `<file name>Import Errors`. You can use this table to troubleshoot what you need to do to fix your original *data source*.
4. After you import and change data properties, you might receive error messages as well. You might need to use some select queries, or check for duplicates or unmatched records.

TIP For information concerning update queries from Step 2, see "Action Query: Update Query." For material supplementing Step 4, see "Queries: Create," "Queries: Duplicates: Remove," and "Unmatched Queries" in the Queries and Filters part of this book.

Import Data: HTML

When you import data, you create a copy of the data in a *table* in your Access database, but you leave the original *data source* intact. You can import an *HTML* table or list data source.

Imported data is copied into your *database* and can be altered. Imported data is an independent copy of the original data.

Steps

1. To import data, choose File, Get External Data, Import.
2. In the Import *dialog box*, select HTML Documents (*html;*.htm) from the Files of Type *list box*.
3. Double-click the file of interest using the Look In list box. The Import HTML Wizard runs.
4. On the first steps of the wizard, choose whether the first row has headings, whether you want to import into a new table or existing table, what the field names and data types should be, and whether you want Access to add a *primary* key. Choose Next after you make the choices on each screen.
5. On the last step of the wizard, type a name for the table and choose Finish.

NOTE The Advanced button on every step of the Import HTML Wizard enables you to see or change the choices you made for the preceding Step 4, as well as identify delimiters and symbols for dates, times, and numbers, and save this specification or retrieve another.

Import Data: Spreadsheet

When you import a spreadsheet (Excel or Lotus 1-2-3 data files), you have the option of importing a range or an entire sheet. You first must follow the steps earlier in this section ("Import Data: 1st Steps") to choose an Excel or Lotus 1-2-3 spreadsheet file. The spreadsheet must be in the standard database format, with each row being a separate *record* and each column a different *field*.

Steps

1. After choosing the spreadsheet file, Access brings up the Import Spreadsheet Wizard. Choose to list worksheets or ranges and then select the appropriate part of the file; choose Next.
2. Identify whether the first row of the *data source* contains *field* names; choose Next.
3. Choose to store data in a New *Table* or choose drop-down arrow for In an Existing Table; choose Next.
4. Click in each field, type the Field Name, the Data Type, whether the field should be Indexed, or Skip the field; choose Next.
5. Decide whether you want Access to add a *primary key* or if you want to choose your own; choose Next.
6. On the final step of the Import Spreadsheet Wizard, give the table a name and choose Finish.

Import Data: Text

Text data can be from many sources, including mainframes. If your data is not in one of the other sources, this might be the only option for you to move your data from your program to Access. Text is often identified with quotes and the fields separated by commas. This is called a delimited text file. Another option is for every field to be a set number of characters. This text file is called fixed width. You first need to follow the steps earlier in this section ("Import Data: 1st Steps") to choose a Text file.

Steps

1. After choosing the text file, Access brings up the Import Text Wizard. Choose whether your file is delimited or fixed width; choose Next.
2. Show where columns break, whether first row contains field names, choose characters that delimit fields, and identify text; choose Next.
3. Choose to store data in a New Table or choose drop-down arrow for In an Existing Table; choose Next.

4. Click in each field, type the Field Name, the Date Type, whether the field should be Indexed, or Skip the field; choose Next.
5. Decide whether you want Access to add a *primary key* or if you want to choose your own; choose Next.
6. On the final step of the Import Text Wizard, give the *table* a name and choose Finish.

NOTE The Advanced button on every step of the Import Text Wizard enables you to see or change the choices you made for the preceding Steps 2 and 4, as well as identify delimiters and symbols for dates, times, and numbers, and save this specification or retrieve another.

Import Data: Word

Although it is more rare than exporting to Word and importing from other file formats, there might be an occasion when you need to import text from Word into an Access *database*. The text needs to be in tab or *table* format. Each column is a *field* and each row is a *record*. You might need to design a table first in Access to accept Word's data. (See "Database: Create Blank" in the Table and Database Design part of this book.)

Steps

1. In Access, design the table structure first by creating fields in the same order as the columns in the Word document. Be sure the *data types* match the data in the Word columns.
2. Launch Word and open the file with the table or tabbed information. Select the data. Do not include any column headers in the selection.

3. Choose the Copy button on the toolbar.
4. Return to Access, go to the *Database window* and double-click the table you designed in Step 1.
5. Choose Edit, Paste Append to bring in the data from Word.

Links to External Data: 1st Steps

The process of linking to a *table* in Access is similar in to importing a table. (See "Import Data: 1st Steps.") With linking, the original table serves as the *data source* and only a reference to that table is contained in your Access database. When you link to a table, you can view and often also modify the data in that table. Access takes care of the details of opening the table and saving it in the appropriate data format. Linking can be contrasted with importing. When you import a new table, a copy of the table is created in the Microsoft Access format. The source table is left intact.

Steps

1. Choose File, Get External Data, Link Table.
2. In the Link *dialog box,* select the appropriate file format in the Files of Type drop-down list; then locate the file of interest using the Look In *list box.*
3. Select the table or spreadsheet, then choose the Link button.

What happens next depends on the data source you selected. See the following *sections* for notes on the various *data types.*

For Access, unencrypted Paradox tables, or spreadsheets, Access tables are imported directly. For an encrypted Paradox table, you will be prompted for a password. A linked Access table has an arrow with the icon in the Tables tab of the *Database window*. Paradox shows a Px icon.

Links to External Data: dBASE and FoxPro

When you link to dBASE and FoxPro, an *index* is requested. Normally, that index is the primary index, but it can also be candidate indexes for these two database programs. To start, first follow the steps in the earlier task, "Links to External Data: 1st Steps." After these initial procedures, complete the following steps.

Steps

1. After you select the dBase or FoxPro file, Access opens the Select Index Files *dialog box.* Choose the FoxPro index (.CDX or .IDX) file or dBASE (.MDX or .NDX) file. If no index exists, choose the Cancel button.
2. Enter the index that identifies each *record* in the Select Unique Record Identifier dialog box; choose OK.

When you link to a dBASE *table*, Access' *Database window* shows the dB symbol, FoxPro shows a fox icon.

Links to External Data: Excel

Before you link to an Excel file, the data must be in the appropriate format for a *database*. Columns will identify fields (with the *field* name usually at the top row) and rows indicate records. To start, first follow the steps in the earlier task, "Links to External Data: 1st Steps." After these initial procedures, complete the following steps.

Steps

1. After you select the Excel file, Access opens the Link Spreadsheet Wizard. Choose the worksheet or range that you want to link; choose Next.
2. Identify if the first row contains names for the fields; choose Next.
3. On the final step of the wizard, give the *table* a name and choose Finish.

The Tables tab of the *Database window* shows a linked Excel spreadsheet indicated by an Excel X icon.

Links to External Data: HTML File

When you link data, you store a reference to that data *object* in its original location, and generally you can modify or update the data from within Access. HTML linked data is read-only. You cannot change the data from within Access.

Steps

1. To link the data, choose File, Get External Data, Link.
2. In the Link *dialog box*, select *HTML* Documents (*html;*.htm) from the Files of Type *list box.*
3. Double-click the file of interest using the Look In list box. The Link HTML Wizard runs.
4. Choose whether the first row of the HTML file contains headers; choose Next.
5. If desired, click each column and type new *field* names in the Field Name text box, change Data Type in with the drop-down list, or choose if you want to Skip the column and not import it.
6. On the last step of the wizard, give the table name and choose Finish; choose Next.

Access imports or links to each *table* or list in an HTML file as if it were an individual table. You will need to repeat this procedure if your HTML file contains two or more tables or lists in it.

NOTE The Advanced button on every step of the Link HTML Wizard enables you to see or change the choices you made for the preceding Step 5, as well as identify delimiters and symbols for dates, times, and numbers, and save this specification or retrieve another.

Links to External Data: Text

Linking to a text file involves the same steps as importing to a text file. First, follow the steps in the earlier task, "Links to External Data: 1st Steps." After these initial procedures, complete the following steps. You might need to use this procedure rather than import the data if you have other programs that use this text file.

Steps

1. After choosing the text file, Access brings up the Link Text Wizard. Choose whether your file is delimited or fixed width; choose Next.

2. Show where columns break, whether first row contains field names, choose characters that delimit fields, and identify text; choose Next.
3. Click in each *field*, type the Field Name, the Date Type, whether the field should be Indexed, or Skip the field; choose Next.
4. On the final step of the Link Text Wizard, give the *table* a name and choose Finish.

The Tables tab of the *Database window* shows a linked text file indicated by a small notebook icon.

For details on the Import Text Wizard, see also "Import Data: Text."

NOTE The Advanced button on every step of the Link Text Wizard enables you to see or change the choices you made for the preceding Steps 2-3, as well as identify delimiters and symbols for dates, times, and numbers, and save this specification or retrieve another.

Links to External Data: Removing

If you no longer need to view the data from a linked file, you can delete the link. Deleting the link does not delete the data—it only deletes the access to the file.

Steps

1. Select the *linked table* in the *Database window.*
2. Press the Delete key on your keyboard.
3. When prompted, choose Yes to confirm removing the link.

Links to External Data: Updating

If the source files for the links move, you will not be able to view or edit the information in the files unless you update the location for the links.

Steps

1. Choose Tools, Add-Ins, Linked Table Manager.
2. In the Linked Table Manager *dialog box*, choose which files you want to update. Click the Select All button to choose all files.
3. For each file you select in Step 2, Access will prompt you for a location. Choose the folder and double-click the file name. When finished, choose OK.

NOTE If you want Access to ask you for the file locations each time you open the *database*, check Always Prompt for a New Location on the Linked Table Manager dialog box.

MDE File: Removing Access to Programming

If you distribute *database* applications to other users, you might want to remove some options to keep users from modifying your work. An MDE file removes the capability to design or edit *forms*, *reports*, and *modules* (*VBA* programming). The database also runs quicker because it is compiled and compacted during the process of making the MDE file.

CAUTION Retain your original database file. This is where you will make design changes. The design of MDE files cannot be modified (and you will have to re-create and redistribute your MDE file when you make a change).

Steps

1. Choose Tools, Database Utilities, Make MDE File.
2. In the Save MDE As File *dialog box*, choose a location and name for the MDE file; choose Save.

Access temporarily closes your database file and then reopens the original file. To open the MDE file, choose the Open database button on the toolbar and under Files of Type, choose MDE files (*.mde). Double-click the MDE file name in the file list.

Replication: Create Replica

There are a number of scenarios in which you might want to create a replica of your database. If you work on a laptop, you would want a copy of your company's database. If you create and use your replica, the changes you make on your laptop are replicated into the main database when you synchronize the replica. (See "Replication: Synchronize.") You might also want to use replication for distributing updates of your software development or for backing up the database.

When you make a replica, you will have two files: the Design *Master* and the Replica. You can change the design of the Design Master but not of the Replica. You can change data in either of the files.

Steps

1. Choose Tools, Replication, Create Replica.
2. Access asks if you want to close the database to create the replica. Choose Yes.
3. Access asks if you want to make a copy of the database. Because something may go wrong during the process, choose Yes.
4. In the Location of New Replica *dialog box*, choose the folder and file name for your replica; choose OK.

When finished, the Design Master opens. When you open up either the Design Master file or a replica, Access indicates Design Master or Replica in the Database window title bar.

Replication: Recover Design Master

One of the benefits of using the *replication* feature is that if your Design Master is damaged you can use one of the replicas as backup and upgrade it to the Design Master.

> **CAUTION** If you made design changes to your Design Master since the last time you synchronized, these design changes will not be

in the replica. For this reason, do not recover the Design Master until you have attempted to repair it. (See "Database: Repair Closed Database.")

Steps

1. Open a Replica database.
2. Choose Tools, Replication, Recover Design Master.

Replication: Resolve Conflicts

To do this task you must first synchronize the Design *Master* and Replica. (See "Replication: Synchronize.") If you made a change to the same *record* in the Design Master and a Replica, there will be a conflict. Which change do you want to keep?

You need to resolve conflicts from the replica. You can resolve conflicts directly from the menu as listed here or you might be finishing another procedure. If you are at the end of synchronizing replication and Access is prompting you to resolve conflicts, you will be at Step 3. When you open the replica, you might also be prompted to resolve conflicts at Step 3.

Steps

1. If necessary, open the Replica *database*.
2. Choose Tools, Replication, Resolve Conflicts.
3. If there are any conflicts, Access opens the Resolve Replication Conflicts *dialog box*. Each *table* with a conflict is listed in this box. Click a table and then the Resolve Conflicts button.
4. The dialog box opens with two columns. The first column shows the database you have on-screen. The second shows the conflict with the Replica or Design Master. To keep the data from the open database, choose Keep Existing Record. To use data from the other database, choose Overwrite with Conflict Record.
5. When you have resolved the conflicts, choose Close. You should resolve conflicts in all tables, but you can close this dialog box and repeat this task at a later time.

NOTE It is possible that changes were made to different *fields* in the same *record* and that you want information from both *databases*. In Step 4, you can Copy (Ctrl+C) and Paste (Ctrl+V) items back and forth between the records. You can also type in the record you want to keep.

Replication: Synchronize

When you want to check for conflicts with the Design Master and Replica, you first need to synchronize the two database files. You must first have created a Replica (see "Replication: Create Replica") before proceeding with these next steps.

Steps

1. Choose Tools, Replication, Synchronize Now.
2. The name of the Design Master or Replica should appear in the Synchronize Database *dialog box*. If you have more than one replica, use the drop-down box to choose another; choose OK.
3. Access asks if you want to close and reopen the database to see the changes; choose Yes.
4. If you have any conflicts between the two databases, Access will let you know.

If you are in the Replica, you can choose to resolve the conflicts now or later. (See also "Replication: Resolving Conflicts.")

Replication: Using Briefcase

With the Briefcase Replicator, you can reproduce an Access database and transfer that file to or from another computer. The database is converted to a Design Master, and a *replica* is created. This method is used to work with a replica database on a laptop. When you connect the laptop with the replica to a network or computer with the original copy, you can synchronize the changes made in both copies so that both databases are updated.

Drag the database into the Briefcase file on your desktop, a Design *Master* and the replica are created. On a *server*, the Briefcase may contain replicas for each use in the office. You cannot distinguish between the Replica or the Design Master by looking at the file name. However, when you open the file, the title bar of the Database window will include Design Master or Replica.

Steps

1. Double-click the Briefcase icon on your desktop.
2. Click the replica icon of the database.
3. Choose Briefcase, Update Selection.
4. Choose the Update button to begin synchronization.

Save File

Unlike Word, Excel, and other programs, you do not have to constantly save your file to avoid losing changes. When you move off a *record* (in a datasheet or *form*), any changes to the data are automatically saved. You can save before you move off an edited record, but this is unnecessary because even the process of closing the *table*, *query*, or form will automatically save changes to the record. However, if you are designing any *object* (rather than inputting data), you will need to save your file for the changes to be accepted. The design of any object (table, query, form, report) needs to be saved if you want to see the changes again.

Steps

1. To save any changes, click the save button on the toolbar.

If the save button is dimmed, there is nothing to save.

Security: Create Secure Workgroup

User-level security limits particular objects in a *database* that a user or group of users can read or write to. Here, a user account is created and a username and password is associated with it. Groups of users can be given specific privileges, and users can be associated with accounts. This information is stored in a *workgroup* information file.

The workgroup information file that comes with Access (SYSTEM.MDW) is not secure because every copy of Access has this file. Before you implement security, you need to create and join a new workgroup.

Steps

1. Exit Access. Find and double-click the file WRKGADM.EXE. In Windows 95, it is in the Windows\System folder. In Windows NT, it is in WinNT\System32 folder.
2. In the Workgroup Administrator dialog box, choose Create. Type your name and organization and any combination of up to 20 characters in the Workgroup ID *text box*; choose OK.
3. In the Workgroup Information File dialog box, change the name of the file. Choose Exit when done.

> **CAUTION** Write down the name, organization, and Workgroup ID, and keep this information in a secure location–you will need it if your file is damaged and has to be re-created.

> **CAUTION** Backup your workgroup information file when changes are made. If the file is damaged you won't be able to open your databases.

Security: Database Encryption/Decryption

When you encrypt a *database*, you scramble its data and definitions, making the file unreadable to anyone trying to decipher the data from another program. You use *encryption* in conjunction with user-level security. (See "Security: User Level.")

Encryption also compacts the database file. When you decrypt a database, a reverse algorithm unscrambles the database and makes it available for use. In order to encrypt a database, you must have exclusive or single-user use of the database file. For exclusive use, check the Exclusive box on the Open dialog box when you open the file. (See "Database: Open" in the Database Essentials part of this book.)

Steps

1. Launch Access, but don't open a database in it. Make sure no other users have the database open.
2. Choose Tools, Security, Encrypt/Decrypt Database.
3. Select the database you want to decrypt.
4. Or, select the database you want to encrypt and enter a name and location for that database.

   When you supply the same name and location for the database you are encrypting, Access replaces the original database with the encrypted version.
5. Choose OK.

NOTE When user-level security has been assigned in a database, you must have a Modify Design permission (see Tools, Security, User and Group Permissions) for any and all tables in a database in order to encrypt or decrypt the database successfully.

Security: Database Password

You can secure a *database* by creating a password that allows the user full access to the database file. When password access is on, a user supplies a password to open the file. The password is encrypted and secure.

CAUTION If you set a password for opening a database, you must remember the password. If you forget that password, you will lose access to your file.

Steps

1. Close the database and end any other user sessions in a multiuser Access database.
2. Create a backup copy of the database. Store the file in a secure location.
3. Choose File, Open Database (Ctrl+O), or click the Open button on the toolbar; click the Exclusive *check box*; then choose the Open button.
4. Choose Tools, Security, Set Database Password.
5. Enter your password in the Password *text box*, then enter it again in the Verify text box. Choose the OK button.

   If the two passwords match, Access enters the password for overall database file access and requires it the next time you open the file.

> **CAUTION** If you set a password for opening a database, you will not be able to synchronize databases using *replication*. (See "Replication: Create Replica.")

You can also create user-level security that limits the particular objects in a database that a user or *group* of users can read or write to. (See also "Security: Limit User Input.")

Security: Limit User Input

Access provides you with a number of different options for securing a database. To limit user input, you must create and define user-level security in your *database*. This provides password access based on a username through a challenge/response mechanism.

You can use the User-Level Security Wizard to define which features and database objects can be used by which users. For information, choose the Help button of the User-Level Security dialog box. After that point, only users with an Administrative permission level can perform the most sensitive functions such as database *replication*, password creation, and so on.

Information about user *group permissions*, accounts, and access privileges are stored in the *workgroup* information file (see "Security: Create Secure Workgroup"), and are opened when you log on. You must have Administration privileges to accomplish this procedure.

Steps

1. Open the database, then choose Tools, Security, User and Group Permissions.
2. Click users or groups on the User/Group Name list on the Permission tab to select to whom you want to apply an access privilege or restriction.
3. Click the type of *object* in the Object Type drop-down *list box*, then click the name of the specific object in the Object Name box.
4. In the Permissions section, click on or off the permissions you desire; then choose Apply. Depending on the object type, the permissions include the following: Open/Run, Read Design, Modify Design, Administer, Read Data, Update Data, Insert Data, Delete Data.
5. When you are done adding or removing permissions, choose OK.

Security: User-Level

To help you set user-level security for your database, Access offers you the User-Level Security Wizard. This wizard will help you start defining accounts and privileges. You must first join a secure workgroup or create a new workgroup information file before you complete this step. (See "Security: Create Secure Workgroup.")

Steps

1. Choose Tools, Security, User and Group Accounts.
2. Select the Admin user account on the Users tab. Then click the Change Logon Password tab.
3. Click the New Password *text box*, enter a password, then enter that same password in the Verify text box. Choose OK.

4. Select the User-Level Security Wizard from the Security submenu of the Tools menu.

   The wizard creates a new database, exports the objects from your current database to it, revokes all *permissions* for access to the objects, and then encrypts the new database file. The Admin group has access, but the Users group has no access to the database.

When you finish running the User-Level Security Wizard, you will want to add new users and groups and then modify permissions for each of the objects in the database. (See "Security: Limiting User Input.")

Queries and Filters

Queries and filters are primary ways to find and organize your data. A *filter* is saved with a *table* and can't be reused for other objects unless you save it as a *query*. Queries can be used to answer questions themselves, but can also be used as the foundation for forms and reports.

Creating queries and filters involves tasks such as sorting data, choosing data (setting *criteria*), and selecting *tables* and *fields*. Queries are more versatile than filters and you can use them to mass update, delete, and add records to a table. You can also do substantial calculations with queries.

NOTE For more on the calculation capabilities of queries see the Calculations part of this book.

Most of the following procedures start in Query *Design View*. You can enter this view by selecting an existing query on the *Database window* and choosing the Design button. You can also get to the design view by selecting New on the Queries tab of the Database window and choosing Design View.

Action Query: Append Query

An append query provides a method for adding records to one or more tables. This is useful when you want to transfer records from one table, or set of related tables, to another. You can also use the append query to write data to the same fields in matching records between two tables. For notes about *action queries*, see "Action Query: Create" first.

Steps

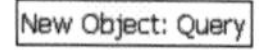

1. In the *Database window*, highlight the table or query for the basis of the append query and choose Query from the New Object button on the toolbar. The New Query *dialog box* is displayed. Click OK to accept the default.

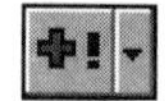

2. Click the Query Type button on the toolbar and select the Append Query option. Enter the name of the target table in the Table Name box. Click either Current Database or Another Database to specify the target table; then choose OK.
3. Drag the fields from the *Field* List that you want to append to the Query Design *grid*, along with any fields you will use for selection criteria.
4. Enter the criteria for creating the result set in the Query Design grid.

5. Click the View button on the toolbar to preview the records to append.

6. Click the Run button to append the records to the table(s) you specified.

NOTE If you want the target table to automatically add new *AutoNumber* values, do not drag the AutoNumber field onto the Query Design grid. To copy the AutoNumber values from the source table, drag the AutoNumber field onto the Query Design grid. If the target table already has AutoNumbers that match the source table, the Append Query will not append those records when you Append to the AutoNumber field.

Also, when all fields have the same name in both tables, drag only the asterisk for the table to the Query Design grid.

Action Query: Create

An *action query* collects records that meet your search *criteria*, and changes the data contained in those records in a single step. Access allows four different action queries: delete, update, append, and make-table query. A delete query removes the groups of records returned from your query from your table. An update query alters the information contained in your result set and writes the changes back to your table. An append query adds the records from your result set to your table. Finally, a make-table query creates an entirely new table from your result set.

> **CAUTION** Because action queries modify your data, it is a good idea to first create a select *query* with the *fields* and *criteria* you want. View the results of the query to make sure you have the correct records. Then, turn the select query into an action query by selecting one of the options on the Query Type button on the toolbar.

First follow the steps to create a select query. (See "Query: Create with Design View" or "Query: Create with Wizard.")

Steps

1. In your query's *Design View*, enter criteria, add a sort order, and create any calculated fields. Click the *Datasheet View* button to make sure your criteria are OK.

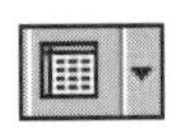

2. Return to the design view by clicking the Design View button.

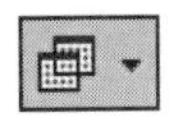

3. Turn the query into an action query by clicking the drop-down arrow on the Query Type button and choosing one of the four action query types (Make-Table, Update, Append, Delete).

4. If prompted, identify the target table. Click the Run button to perform the action query.

5. Click the Save button on the toolbar. Enter a name in the Save *dialog box*, then choose OK.

The action query will appear on the Queries tab of the *Database window*. To indicate that it will run when opened, the icon next to the name includes an exclamation point.

> **CAUTION** Be careful when you double-click or choose the Open button for an action query. The query runs every time. You might want to delete action queries when you no longer need them to avoid accidentally updating your data. You can also hide the query by choosing the hidden *object property*. (See "Database Object: Properties" in the File Management part of this book.)

Action Query: Delete Query

The *delete query* enables you to remove a set of records from the *table* you specify. If you have already created a *relationship* that enforces referential integrity with *cascade deletes*, you will only need to delete records from parent table. (See "Relationships between Tables" in the Table and Database Design part of this book.) The records from the related *child* table will delete automatically.

Steps

New Object: Query

1. In the *Database window*, highlight the table or query for the basis of the delete query and choose Query from the New *Object* button on the toolbar. Click OK.

2. Drag any fields you need to identify records into the design *grid*. Then click the Query Type button on the toolbar and select the Delete Query option.
3. Enter any criteria for deleting records, and they appear under `Where` in the Delete cell.

4. Click the View button on the toolbar to preview the records to be deleted.

5. Click the Run button to delete the records from the table.

After closing the *dialog box*, the records in your result set are removed from the table you specified.

Action Query: Make-Table

The make-table query enables you to create a table for export; it provides the basis for a *report*; it provides a method for making backups; and it gives a snapshot of your data at a point in time. The make-table query also enables you to improve the performance of your forms and reports by working from a set of records stored to disk that don't have to be retrieved from a large data set or from a network. You can also copy a table from the *Database window* and if necessary, delete or add any additional fields you want. (See "Database Object: Copy" in the File Management part of this book.)

Steps

1. In the Database window, highlight the *table* or *query* for the basis of the make-table query and choose Query from the New Object button on the toolbar. Click OK.

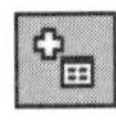

2. Drag any *fields* you need to identify records into the design *grid*. You can also add an additional table and any other fields from the second related table if you want to use fields from more than one table. Then click the Query Type button on the toolbar and select the Make-Table Query option.

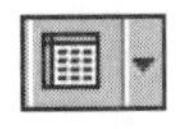

3. Enter a name in the Table Name *text box*, select either the Current Database or Another Database *option button*, then choose OK.

4. Enter any *criteria* for choosing *records* in the Criteria row. Click the View button on the toolbar to preview the records to be included.
5. Then Click the Run button to create the new table.

After dismissing the *dialog box* indicating that a new table will be created, Access writes your result set to disk as a table in the database you specified.

Action Query: Update Query

An update query can make *global* changes to selected records in a *table* or a set of related tables. This type of query is useful for replacing information quickly.

A common example for an update *query* would be where you would increase the price for an item. In the Update To cell under the price *field* in the Query Design *grid* you would type the *expression* **[Price]*1.02** (to increase the price by 2%). For more information on calculations, see "Calculated Fields: Queries Create" in the Calculations part of this book.

Steps

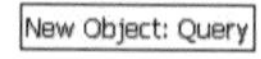

1. In the *Database window*, highlight the *table* or query for the basis of the update query and choose Query from the New *Object* button on the toolbar. Click OK.

2. In the Query *Design View*, click the down arrow next to the Query Type button on the toolbar, then select the Update Query option.
3. Drag the fields from the Field List to the Query Design grid that will be in the new table. Enter the criteria for your result set, and any sort you want.

4. In the Update To cell, enter the expression or value to be used as a replacement for the field(s) selected.

5. Click the View button to see a list of records that will be updated. Then click the Run button on the toolbar.

After closing the *dialog box*, Access replaces your old data with the new values in the result set you specified.

Criteria: Blanks, Nulls, and Empty

When you create select or action queries or use the Advanced Filter/Sort option to create a *filter* for a *table*, you often might want to see which records have no values. For example, you might want to find all addresses without zip codes so you can look them up before you do a mailing. You may also want to find which fields have *zero-length strings*.

When you use a *null field* in a calculation, the result of a calculation is null. You can use the NZ *function* to convert nulls to zeros. (See "Blanks, Empty, and Null: Work With" in the Calculations part of this book.)

NOTE For a field to be capable of accepting zero-length strings, that field *property* must be set to Yes. (See "Data: Blanks, Nulls, and Zero-Length Strings" in the Table and Database Design part of this book.)

Steps

1. In *Design View* of a *query*, click in the *criteria* row under the desired field.
2. To find all *records* with no entry, enter **Null**. Access will translate this to `Is Null`. If you want to find all records except blanks, type **Not Null** (which Access enters as `Is Not Null`).
3. To find records with zero-length strings, enter **""** (two quotes with no space).
4. In the Field cell of the design *grid*, if you are calculating values that have nulls in some of the fields, enclose each field name in the `NZ([`*`Fieldname`*`])` function.

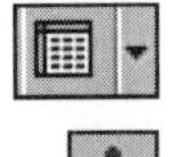

5. Choose the *Datasheet View* button to see the results of the query or choose the Run button to update records if the query is an action query.

TIP To display zeros for a numeric field that has nulls, type the following in the Field cell of the Query Design grid: **NZ([*Fieldname*])+0**.

NOTE When you sort ascending on a field with Nulls, the records with the Null fields display first.

Criteria: Date

When you are working with date *fields*, there are some *criteria* you might want to keep in mind. You can choose to show just today's date or a specific month, day, or year. Another option is to include a range of dates.

Steps

1. In *Design View* of a *query* or *filter*, click in the criteria row under the desired field.
2. If you want to enter a specific date, type the date. Regardless of the format for the date, you can enter the date in its simplest format for the criteria: For example, **1/1/98**. When you leave the criteria cell Access translates this to `#1/1/98#`.
3. If you want to find all records with today's date, type **Date( )**. If you want all those after today's date, type **>Date( )**. If you want all those up to and including today's date, type **<=Date( )**.
4. If you want all records between two days use the Between And *expression* as in the example: **Between 1/1/97 and 3/5/98**.
5. To find all records for a specific month, year or day, use the * (asterisk). **1/*/98** finds all records in January 1998. ***/*/92** finds all records in 1992.

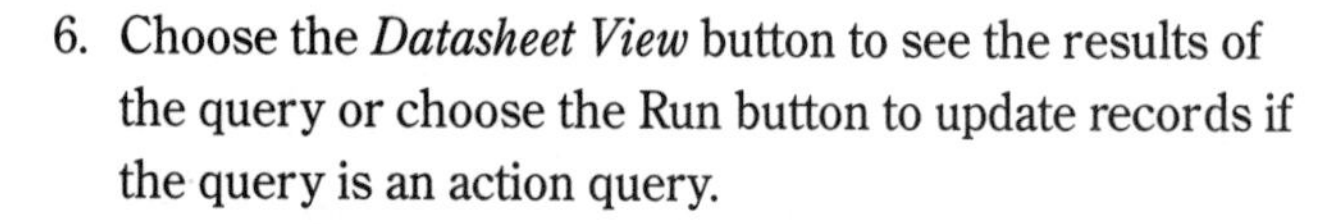

6. Choose the *Datasheet View* button to see the results of the query or choose the Run button to update records if the query is an action query.

For date *functions*, see also "Functions: Date" in the Calculations part of this book.

Criteria: Multiple

If you are searching for data that meets more than one criteria, you can use the *Query* Design *grid* or the keywords **AND** and **OR**.

To enter *criteria*, be sure you are in the Design View of a query or *filter*.

Steps

1. To set criteria for multiple fields where all criteria must be met (for example, **City is Denver** and **Address includes Broadway**), type the *expression* for the first *field*, move to

the second field in the same criteria row and type the second expression. Repeat for all necessary fields.

2. To set criteria for multiple fields where any criteria can be met, type the expression for the first field, move down to the next criteria row (labeled `Or`) and type the second expression under the second field. Move down again if there is a third criteria.
3. If you are looking for multiple possibilities in the same field, type in one criteria cell and type **OR** between each expression (for example: **CO or NE**). If you have many entries you can use the **IN** keyword (for example, **IN(CO, AL, NE, KS)**.
4. If one field must meet two criteria use the **AND** keyword (for example **>5 AND <10**).

5. Choose the Datasheet View button to see the results of the query or choose the Run button to update records if the query is an action query.

Criteria: Numeric

When you are looking for numeric data, there are some handy expressions for use with numeric *criteria*. To enter criteria, be sure you are in the criteria cell of the *Design View* of a *query* or a *filter*.

Steps

1. Type the number in the criteria cell to see just this value.
2. Type **<*Number* or <=*Number*** to see all numbers less than or less than or equal to the number.
3. Type **>*Number* or >=*Number*** to see all numbers greater than or greater than or equal to the number.
4. Type **Between *Number1* and *Number2*** to find all numbers between two numbers (including both numbers).
5. Type **>*Number1* and <*Number2*** to find all numbers between two numbers (not including both numbers).

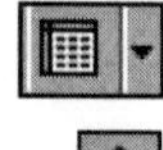

6. Choose the *Datasheet View* button to see the results of the query or choose the Run button to update records if the query is an action query.

Criteria: Specify

You can enter selection *criteria* into *filters* and into queries. Queries are more generally useful in that they can work with related tables of *records* and direct the output of the result set to several different places. Filters apply only to the current *table* or *query* and cannot be used elsewhere.

Steps

1. Move to the criteria row and enter the *expression* into the design *grid* of the Query or Filter.
2. If you cannot see the entire criteria, press Shift+F2 to expand the cell into a window. Choose OK when finished editing the criteria.

3. If you want to enter complicated criteria, click the Build button on the toolbar and use the Expression *builder*.

Access allows for a wide range of values and expressions, and the Query *Design View* is a powerful tool for composing queries and applying criteria for selection. For some of the criteria types, see the other Criteria *sections* in this part. (See also "Expression: Create with Builder" in the Calculations part of this book.) Access translates the query into *SQL* and applies it to the appropriate *data sources* (tables and grids) that the query operates on.

Criteria: Text

Most of your data will be text *data type*. There are some handy expressions for use with text criteria. To enter criteria you need to be in the criteria cell of the *Design View* of a query or a *filter*.

Steps

1. Enter in the complete text match you want. Access puts quotes around the *expression*.

2. Include the asterisk (*) wild-card character for any text you are not sure of. A single asterisk can take the place of any number of characters. You can also use multiple asterisks in one expression. **Jo*ns*n** will find Johnson, Johanson, Jonsen, and Johnsen. Access enters **Like "Jo*ns*n"** in the criteria cell.
3. Enter **Not** and then the text you don't want to match. **Not NY** will find all states except NY.
4. Use the question mark (**?**) as a wildcard character for one letter. For example, **C?** would find CO, CT, and CA.

5. Choose the *Datasheet View* button to see the results of the query or choose the Run button to update records if the query is an action query.

Criteria: Use Another Field

In some instances you want to use one *field* in a *criteria* for finding *records* based on another field. For example, you might want to find all records where the Promised Date is less than the Shipped Date and send the clients an apology.

Steps

1. In *Design View* of a *query* or *filter*, move to the criteria row of the field.
2. Type any operators and then the second field's name in square brackets. For example, **<[ShippedDate]**.

3. Choose the Datasheet View button to see the results of the query or choose the Run button to update records if the query is an action query.

Duplicates: Find

One of the most frustrating parts about managing data is trying to dispose of duplicates. Access can show which records have exact duplicates. You can then decide which *record* to delete. Before you create a *primary key* on a *table* with existing data, you also need to search for and remove duplicates.

Steps

1. On the Queries tab of the *Database window*, choose New and double-click Find Duplicates Query Wizard.
2. On the first step of the wizard, double-click the table or query.
3. Double-click the *field* (or combination of fields) that will identify duplicates; choose Next.
4. Double-click any additional fields you want to display in the query; choose Next.
5. Give your query a name and click the Finish button.

The query will list only duplicated records in the table. You can modify the fields or delete the unnecessary records. (See "Records: Delete" in the Database Essentials part of this book.)

TIP Access cannot show you which records have close matches. For example, if you have `491 Fox St` and `491 Fox Street`, Access will not show these as duplicates. You might want to develop standard rules for entering data (always spell out or use abbreviations, for example).

Duplicates: Remove

You can delete duplicates one at a time from the result of a Find Duplicates Query Wizard. (See "Duplicates: Find".) However, if you have many duplicates, you might want to use the following procedure. This procedure does not allow you to choose which *record* of the two duplicates you want to delete.

Steps

1. In the *Database window* select the *table* and click the Copy and Paste buttons on the toolbar. When prompted copy the structure only and give the new table a name.

2. Open the new table in Design View, hold down Ctrl, click the *field*(s) with duplicated information, and click the *Primary Key* button on the toolbar. Save and close the new table.

New Object: Query

3. Select the first table and choose Query from the New Object button. Include all fields from the table in the query *grid* by double-clicking the asterisk in the Field List.

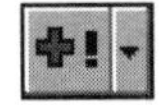

4. Choose *Append Query* from the Query Type button and enter your new table name.
5. Click the Run button to run the query and answer Yes to the prompts.

This query works because the primary key in a table cannot be duplicated. After you view your second table to make sure the information is correct, you can delete the first table and rename the second. (See "Database Object: Delete" and "Database Object: Rename" in the File Management part of this book.)

Filter Data: Advanced Filter

The most complex filters you can create enable you to both *filter* and sort *records* in a single operation for a single *table* or *query*. The Advanced Filter/Sort window is similar to the Query *Design View* in construction in that you work in a design *grid* where you specify the criteria used to filter your records and the sort order. The Advanced Filter/Sort feature can operate on tables or queries, but cannot provide related tables.

Steps

1. Open a table, query, or *form* in the *Datasheet View*, or a form in the *Form View*.
2. Choose *Record*, Filter, Advanced Filter/Sort.
3. Enter the *criteria* and sort you want in the design grid.

4. Click Apply Filter on the toolbar.

Filter Data: By Form

If you want to select a set of records in a datasheet or a *form*, the simplest way to do this is to set a *filter*. A filter is a single set of *criteria* that can be applied to your data set. When you apply another filter to a result set from a previous filter, you narrow your result set even further.

Access remembers your last filter in a session and lets you reapply it at any time. If you apply a filter to a *table* or *form*, Access remembers that filter until you apply a new one. Filters applied to *queries* are not entered into the query *grid*, but can be applied later separately. You can also sort filtered *records*. You might find that filters provide much of the find and query capability you need in your work.

Steps

1. Open a table, query, or form in the *Datasheet* or *Form View*.
2. Click the Filter By Form button on the toolbar to open a Filter By Form window.
3. Click the *field* you want to filter by and enter the selection criteria that records must match to be returned in a result set.
4. To enter a value to search for, select that value from the list in that field; or enter the value manually.
5. To enter a value of a *check box*, *option button*, or *toggle button*, click that button. Entering a value in two fields on the same line in the Look For tab (see the bottom of the window) requires both values to be matched in the result set.

6. To perform a filter based on alternative values, click the OR tab at the bottom of the window and enter additional criteria. Click the Apply Filter button on the toolbar to perform the selection.

NOTE Check boxes display three states: checked (on), not checked (off), and mixed state (grayed). Make sure you place a check mark into the condition you want. Also, you can select a field based on the conditions Is *Null* or Is Not Null.

You can reapply the filter by clicking the Apply Filter button at a later time. You can use the Remove Filter button to remove your current filter.

Filter Data: By Selection

You can *filter* the records shown in a *form*, *subform*, or datasheet by applying a Filter By Selection. When you click the toolbar button, all records that match your selected *field* display. This procedure is very simple to use, but more limited than Filter By Form. (See "Filter Data: By Form.")

Steps

1. Open a *table*, *query*, or form in the *Datasheet View*, or a form in the *Form View*.
2. Select the *record* that has the value you want to limit in a form or datasheet.
3. Click the insertion point in the *field* (this will cause the entire field's contents to be the *criteria* for the filter).

4. Click the Filter by Selection button on the toolbar.

NOTE As mentioned in the preceding Step 3 you can click in a field (with no text selected) to have Access use the entire field for the filter. You can also select part of a field starting with the first character to return records where the value in that field also starts with those characters. Another option is to select any value after the first character in a field to return all or part of a value in that field with the same characters.

Filter Data: Filter With Shortcut Menu

Access lets you enter a filter directly into a *field* on a field's shortcut menu as a filter request.

Steps

1. Open a *table*, *query*, or *form* in the *Datasheet View*, or a form in the *Form View*.

2. Right-click a field and enter a value or *expression* in the Filter For *text box*; then press Enter.

By successively filtering, you can narrow your result set. You can press Tab while still in the Filter For text box in Step 2 to apply the filter and add a new filter criteria as well.

Filter Data: Save as Query

After working with a *filter* you might want to use it again under different circumstances. You can save the filter as a *query*.

Steps

1. Create a filter from any of the methods mentioned in the filter tasks in this part of the book.
2. Go to the filter design window by choosing *Record*, Filter, Advanced Filter/Sort.
3. If desired, modify the filter *grid* and click the Save As Query button on the toolbar.
4. Enter the name of the query in the Save As Query *dialog box*.

If you want to use the specification from this query in a filter again, go to the filter design grid by choosing Record, Filter, Advanced Filter/Sort, click the Load from Query button and double-click the query name.

This query now appears on the Query tab of the *Database window*. You can use it like any other query. One difference is that all fields are displayed rather than just the fields that are in the grid. This is because the Output All Fields *property* is set to Yes.

List of Values

Sometimes you want to just see a list of all the different values in one *field* with none of the items duplicated. You might want to create a lookup *table* with these values, in which case you could create this query and then turn it into a Make-Table Query (see "Action Queries: Make-Table Query") and use the table in a *lookup column* (see "Lookup Column: Create with Wizard" in the Table and Database Design part of this book).

Steps

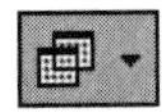

1. In the *Database window*, select the table or query from which you want to find the values. Choose Query from the New Object button on the toolbar.
2. Right-click the mouse button on the query's title bar and choose Properties on the shortcut menu. The Query Properties sheet opens.
3. Change the Unique Values *property* to Yes.
4. Double-click in the Field List the one field for which you want to see values.
5. Close the Property sheet, save, and run the query.

Query Design: Expand Column

At any point during *query* design you might not have enough room to see your *field* or *criteria*. You can change the column width temporarily to see what you need at the moment, or you can permanently widen the column.

Steps

1. If you permanently want to see a wider column width, move to the gray border above and between two field names. The mouse pointer will be a double-headed arrow. Drag the mouse to the right to increase the column width.
2. If you want to temporarily see the entire entry, press Shift+F2 to open the Zoom window. Choose OK when you are done viewing or editing.

Query Parameters: Prompt for Input

When you want one query to work as many, consider using a parameter query. For example, suppose you need all the same information but want to change the salesperson each time you run the query. When you create a *parameter* query, Access will prompt you each time you run the query. This is true even when you open a *form* or *report* based on this *query*.

Steps

1. Create the query with all the fields and other criteria you want and open the query in *Design* View.
2. Move to the criteria *grid* under the *field* you want to check. Type an open square bracket, any text you want for the prompt, and a close square bracket. For example, type **[Enter the salesperson's name:]**.
3. You might have more than one prompt and need to change the order of the prompts or define a *data type* for the prompt (so Access displays a warning if the wrong data is entered in the prompt). Choose Query, Parameters. Enter the exact text of your prompt and choose a data type for each prompt.

4. Click the Run button. Access will show a *dialog box* with whatever prompt you added. Enter your text.
5. Save and close your query.

Whenever you run the query (including just opening it) Access will display a dialog box with the prompt you created.

TIP Enter the keyword **Like** before your prompt if you want to use wildcards.

Query: Add Field

When you edit or build a query you might need to insert fields in the appropriate place on the *grid*. Open up any query in Design View to add a *field*.

Steps

1. To add a field at the end of the query grid, double-click the field.
2. To add a field between two existing fields, drag the field name from the *list box* onto the right field.

3. To add all fields in the grid, first clear the grid if necessary with Edit, Clear Grid. Double-click the asterisk (*) in the Field List.
4. If you want to add all fields to the grid and you are going to use sort or criteria from any of the fields, double-click the title bar of the list box and drag from one of the fields to the grid.

Query: Add Table

You can use more than one *table* in the *query*. In almost all cases the tables need to be related. Open up any query in Design View to add a table.

Steps

1. In Query *Design View*, click the Show Table button on the toolbar.
2. Double-click each table or query you want to add; choose Close when done.
3. If necessary, draw a *join* line between the two related fields in the *Field* Lists. Generally, you will be drawing a line between two fields with the same or similar names (for example, EmpID and Employee ID).
4. Double-click fields from any of the Field Lists to add them to the design *grid*.

For more details on the joins, see "Tables: Combine with Join" and "Tables: Create a Self Join."

NOTE If you accidentally add a table twice to the design grid, click in the table and press the Delete *key* to remove it. Don't forget that you may not see all the tables. Use the scroll bars in the upper part of the grid to see if you have any more tables hiding in the grid.

Query: Change Column Heading Names

When you make calculated columns in a query, you will probably want to add a column name instead of the Expr headings that Access defaults to.

Steps

1. In Query *Design View*, click before text in any *Field* cell.
2. Type the new column name and a colon (:).

Query: Create with Design View

Queries are recipes for finding, selecting, and sorting data in tables. Access stores the definition of a *query*, runs the query, and returns a result set when the query is requested. Queries can be used as the underlying *data* set for *forms* and *reports*. Queries can also be used to select, append, delete, and update *records* in the *database* (see the appropriate "*Action Query*" sections).

You create a new query using either the Query Wizard or the Query Design window. Both are relatively easy to use, though the Query Wizard will walk you through the process step-by-step. The Query Design Wizard provides you with additional options. (See "Query: Create with Wizard.")

NOTE You can select records by applying a *filter* and sort those records. Access 97 remembers the last filter you applied without you having to re-enter it (see the Filter tasks earlier in this part). This is an alternative to running some queries.

Steps

1. Click the Query tab in the *Database window*, then choose the New button. Select Design View in the New Query *dialog box*; then double-click the table(s) you want from the Show Table dialog box, choose Close.

   If you add related tables, Access will automatically create *join* lines between the tables.

   To create a *relationship* between two tables, drag the *key field* of the parent tables to the related *field* of the *child* table.
2. Double-click any fields from the Field Lists for each table you want as part of the query.

3. Click in the Sort row and select Ascending or Descending for any field that you want to sort.

   Fields are sorted in their order from right to left, the left field being the primary sort key. To re-order the fields, click and drag the column header.

4. Uncheck the Show *check box* for any field you want to hide in the Query.

   Fields can be used in queries that do not appear in the query output.

5. Enter any *expression* in the criteria cell for that field. Click Save in the Query Design toolbar. Enter the name of the *form* in the Query Name *text box* of the Save As dialog box, then choose OK.

See the *Criteria* sections of this part for examples of criteria. When you run a query, the data you see reflects the data that conforms to your query at runtime. You can update, delete, or append the data in a result set for most queries. (See "Updatable Queries.")

Query: Create with Wizard

The Query Wizard is easier for novices to create queries but provides less flexibility than Query *Design View.* (See "Query: Create with Design View.")

Steps

1. On the Query tab of the *Database window*, choose the New button and choose Simple Query Wizard.
2. Choose a *table* or *query* from the Table/Query drop-down box.
3. Double-click any *fields* you want as part of the query. Repeat Steps 2 and 3 for additional tables if necessary; choose Next.
4. If you want to see every *record*, click the Detail *option button*.

If you want to only see summaries of the records such as totals or counts, choose the Summary Option button and choose the types of summaries you want; choose OK.

5. On the next choices in the wizard choose any additional options for grouping your data and naming your query; choose Finish when done. Save and close your query.

Query: Delete Field

To remove a *field* from a *query* you need to be in Design View. If that field is needed in sorting or *criteria*, uncheck the Show box in the design *grid*.

Steps

1. In the query or *filter* design *grid*, click the black down arrow mouse pointer on the gray field selector above the field name and press Delete.
2. To remove all fields, choose Edit, Clear Grid.

Query: Description

If you want to explain your query in more detail than the field name allows, you can use the Description *property*.

Steps

1. If you are in the *Database window*, right-click the query name, choose Properties, and type the text in the Description *text box*.
2. If you are in Query *Design View* and the properties window is not in view, right-click the gray background behind the Field List(s) and choose Properties. The Query Properties dialog box opens On the General tab type the text in the Description text box.

Query: Editing

When you want to edit the design of a query, you need to go into Design View. You might want to add more fields, delete fields, change your criteria, or change other query properties.

NOTE You can edit the data in most queries the same way you edit a table. (See "Data: Edit" in the *Database* Essentials part of this book.)

Steps

1. On the Query tab of the *Database window*, select the *query* and choose the Design button.
2. Select any *criteria expression* and press the Delete *key* to remove it or type a new expression.
3. Change a *field* by clicking the drop-down arrow in the field box and choosing a different field name.
4. If you want to use the same fields but a different *table*, add the other table with the Show Table button and change the table name in the design *grid* for each field, and then click in the old table Field List and press the Delete key.

NOTE If the table name row does not appear in the Query Design grid, choose View, Table Names.

Query: Format Field

Often when you create a calculation *field* (see "Calculated Fields: Queries" in the Calculations part of this book), the data is not formatted the way you might want. You might also want to change the format of a field to be different than the Format *property* of the field in the underlying *table*. (See "Data: Format" in the Table and *Database* Design part of this book.)

Steps

1. In Query *Design View*, right-click the field you want to format and choose Properties.
2. Click in the Format property *text box* and choose one of the formats from the drop-down list.

   You can also type customized formats in the Format box. Some examples include: For a required text character, type @ and the required text characters. For example, if you want the word `Unknown` displayed when there is nothing typed in the field, or `No Value` when two quotes have been typed in the field, type **@;"Unknown";"No Value"**

For dates, type **mmm**, or **mmmm** to see just the month (abbreviation or full name) or **yyyy** to see the year.

NOTE For text you can also type **>** to change the entry to be all caps or **<** for all lower cases. For a description of customized format characters, click in the Format property and press F1.

Query: Hide and Show Columns

Sometime you will need to use a *field* but not want to see it displayed in the query datasheet.

Steps

1. If you are in *Datasheet View*, right-click the column and choose Hide Columns from the shortcut menu.

   To redisplay the column choose Format, Unhide columns, pick the column, and choose Close.

2. If you are in Design View, uncheck the Show box in the design *grid*. Recheck the box to display the column again.

Query: Move Column

You can move a column either in the *Datasheet View* or Query *Design View*. Once you've changed the column order in Datasheet View for a query, you need to change it in Datasheet View each time rather than depend on Query Design View.

Steps

1. In either Design View or Datasheet View, move the mouse to the column or field header until the mouse pointer becomes a black down arrow. Click and release the mouse to select the column.
2. With the mouse pointer still on the column header (it is now a white arrow), drag the column to the new location.

Query: Properties

There are a number of useful properties that you can set as part of a *query*. These properties help you control the number of *records* returned in your view of the result set, optimize performance, and specify other useful options.

Steps

1. Open a query in *Design View*.
2. Click a *field* in the Field row, a Field List in the data environment, or elsewhere on the Design View window to select the query.

3. Click the Properties button on the toolbar to display the *Property* sheet for the selected object.
4. Add your properties or *expressions*; then close the Property sheet.

Both the query and field have a Description property for notes or comments. The field also has a *Caption* property that shows as the column header or becomes the default *label* for forms and reports. The Format property on the field changes the way data is displayed. (See "Query: Format Field.") The field's *Input Mask* property works the same as for fields in a table. (See "Input Mask: Phone Number and Other Entries" in the Table and Database Design part of this book.)

Query: Run

You can run a query from Query Design View or directly from the *Database window*.

> **CAUTION** Be careful when you run action queries—they will update or delete data. These queries are indicated with an exclamation point (!) as part of their icon in the Database window.

Steps

1. From the Query tab of the Database window, double-click the query name to run it.

2. From the Query Design View, click the Datasheet View button to show the results of a select query or preview the results of an *action query*.

3. From the Query Design View, click the Run button to execute the action query. This button functions the same as the Datasheet View button for select queries.
4. From Datasheet View, if you want to requery (perhaps you want to redisplay the input box for a parameter query), press Shift+F9.

Query: Show All Fields

No matter which *fields* are used in the *grid*, a filter shows all fields. When a *filter* is saved as a *query*, all fields also display. When you create a new query through *Design View* or through a wizard, only those fields you use in the grid (and that have the Show box checked) display in *Datasheet View*.

Steps

1. Select the query in the *Database window* and choose the Design button.
2. If the Properties window is not displayed, right-click the gray background behind the Field Lists(s) and the title bar of the query, and choose Properties. The Query Properties sheet opens.
3. Change the Output All Values *property* to Yes.

Query: Sort Columns

You can apply a sort order to the result set of a query in either *Form* or *Datasheet View*. You can also sort the result set of a filter or an advanced filter/sort.

The sort order for a query is usually determined by the Sort row of the Query Design *grid*. You can sort the query independent of the *property*, however, with the following steps.

Steps

1. Click the column(s) or field(s) you want to sort on.

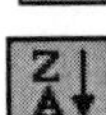

2. Click either the Sort Ascending or Sort Descending buttons on the toolbar.

NOTE If your sort is more complex (with multiple non-adjacent fields) choose Records, Filter, Advanced Filter/Sort and create your filter.

The primary sort *key* is the leftmost sorted column in the *Query* Design grid. A sort order is saved with the datasheet or *form* and reapplied when you open it.

To remove the sort, go into *Design View* for the query, click the right mouse on the gray background behind the *Field* List(s) and choose Properties. The Query Properties sheet opens. Delete the text in the *Filter* By property.

SQL Statements: View

SQL stands for *Structured Query Language*. This is the underlying language that Access uses to create its queries, filters, and select data for reports. Most of the time you do not have to see the actual SQL statements because Access builds them for you in design grids. In a few cases you have to work with SQL if you want to perform some features of Access (see "Tables: Combine with Union Query" especially).

Steps

1. Open a query in Design View.
2. Click the View button on the toolbar and choose SQL View. The SQL window opens where you can copy or edit the text instructions for the query.

Keywords in the query include the type of query (SELECT, DELETE or, for Append, INSERT INTO), source of data (FROM), criteria (WHERE), and sort (ORDER BY). Fields are indicated by the name of their table, a period, and their field name. If field names include spaces, they are enclosed in square brackets.

Subqueries: Create

Once in awhile you might want to create a *query* that uses the results of another query to run. One option is to create a query and then use that query as the basis for the next query. Another option is to copy the *SQL* statement and place it in a *Criteria* cell.

You might need to find the average price for all products and then find all products that exceed the average price.

Steps

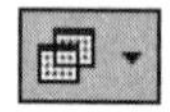

1. If you want to have both query and *subquery* listed in the *Database window*, highlight the first query name in the Database window, click the New Object button and choose Query. Create the second query using the first queries fields.
2. If you want to have only one query in the Database window, first create the subquery with only one field and one *record* as an output (create a Totals Query with no grouping). Display the subquery in SQL view and copy all text. Create the main query and move to the Criteria row under the field. Type any *operator* (such as =, <, >), then type an open parenthesis, paste the SQL statement, and then type a close parenthesis.

Table Names: Display

When you are designing a query with multiple tables, the *grid* can be confusing unless you have table names displayed.

Steps

1. In Query *Design View*, choose View, Table Names to turn the names on or off.

Tables: Combine with Join

When you have two tables that are related to each other (for example, if you have Customers and Orders tables), you might want to see fields from both tables. In the Order table you have a Customer ID but no other customer information. To see the customer name and phone, as well as order information, you can *join* two tables together in a query.

Steps

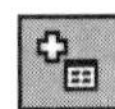

1. From the *Design View* of a *query*, click the Show Table button to add additional table(s), double-click the *child* table(s) you want and choose the Close button.

   Access will use any *relationship* you created in the Relationships window.

2. To create a relationship between two *tables*, drag the *field* of the parent tables to the related *field* of the child tables. A line appears between the two tables. Generally, you will be dragging the primary *key* from the parent table (which is in bold) to a non-primary field in the child table.
3. To set the join *properties*, right-click the line and choose Join Properties.
4. The default is the first choice, which only shows *records* where both joined fields have data. (This is called an *Inner Join.*)

   Choose the second choice to see matched records and all records from the parent table without a match in the child table. (This is called a Left *Outer Join.*)

   Choose the third choice to see matched records and all records from the child table without a match in the parent table. (This is called a Right Outer Join.)

5. Choose OK and finish building the query by adding any fields, sort options, and criteria you want.

6. Click the Run button to run the query.

NOTE If you design your database relationships (see "Relationships Between Tables" in the Table and Database Design part of this book) with *referential integrity* checked, the Right Outer *Join* should yield the same results as the Inner Join because there should be no "orphan" records in the *child* table.

TIP To find all records that have no match, create a query with both linked fields and choose a Left Outer Join or Right Outer Join. Under one of the fields set the criteria to Is *Null*. You might want to create this type of query before you create relationships with existing data to see which records you need to delete.

Tables: Combine with Union Query

The *join query* in the "Tables: Combine with Join" task combines related *records* and adds additional *fields* when you have an additional *table*. In some cases, you do not have related records and yet all fields of two tables are identical. This can be the case when you have a current table and an historic table. When you combine the two tables you want to see one record set below the other. You do this through the Union Query, which must be written in *SQL*. Luckily, you can use the Query *Design View* and then paste the results.

Steps

1. Create a query with the first table. Use field names that are the same in both tables. Click the View button and choose SQL View.

2. Select the entire SQL statement if not already selected, and click the Copy button.

3. Close the query without saving it. Create a query with the second table and the matching fields. Click the Design View button and choose SQL View.

4. Move to the end of the SQL statement and press Enter. Type **UNION**. Press Enter again and click the Paste button to paste the SQL statement from the first query.
5. Click the Run button to run the query.

NOTE If there are any duplicate records (all fields), they do not display in a Union Query.

QUERIES AND FILTERS

Tables: Create a Self Join

When you have a *field* in the *database* that refers to another field in the same database, you can create a *self-join* where you join the database to itself to display the information you want. This can occur, for example, when you have an employee database where one field is the employee ID of the employee's supervisor and the supervisor is in the same database. Instead of the supervisor's ID, you want to see the supervisor's name.

Steps

1. In Query *Design View*, select all the fields you want from the table.

2. Click the Show Table button and double-click the same *table* so you have two Field Lists from the same table; click Close to return to the design grid.
3. The second table name is identical to the first table name with the number 1 added. To avoid confusion, right-click in the second Field List and enter a name in the *Alias property* to give your second table a name.
4. Drag from the field in the first table that is related to the field in the second table to create a join. These fields will be different names but have the same *data type*.
5. Finish building the *query* by adding any fields, sort options, and criteria you want.

6. Click the Run button to run the query.

Top Value Query

If you want to see the top (or bottom) five salespeople or top 10% of customers, you can create a Top Value query.

Steps

1. Create a query with all fields you want to see, especially the field that you will use to rank the records. Go to Design View of the query.

2. Click in the ranking field. For top values, choose Ascending in the Sort row. For bottom values, choose Descending in the Sort row.

3. Click the Top Values button and choose one of the items in the list or type a value if it is not one of the drop-down choices.
4. Click the Run button to run the query.

Unmatched Query

As you are designing your *database* you might need to check how data from two existing *tables* are related. This will be especially true if you plan on creating a *relationship* between the tables and enforcing *referential integrity.* (See “Relationships between Tables” in the Table and Database Design part of this book.)

Steps

1. In the Query tab of the *Database window*, choose the New button and choose Find Unmatched Query Wizard.
2. Double-click the table where the parent *records* are located.
3. On the next screen, double-click the table where the *child* records are located.
4. On the third screen, choose the name of the related field in both lists and choose the <=> button; choose Next.
5. On the next two screens, choose which fields you want to display and the name for your *query*; choose Finish to create the query.

The query will only display records from the first table because there aren’t any related records from the second table. You can edit these records or delete them from this query. (See “Records Delete” in the Database Essentials part of this book.)

Calculations

You can use calculations and *expressions* throughout Access in all *objects—tables, queries, forms, reports,* and even *macros* and *modules.* Calculations can help you find all sorts of statistics about your data—from averages, sums, and maximums, to standard deviations and present value. You can even combine text fields together in one *field.* You can type calculations directly or use the Expression Builder to help you.

In a query, calculations can be done by creating a new field based on the values of other fields in the query *grid.* You can also create grouping types of queries with crosstab and total queries.

In forms and reports, you generally add *text boxes* for calculations. These text boxes, as well as everything else on the form or report, are called *controls,* You learn more about forms and reports in the next part of this book, "Forms and Reports."

Blanks and Nulls in Calculations

When you run a query, form, or report with calculations, you might see a blank when you expect a value. This happens when you have a *null* value that is part of any expression; then, the result of the expression evaluates to null. Criteria for nulls are discussed in "Criteria: Blanks, Nulls, and Empty" in the Queries and Filters part of this book.

Steps

1. If the expression is in a form or report, open in *Design View.* Double-click the control containing the expression to open the Properties sheet. Click in the Control Source *property* (on the Data tab).

If the expression is in a query, open the query in Design View and click in the field with the expression.

2. If necessary, press Shift+F2 to zoom and see the whole expression.
3. If your *expression* evaluates to a numeric value and one of your *fields* is *null*, the whole expression evaluates to null. You can use the `NZ` *function* to convert any field to another number. Click before the field name and type **NZ**. Enclose the field name in parentheses. For addition and subtraction, use `NZ(Fieldname)` to convert null values to zero. For multiplication and division, use `NZ(Fieldname,1)` to convert null values to 1.
4. If your expression includes any text strings, use the & operator instead of + (or the entire expression will evaluate to null when any value is null). For example, type **[Field1]&" "&[Field2]**.
5. If you don't want extra spaces in text strings, you might need to use Is Null. The `IsNull` function tests if a value is null. For example, to avoid having two spaces if someone does not have a middle name, use the following expression: `Name: [Firstname] & " " & IIf(IsNull([Middlename]),"",[Middlename] & " ") & [Lastname]`
6. When finished, display and then save the form, report, or query.

NOTE In a Totals *Query*, Access does not include null values for *aggregate functions* such as Sum, Count, and Average. If you want to count all records including nulls, use `Count(*)`.

Calculated Fields: Forms and Reports—Create by Typing

You can enter a calculation in a *form* by typing it or using the Expression Builder. When you enter a *field* name that includes spaces as part of the expression, you must include square brackets around the field name. Access will automatically put brackets around field names with no spaces.

Steps

1. In *Design View* of a form or report, click the *Text Box* tool and then click the form or report and type an equal sign (=).
2. If you are including a *function*, include the function name with parentheses (*arguments* might or might not go inside parentheses).
3. If the next part of the expression is a field, include field in square brackets, as in `[Fieldname]`.
4. If you are doing arithmetic operations, include + - * /, or if you are combining text, include the ampersand (&).
5. When finished, click outside the text box.

NOTE Only *controls* that have Control Source properties can take an expression with a calculated result. Expressions can be any valid Access function or *operator*, values, fields, or identifiers, and must start with an equal sign.

CALCULATIONS

Calculated Fields: Forms and Reports—Edit Expression

After you type an *expression* in a *text box*, you can click the text box and try to edit the expression. This is okay if the expression is short, but if the expression is long you will not be able to see the entire formula.

Steps

1. Open the *form* or *report* in Design View.
2. If the *Property* sheet is not displayed, right-click the text box, choose Properties, and click the Data tab.
3. Click the Control Source property and edit the expression or press Shift+F2 to zoom. When done with the zoom window, choose OK.
4. Save and close the form or report.

Calculated Fields: Queries—Create by Typing

Because you do not want to store unnecessary data in a *table*, you often need to do calculations in a *query*. To create a calculated *field* in a query, you use a Field cell in the Query Design *grid*. Calculated fields in a query are not stored to disk, but are recalculated at the query's runtime.

Steps

1. Open the query in *Design view* and click an unused Field cell.
2. Type the name for the field followed by a colon (**:**).
3. If the next part of the *expression* is a field, include field in square brackets, as in `[Fieldname]`.
4. If you are doing arithmetic operations, include + - * /, or if you are combining text, include &.
5. Repeat field names and operators as much as necessary, and then click outside of the field box. If there is a *syntax* error, Access will give you a warning message.

NOTE To edit the expression, click the Field cell. If necessary, press Shift+F2 to zoom to a larger window.

Calculations: Average of Values

The AVG *function* returns the average (mean) of the values in a number field. Unlike Excel's Average function, you have only one expression (which is a fieldname) in the parentheses rather than multiple cells.

Steps

New Object: Query

1. In the *Database window*, click the table or query on which you want to base the new query and choose Query from the New Object button on the toolbar. Double click any fields in the Field List you will use for the query.

2. To find an average of one value for an entire *table*, create a *query* with just that field. Click the Totals button on the toolbar and choose Avg in the Total row.

3. To find an average of one value for a selected set of records, create a select query and choose criteria for which values you want to select. Include the number field in the Query Design *grid.* Uncheck the show box for all fields except the number field. Click the Totals button on the toolbar and choose Avg in the Total row.
4. To find the average for a group of values, create a query and put the field(s) you will *group* in a column and the numeric field to average in another column. Click the Totals button on the toolbar and choose Avg in the Total row of the numeric field. The grouping field(s) has Group By in the Total row. This query will not show the detail for each *record*, just the averages for the groups.
5. Save the query and click the Run button on the toolbar.

NOTE To show the detail and the average of these groups in a *report*, create a report that is grouped on a field. In the report's group footer, add a *text box* and type **=Avg([*Fieldname*])** where ***Fieldname*** is the numeric field to average.

CALCULATIONS

Calculations: Count of Items in List

The easiest way to see a count of all records (or selected records) in a *table* is to look at the navigation buttons at the bottom of a table or *Query* window after the word `of`. You can also look at this number for filtered records—more specifically, you can find a count of the numbers of each item in a *group*.

Steps

1. From the Query tab of the *Database window*, choose New and choose *Design View*.
2. Click the Totals button on the toolbar.
3. Double-click the *field* you want to group by (the Total row defaults to Group By).

4. Double-click a field where every *record* has a value (the *primary key* is a good choice). Choose Count in the Total row.
5. Run the query, save, and close.

Calculations: Date

Date fields are common in *databases*. With these fields, you can find today's date (or a date relative to today's date such as 60 days after). You can also find the difference between two dates, or the year or month portion of the date.

Steps

1. If the *expression* is in a *form* or *report*, open in *Design View*. Double-click the *control* containing the expression to open the Properties sheet. Click in the Control Source *property* (on the Data tab).
2. If the expression is in a *query*, open the query in Design View and click in the field with the expression.
3. If the expression is for a *field* in a *table*, open the table in Design View. Click in the field you want to change. In the lower half of the window go to the Default Value or *Validation* Rule property.
4. If the expression involves more than one field in a table, open the table in Design View. Right-click the title bar of the table and choose Properties. Click in the Validation Rule box.
5. Type one of the expressions listed in the following section. When finished, save and display the table, query, form, or report.

Using Date and Time Expressions

You can create both simple and complex expressions for use in tables, forms, queries, and reports. An expression takes a set of values, symbols, operators, or identifiers and evaluates it to produce a result. The following list illustrates how and when to use date and time expressions.

- **Date()** You enter today's date as **Date()**. This is often the Default *property* in the *Table* Design *grid* or *Form* Design property of a *control*. This also is combined with an *operator* such as `<Date()` as the *Validation* Rule property *expression* or in the criteria cell of the *Query* Design grid. In the *Field* cell of Query Design grid, `Date()` is often combined with other date fields as in `DaysLate: Date()-[DueDate]`. Use `Now()` if you need to include the current time.
- ***DateDiff(interval, date1, date2)*** If you want to find the difference between two dates in weeks or months, use `DateDiff(interval, date1, date2)`. Enclose the `interval` argument in quotes such as `"ww"` or `"m"`. See the upcoming note for options on the interval. You would generally use this *function* in a Field cell of the Query Design grid or in the Control Source property of a calculated control on a form or *report*.
- ***DateAdd(interval, number, date)*** If you want to find a date in the future, use `DateAdd(interval, number, date)` in the same places and with the same values for interval as `DateDiff`. `Number` is the number of intervals.
- ***DatePart(interval,date)*** To convert a date field to the month or year portion of the date (or any other interval below), use `DatePart(interval,date)`. When you use this function, it is often in the Field cell of Query Design grid of Total and Crosstab queries.
- ***Format(expression,fmt)*** If `DatePart` doesn't give you enough options, you can also use `Format(expression, fmt)` where `expression` can be a date field and `fmt` can be the same as interval below with additional choices (`y` = year; `yy`=year with 2 digits—97 or 01; `yyyy` = four-digit year; `m` = month number; `mm` = month number with leading 0; `mmm` = month abbreviation; `mmmm` = full month name). You enclose the `fmt` value in quotes also. Format is often used in Total and Crosstab queries.

NOTE The interval options for the `DateDiff`, `DateAdd`, and `DatePart` functions include `yyyy` (Year), `q` (Quarter), `m` (Month), `y` (Day of year), `d` (Day), `w` (Weekday), `ww` (Week), `h` (Hour), `n` (Minute), and `s` (Second). For formatting numbers, see also "Query: Format Field" in the Queries and Filters part of this book, and "Format: Numbers and Dates" in the Forms and Reports part of the book.

Calculations: First and Last Values

When you want to see the first or last value in a list, you can use the `First` and `Last` functions. You need to sort the list or the results of these functions will be arbitrary.

Steps

1. On the *Query* tab of the *Database window*, choose the New button and double-click *Design View*.

2. In Query Design view, click the Totals button.
3. Double-click the *field* to sort and choose *Group* By in the Total row.
4. Double-click the field to find the order, and choose First or Last in the Total row.
5. View, save, and close the query.

NOTE You can also see `First` and `Last` values in a *report*. Create a report that is grouped by one field. In the Group Footer section, create a calculated *control* and use the `First` or `Last` functions.

Calculations: Maximum and Minimum

The Maximum and Minimum functions help you find the highest and lowest values of a *field*. You can also find these values by sorting a *table* on the field of interest Descending or Ascending and looking at the first *record*. Unlike the `Avg` or `Sum` functions, the field you are finding the maximum or minimum value of can be a text or date field in addition to a number *data type*. The following items show just the maximum (MAX) *function*. You can use these identically with the minimum (MIN) function.

Steps

1. From the Query tab of the *Database window*, choose New and choose *Design View*.
2. Click the Totals button on the toolbar.
3. Double-click the *field(s)* you want to include in your query. To find the maximum of one value for an entire table, create a *query* with just that field. Choose Max in the Total row.
4. To find the maximum of one value for a selected set of records, choose *criteria* for the values that you want to select. Include the evaluation field in the Query Design *grid*. Uncheck the show box for all fields except the evaluation field. In the evaluation field, choose Max in the Total row.
5. To find the maximum for a group of values, insert the field(s) you will *group* in a column and the evaluation field to maximize in another column Choose Max in the Total row of the numeric field. The grouping field(s) has Group By in the Total row. This query will not show the detail for each record.
6. When finished, display and then save the query.

NOTE To show the detail and the maximum of these groups in a *report*, create a report that is grouped on a field. In the report's group footer, add a *text box* and type **=Max([*Fieldname*])** where ***Fieldname*** is the numeric field to maximize.

Calculations: Percent

Percent means per 100. When you look for percentages, you are often dividing a *field*'s value by the total of all values for that field. Normally when you divide, the result is first in decimal notation (for example, 0.345). When you format the number as percent, Access multiplies the number by 100 and displays a percent sign (34.5%). You can calculate a percent of the whole in a *report* or *form*.

Another use of percent is to take a percentage of a number. To do the calculation, you multiply the percent times the number (10% * 500 = 50). A common mistake is to assume that a field formatted as percent will not need the decimal point or percentage sign when you enter the number (10 is entered incorrectly instead of .10 or 10%). You can use a *query*, form, or report to multiply a percent. (See "Calculated Fields: Queries—Create by Typing.")

NOTE To increase an amount by a percentage, don't forget to include the amount itself by including a "1" in the multiplier. For example, to increase prices by 5 percent, you would type **[Price]*1.05**. Unlike Excel, you cannot type **105%** in the formula, and you must use the decimal equivalent of the number.

Steps

1. Create a *text box* in *Form* or *Report view*, right-click the text box, and move to the *Control* Source *property*.
2. Type **=[*Fieldname*]/Sum([*Fieldname*])** where ***Fieldname*** is the value for which you want to find the percent.
3. Move to the Format *property*. Choose Percent from the drop-down list of choices. Type the number of decimal places you want in the Decimal Places property.
4. View, save, and close the form or report.

Calculations: Standard Deviation and Variance

Standard deviation (STDEV) and variance (VAR) give you an idea how much your data varies throughout the whole *table*. If you have a small variance or standard deviation compared to the absolute value of the number, then most of your values are close to the mean. If you have a large standard deviation or variance, then the value of your *field* is spread across many numbers. Both functions work the same way ; STDEV is used in the steps of the following task. For variance, replace STDEV with VAR. Both of these functions must be used with number (or currency) fields.

Steps

1. From the Query tab of the *Database window*, choose New and choose *Design View*.
2. Click the Totals button on the toolbar.
3. Double-click the *field(s)* you want to include in your query. To find the standard deviation of one value for an entire *table*, create a *query* with just that field. Choose StDev in the Total row.
4. To find the standard deviation of one value for a selected set of records, choose criteria for which values you want to select. Include the evaluation field in the Query Design *grid*. Uncheck the show box for all fields except the evaluation field and choose StDev in the Total row.
5. To find the standard deviation for a group of values, insert the field(s) you will *group* in a column and the evaluation field to check for standard deviation in another column. Choose StDev in the Total row of the numeric field. The grouping field(s) has Group By in the Total row. This query will not show the detail for each *record*.
6. When finished, display and then save the query.

NOTE To show the detail and the standard deviation of these *groups* in a *report*, create a report that is grouped on a field. In the report's group footer, add a *text box* and type **= StDev ([*Fieldname*])** where ***Fieldname*** is the numeric field to check for standard deviation.

Calculations: Sum of Values

The Sum *function* is the most used function of all. Sum will total all values in a *field*. You can create a query that will sum an entire *table* or show the sum for groups of *records*. In a *query* you cannot show both the sums and the detail of the records. For that purpose, you need to create a report.

Steps

1. From the Query tab of the *Database window*, choose New and choose *Design View*.

2. Click the Totals button on the toolbar.
3. Double-click the *field(s)* you want to include in your query. To find the total of one field for an entire table, create a *query* with just that field. Choose Sum in the Total row.
4. To find the total of one field for a selected set of records, choose *criteria* for which fields you want to select. Include the evaluation field in the Query Design *grid*. Uncheck the show box for all fields except the evaluation field and choose Sum in the Total row.
5. To find the total for a group(s) of fields, insert the field(s) you will *group* in a column and the evaluation field to total in another column. Choose Sum in the Total row of the numeric field. The grouping field(s) has Group By in the Total row. This query will not show the detail for each *record*.

NOTE To show the detail and the total of these groups in a *report*, create a report that is grouped on a field. In the report's group footer, add a *text box* and type **=Sum([*Fieldname*])** where ***Fieldname*** is the numeric field to maximize. You can also type **=Sum([*Fieldname*])** in a text box in the report footer to find the total for all records displayed in the report.

To show the total of values in a *form* (whether you can see all values or not), add a text box to the form footer and type **=Sum([*Fieldname*])** where ***Fieldname*** is the numeric field to maximize. Tabular forms make the most sense for this kind of calculation.

Conversion Functions

If you are using a *form* to prompt for user input, the form can have *unbound text boxes* where you cannot define a *data type*. The same is true for the *VBA* `InputBox` *function*. In these and other programming cases, there might be instances where you have to use conversion functions to convert the data type of your input. The conversion in some cases actually corresponds to the data type and length *property* for numbers.

Steps

1. If the *expression* is in a form or *report*, open in *Design View*. Double-click the *control* containing the expression to open the Properties sheet. Click in the Control Source property (on the Data tab).

   If the expression is in a *query*, open the query in Design View and click in the field with the expression.
2. Position the insertion point directly before a fieldname or control name and type one of the following most common conversion functions: `CCur` (currency), `CDate` (date), `CStr` (text), `CDbl` (Number-double), `CSng` (Number-single), `CInt` (Number-*integer*).
3. Enclose the fieldname in parenthesis.
4. When finished, display and then save the form, report, or query.

Crosstab Query: Create

Crosstab queries enable you to summarize data by two or more variables. These queries are more compact than Total queries. The first column of the result shows one *variable* (called the Column Heading). The first row of the result shows another variable (called the Row Heading). The intersection of a column and row displays the summary of a third variable (called the Value) for only values that match the Row and Column heading. Within reports, you can also use *pivot tables* (see "Pivot Table: Create") to create the same effect.

Row and Column headings are often text or date fields, and the Value *field* is often a number or currency *data type.*

Steps

1. On the Query tab of the *Database window*, choose New and double-click Crosstab Query Wizard.
2. In the first step of the Crosstab Query Wizard, double-click the name of the *table* or *query.*
3. Double-click up to three fields for the Row Headings; choose Next. Double-click one field for the Column Headings.
4. Choose the value you want to summarize in the Fields list, and how you want to summarize it in the *Functions* list (such as `Sum`, `Count`, and so on). If you want a summary of each row, check Yes, Include Row Sums; choose Next.
5. On the last *dialog box* of the wizard, type a name of the query and choose Finish. View the results of the query and save it.

NOTE When you use a date field for Row or Column Headings, you probably want to *group* the values into time units such as month or year. In the Query Design *grid*, change the Field entry from the field name to an *expression* using the `DatePart` *function*. `DatePart("yyyy",`*`DateField`*`)` will group by year. `DatePart("m",`*`DateField`*`)` will group by month number. You can also use the `Format` function.

Crosstab Query: Fix Column Headings

Sometimes the order of Crosstab Headings is not appropriate. For example, if you use the `Format(`*`DateField`*`,"mmm")` *function*, the months will appear in alphabetical order (Apr, Aug, Dec, Feb, and so on) rather than date order.

NOTE The `mmm` indicates abbreviated month names (Apr, Feb, and so on). An `mmmm` would indicate full spelling for the months (January) but would still give an alphabetical order.

Steps

1. Open the Crosstab *Query* in *Design View.*
2. If the properties window is not visible, right-click the title bar and choose Properties.
3. Click the Column Headings *property* and type the order you want the columns to appear, separating each entry with a semicolon (;).
4. View, save, and close the query.

NOTE Access will display all fields in the Column Headings property whether there is data there or not. If you misspell an entry, that column will appear and the correct data will not.

Expression: Operators

Most people are familiar with arithmetic operators: plus (+), minus (-), times (*), and divide by (/). There are also other expressions you will use in criteria and calculations. These include greater than (>), less than (<), greater than or equal to (>=), less than or equal to (<=), and NOT (opposite of the *expression* that follows). Two connectors are OR (which indicates that any of the expressions need to be true for the expression to be true), and AND (which indicates both expressions need to be true for the expression to be true). Use the ampersand (&) to connect text strings.

Arithmetic expressions are evaluated based on *rules of precedence*—that is, the order in which the operations in an expression are carried out. The order is determined by the type of operation, its location in the expression from left to right, and whether the operation is surrounded by parentheses. Parentheses take top priority. Then comes multiplication and division, and finally addition and subtraction. 1+2*3 would first do 2*3 (=6) and then add the 1 to equal 7. (1+2)*3 would evaluate to 9. You can type the expressions or use the expression builder. (See "Expression: Using the Builder.")

Steps

1. Open an existing or new *query* in Query Design View.

2. To create a calculation, click the *Field* row, type a name for the new calculated field and a colon (:), and then type the *expression*. You can also use the build icon to run the expression builder to help you build the expression.
3. To select data, click any of the *criteria* rows (starting with the Criteria row, then use the Or row, and then any blank rows below). Type the expression.
4. Finish building the query, view the results, and save it.

NOTE To create an expression in a *report* or *form*, open the form or report in design view. Choose the Text Box tool on the Toolbox. Start with an equal sign (=) and then type the expression.

Expression: Refer to Controls

Referring to controls is similar to referring to *field* names. (See "Expression: Refer to Field Names.") If the *control* is on the current *form* or *report*, you can just type the control name in square brackets. However, if you are referring to another open form or report, you need to include the *object* type and object name.

NOTE The form or report must be open to access the value from a control.

Steps

1. In an expression, type **Forms** or **Reports**.
2. Type an exclamation mark (also called a *bang*).
3. Type the name of the form or report and another exclamation mark.
4. Type the name of the control.

NOTE If the name of the form, report, or control includes a space, type square brackets around the name. An example is **Forms![*Names and Addresses*]![*Dues Amount*]**.

Expression: Refer to Field Names

Queries, forms, reports, and even tables can refer to *field* names in criteria, calculations, and properties. You might need to use one field name for another field name's criteria. For example, to find all shipped dates that were after the customer's required date, include `>[Required Date]` in the query's criteria row of the shipped date's field.

Steps

1. Move to the appropriate place in an *expression.*
2. Type an open square bracket, the field name, and a close square bracket. An example is **[*First Name*]**.

Access will automatically put square brackets around field names if there is no space in the name. However, it is a good habit to include brackets around all field names.

Expression: Using the Builder

You can use the *Expression* Builder to create both simple and complex expressions for use in tables, forms, queries, and reports. Whenever a field, value, or *control* takes an expression, you will see a build button with an ellipsis (...) on it or you can use the Build button on the toolbar.

An expression takes a set of values, symbols, operators, or identifiers and evaluates it to produce a result. Often the result is a value, be it numeric, text, logical Yes/No, dates and times, and so on. (See "Expression: Operators.")

Steps

1. In the Control Source of a *form* or *report* control, cell on the *Query* Design *grid*, or other *property*, click the build button (...) to view the Expression Builder.
2. To find a field control name to use in the expression, double-click the first column on Tables, Queries, Forms, or Reports and choose the appropriate *object* name. Then double-click the field or control name in the second column.

3. To use an operator (such as plus, greater than, and so on), click the button in the Expression Builder window. If it is a rarely-used operator, double-click the Operators folder in the first column of the lower portion of the Expression Builder. Then choose a category in the second column and double-click the operator in the third column.
4. To use a *function*, double-click Functions in the first column and then Built-In Functions. Choose a category in the second column, and double-click the function in the third column. The function shows `<<place holders>>` where *arguments* should go. Click each placeholder and type your variables, use the Expression Builder items, or delete the placeholder.
5. When finished with the function, choose OK.

NOTE If you don't know the category of a function, choose <All> in the second column of the Expression Builder, and click and scroll in the third column. Type the first few letters of the function to scroll down to those letters.

You can also use functions created in *VBA*. Double-click Functions in the first column and choose the second folder which is the name of your *database*.

Access checks the syntax of your *expression* when you close the Expression Builder to see if it violates any obvious rules; if it doesn't, it allows you to enter that expression. Just because the expression's syntax checks out doesn't mean that you've created the correct expression. But at least you have an expression template interface to speed up your work, and to take much of the drudgery out of entering the symbols and data correctly.

Expressions: Test Values

The syntax you use in an expression is important. In controls on reports and forms, an expression requires the use of a preceding equal sign, but not in queries. Text is often required to be surrounded by quotation marks. In addition to spelling function and field names correctly, make sure you enclose field names with spaces in square brackets. To test an expression, follow these steps.

Steps

1. In the *Table* Design *property*, *Query* Design *grid* cell (Field or Criteria), or *Control* Source or other property on a *form* or *report* control, type the expression.
2. Click outside of the box you are typing in. If you have a syntax problem, Access will often give you a message. Common errors include not enough parentheses, missing one or both of the brackets for field names, or forgetting an operator such as the ampersand (&).
3. Display the table, query, form, or report. Access might give you an error message in the *object*.
4. If your expression was in a field, try entering data in that field. If the expression is calculated using other fields, try entering sample data in those fields.
5. If you still have problems with an expression that includes a function, go back to Design view, double-click the function name, and press F1 to view help for that function.

Functions: Financial

If you need to calculate payments or interest rates, you would probably create a calculated field on a *query* (Field row of Query Design *grid*) or a *form* or *report* (*Control* Source *property* of a *text box* for a calculated field).

Steps

1. In the Control Source of a *form* or *report* control, a cell on the *Query* Design *grid*, or other *property*, click the build button (...) to view the Expression Builder.
2. To use a financial *function*, double-click Functions in the first column and then Built-In Functions. Choose Financial in the second column, and double-click one of the following functions listed in the third column.

3. The function shows `<<place holders>>` where *arguments* should go. Click each placeholder and type your variables (which include field names in brackets). You can use the Expression Builder for field names or other functions. You can also delete the placeholder.
4. When finished, display and then save the form, report, or query.

The following list includes some of the common functions you would use in the preceding Step 2. You will replace the arguments in brackets with field names or numeric values.

- **Payment—Pmt(*rate, nper, pv*)** The amount you need to pay on a car or house loan or money you would get back on a loan.
- **Future Value—FV(*rate, nper, pmt*)** The value in the future when you make a series of payments at one rate.
- **Present Value—PV(*rate, nper, pmt*)** The value in the present of a series of payments at one rate.
- **Internal Rate of Return—IRR(*values*)** The rate your money is earning. Unlike the other three functions, this *function* will probably be in a report's *group* footer or report footer.

CAUTION When you work with financial functions, make sure the `rate` (interest rate) is for the same time period as `nper` (number of payments). So if *nper* refers to monthly payments, you will have to divide the annual interest rate by 12 to get monthly interest.

NOTE These functions show *arguments* that are required. The arguments include `rate` for interest rate, `nper` for number of periods, `pmt` for payment amount, and `pv` for amount (present value) of loan. For more information on each function, highlight the function name in the expression or Expression *Builder* and press F1.

Functions: *IIf*

The `IIf` *function* enables you to test an expression and return one result if the value is true and another if the value is false. The *syntax* is `IIf(expr,truepart,falsepart)`. You would most likely type this expression in the Field cell of a Query Design *grid*. An example might be **IIf([DueDate]>Date(),"Call Now","")**, which says if the value of the DueDate field is greater than today, show the text Call Now, otherwise show nothing (a zero-length *string*).

Steps

1. Click in the Control Source of a *form* or *report* control, cell on the *Query* Design *grid*, or other *property*.
2. Type **IIf**, and an open parenthesis **(**. Then, type an expression that will evaluate to true or false.
3. Type a comma and type what you want to display if the expression in Step 2 evaluates to true. If you want text to display, include the text in quotes.
4. Type another comma and type what you want to display if the expression in Step 2 evaluates to false. Again, if you want text to display, include the text in quotes.
5. Finish the `IIf` expression with a close parenthesis **)**.
6. When finished, display and then save the form, report, or query.

Functions: User-Defined—Use

You use a user-defined *function* just like you use a built-in function. You can use the function in the same places you do any other function. These include a field *property* in *Table* Design *grid*, Field cell to create calculated field in Query Design grid, criteria in Query Design grid or Advanced *Filter* grid, *Control* Source property of a calculated control on a *form* or *report*, and property of a query field or control on a report or form.

Steps

1. Click in the Control Source of a *form* or *report* control, cell on the *Query* Design *grid*, or other *property*.
2. In a Control Source property, type an equal sign. For all expressions, type the user-defined function, an open parenthesis, any *arguments*, and a close parenthesis.

3. If you can't remember the function or *syntax*, click the Build button. Double-click the Functions folder in the first column. Double-click the folder with your *database* name. Single-click the *module* name in the second column. To insert a function with its requested prompts, double-click the function in the third column.

Functions: User-Defined—View

If Access does not have the functions you want, you can create your own in a Visual Basic statement in a *module*. To see examples of user-defined functions, open one of the example databases supplied with Access. The Solutions file provides the richest assortment of functions (see "Database: Examples" in the Table and Database Design part of this book).

Steps

1. To view a *function* created in a module, in the *Database window*, highlight the module name and choose the Design button.
2. In the drop-down box on the right top of the window (the Procedure drop-down *list box*), choose one of the functions. Notice that the procedure beginning with the keyword `Function` has the function name and any *arguments* you need to supply inside the parentheses.

   After some programming statements, you will see the function name repeated, an equal sign, and an expression. This is the definition of the function.
3. Close the module window. If requested, do not save changes you made.

Grouping in Queries

You can calculate expressions based on *groups* of records in a query. To do so, you must establish the grouping by entering the field and selecting Group By in the Totals row of the Query Design *grid*. Then you create an expression on a different field using an *aggregate function* such as SUM, AVG, COUNT, MIN, MAX, STDEV, or VAR.

Steps

1. Double-click each field in the Field List or enter expressions in the Field row of the Query Design grid.
2. If the Totals button has not been clicked, click it now.
3. In the field or field(s) you want to group, choose Group By in the Total row.
4. In fields that you are going to aggregate, choose one of the *aggregate functions* listed earlier—such as SUM, AVG, COUNT, MIN, MAX, STDEV, or VAR in the Totals row.
5. View the query results, save, and close the query.

A calculation is not stored, but rather is evaluated and displayed each time the query is run. You cannot update the results in *Datasheet view*, but you can use the results of a group calculation to update records through an *Update Query*. (See "Action Query: Update Query" in the Queries and Filters part of this book.)

Grouping in Reports

To calculate an expression for a *group* of records on a *report* (see also "Report: Grouping" in the Forms and Reports part of this book"), you must add a *control* on that report and set the Control Source *property*. To sum records, you would type **=Sum([*Fieldname*])** in the Control Source property. To average records, you would type **=Avg([*Fieldname*])**. (See "Calculations: Average of Values.")

Steps

1. Open the report in *Design View*, click the Text Box tool in the *Toolbox*.
2. To sum or average a group of records, add a *text box* to the group header or footer.
3. To sum or average all records, add a text box to the report header or footer.

4. With the text box control selected, click the Properties button on the toolbar to open the Properties sheet. 3/21/97 V&N.
5. Enter the expression starting with an equal sign in the Control Source property box.

Or, click Build and create the expression in the Expression *Builder*.

Pivot Table: Create

A *pivot table* enables you to summarize, analyze, and manipulate data in lists and tables. When you use the *PivotTable Wizard* to create a pivot table, you tell Access which fields in the list you want to arrange in rows and columns. Pivot tables are called such because you can quickly rearrange the position of pivot table fields to give you a different view of the table. You start the Pivot Table Wizard when you create a new *form*.

One useful application of pivot tables is creating summary tables that *group* large categories of data, with totals displayed for each category. A pivot table provides similar information to the Crosstab query. (See "Crosstab Query: Create.")

NOTE Access "cheats" and uses the programming in Excel to create a pivot table. To do this procedure, you need to have Excel installed.

Steps

1. On the Form tab of the *Database window*, choose New, and choose Pivot Table Wizard. Choose OK.

2. After you read the description of a Pivot Table, choose Next and then select the Table or Query on which to base the pivot table. Double-click any fields you want to use in your pivot table. Generally, you will click at least one text or date field and one number or currency field.
3. Access launches Excel where you define the column and row layout of the pivot table. The fields are listed as buttons on the right side of the *dialog box*. Drag into the DATA area the button corresponding to the data field you want to summarize. To arrange items in a field in columns with the labels across the top, drag the button for that field to the COLUMN area. To arrange items in a field in rows with labels along the side, drag the button for that field to the ROW area.
4. To change the aggregate function (count, sum, average) for the data value, double-click the field name in the DATA area, choose the desired function, and choose OK. Then choose Next and Finish.
5. Access returns and shows you the results of the Pivot table in a form. Save and close the form.

NOTE This procedure works with small numbers of categories for rows and columns. The view on the Access form is limited to what you can see on the screen at one time (there is no Page Down). Another alternative is to highlight a table or query; choose Tools, Office Links, Analyze it with Excel; and then run the pivot table directly in Excel.

Pivot Table: Modify

Because *pivot tables* are devices for displaying information, you cannot manually change information in the body of the *table*. You can, however, change the names of the pivot table fields and items. Access doesn't allow you to duplicate names. If you enter an existing field or item name inadvertently, Access will rearrange the pivot table, moving the item with that name to the location where you typed the name. (See "Pivot Table: Create" before you complete this task.)

Steps

1. Open the pivot table *form* in *Form view* and choose the Edit Pivot Table button on the bottom of the form.
2. Choose Data, Refresh Data to refresh the link to Access so that the pivot table will recalculate with the latest data and display any new results.
3. To edit a pivot table field or item name, select that field or item in the pivot table. Type the new name and press Enter.
4. To move a field from a column to row header (or column to row), drag the gray box with the field name to the new location. If your pivot table has too many columns and a few rows, for example, you may want to switch the column and row headers.
5. When finished, choose File, Close & Return to Pivot Form on Excel's menu. View, save, and close the form.

TIP To change additional options for a specific pivot table field, double-click the field button. Choose the options you want in the PivotTable Field *dialog box*; then choose OK.

Running Sum and Count of Records

A *running sum* keeps adding the field instead of giving you the value of the field. You can set the running sum to go over the whole *report* or start again with each change in grouping. If you are working on a budget, for example, you might want to see how the expenses are piling up by date.

NOTE To count the number of records in each *group* or report, create a *text box control*. Set the Control Source *property* to equal 1. Then follow the next procedure to create a running sum.

Steps

1. Open a report in *Design view* and, if not displayed, click the Field List button to display the list of fields in the report.

2. Drag the field that you want a running sum of to the detail section. If desired, move the field's *label*.
3. If the Property sheet is not displayed, right-click the field control and choose Properties.
4. Move to the Running Sum property and double-click to choose Over Group to reset the number when the group changes or Over All for the entire report.
5. View, save, and close the report.

Text: Combining

When you have more than one text field that you would like to combine on a query, *form*, or *report*, use the ampersand (&) *operator*. If you have any constant text, enclose that in quotes. A common example for what you would type is **[First Name]&" "&[Last Name]**.

Steps

1. Create a *text box* in Form or Report *Design view*, right-click the text box, and move to the *Control* Source *property*. Or go to the Field cell in a Query Design *grid*.
2. Type = in a form or report control, or the name of the column header and a colon in a query.
3. Type the field name in square brackets.
4. Type a space and an ampersand (**&**).
5. If you have any connecting text (including spaces), type the text in quotes. Repeat Steps 3 and 4 as often as necessary. View your *object*, save, and close.

Text: Displaying Parts

Sometimes you only need to use some of the characters of a text field on labels, reports, or queries. Several functions enable you to choose which portion of an expression you want.

Steps

1. Click in the Control Source of a *form* or *report* control, cell on the *Query* Design *grid*, or other *property*.
2. Type one of the expressions from the following section.
3. When finished, display and then save the form, report, or query.

Specifying Data with Functions

Access 97 functions can display specified portions of data within your expressions. These functions include:

- **Left(*stringexpr,n*)** Takes the `n` number of characters from the left side of the `stringexpr`.
- **Right(*stringexpr,n*)** Takes the `n` number of characters from the right side of the `stringexpr`.
- **Mid(*stringexpr,start,length*)** Takes out the middle of the `stringexpr` beginning at `start` for `length` characters.
- **InStr(*stringexpr1,stringexpr2*)** The simplest *form* of this function returns the starting position of where a `stringexpr2` begins in `stringexpr1`.
- **Trim(*stringexpr*)** Removes any spaces at the beginning and end of the *string* expression. To remove leading spaces, use `LTrim`; to remove trailing spaces, use `RTrim`.

Forms and Reports

You use *forms* mainly for inputting data and for viewing the data on-screen. You use *reports* for printing lists and summaries of your data (including charts). You construct forms and reports similarly.

The elements you add to a form or report are called *controls*. Controls can be graphics, text labels, pictures, and other *static* elements that do not change as you move from *record* to record; as well as *text boxes* that do change when you move from record to record. Controls can also be used to display or enter data, or perform and display calculations. Controls can be buttons that perform actions; containers like *subforms* (datasheet grids of related records to the main form); or objects that make data entry or viewing easier, such as ActiveX calendar, spinner, and other custom controls.

In most instances, you add a control to a form or report by dragging a *field* name from the Field List or by using the *Toolbox* in Form *Design View* or in Report Design View. You place each control on a *section* within a form or report. Depending on the section, the control will be seen once, on every page, every time a *group* changes, or for every record.

Chart: Axes Modify

On the horizontal(X) or vertical(Y) *axis*, you can change the scaling (minimum and maximum numbers) and values where tick marks appear. You can also format fonts and numbers on the axes, and determine the patterns you want for the lines.

Steps

1. In *Design View* of a *report* or *form*, double-click the *chart* to open Microsoft Graph.
2. Right-click one of the axes and choose Format Axis.
3. Change the weight, style, and color of the axis line or style of tick marks by choosing the Patterns tab and making your selections. Change the maximum or minimum numbers or location of tick marks on the value axis by choosing the Scale tab. Change the format of the labels on the axes by choosing the Font and Number tabs. Align the labels up and down or diagonally on the axis by choosing the *Alignment* tab and making the appropriate changes. Choose OK when finished.

> **CAUTION** When you are selecting objects in a chart, be careful which object you select and then right-click. Since the objects are so close together, you may need to click more than once to get the correct object selected. If you have problems selecting the correct object, you can also use the Chart Objects drop-down button on the toolbar.

Chart: Colors Display

You can change the colors or patterns that appear for each bar or line series on your chart. You can make an individual series stand out more than usual by using Access's default color.

Steps

1. In Design View of a report or form, double-click the chart to open Microsoft Graph.
2. Select bar or line series or a pie slice: To select an entire data series, click any point in the series; to select an individual point in the series, click the data point twice (not a double-click); to change all data points for all series, click outside the chart to select the entire chart.
3. Right-click the selected *object* and choose the format option.

4. Make choices for the Border, Area, or Markers on the Patterns tab. Choose OK.

Chart: Create

Charts enable you to present data in graphical form. When you create a chart, the data used to create the chart is automatically linked to the chart. When the data changes, the chart is updated to reflect those changes. Access provides many features for creating and formatting charts. The *Chart Wizard* leads you step-by-step through the process. You can change chart types, add elements to a chart (such as titles or legends), and format chart elements (such as numbers, fonts, and styles).

You can launch the Chart Wizard from the *Database window* by selecting the New button from the Forms tab or the Reports tab. In the *Design View* of a *report* or *form*, you can also launch the Chart Wizard by selecting Insert, Chart and dragging the mouse pointer to draw the area where you want the chart to be placed.

CAUTION Try not to add too many data points to your chart. It can be confusing to read. Be especially careful if you plan on turning your chart into a slide or overhead. Too many items on the page will be difficult to see at a distance.

Steps

1. From the Reports or Forms tab of the Database window, click the New button. Select the *table* or *query* source for the data from the drop-down button and double-click Chart Wizard.
2. On the next two steps of the Chart Wizard, choose the fields to be charted and the chart type and choose the Next *command button* after completing each step of the wizard.
3. The Chart Wizard then enables you to choose the layout for your chart. To change the location of what will be

graphed, you can drag the name of a *field* to the Data box (value axis), the Axis box (category axis), or to the Series box.

4. Double-click a number field in the Data box and choose whether you want to sum, average, count, or find the maximum or minimum of each value.
5. Double-click a date field in the Axis box to determine how you want to *group* dates (years, months, and so on) and if you want to select specific data. Choose Next.
6. On the last (finish flag) step of the Chart Wizard, give the chart a title, decide whether you want a legend and whether you want to go to Design View. Choose Finish.

Chart: Data Labels

You can attach labels to data points on your *chart*. This can help the viewer interpret the data in a chart more easily. Data *labels* can represent the value for that data point or the category axis label associated with the data point. You can attach data labels to individual data points, a single data series, or all data points in a chart.

> **CAUTION** Only attach labels to charts with small numbers of data points or attach labels to only some of the points. Otherwise, your chart will become too crowded and difficult to read.

Steps

1. In *Design View* of a *report* or *form*, double-click the chart to open Microsoft Graph.
2. Select the data point(s) to which you want to add labels: to select an entire data series, click any point in the series; to select an individual point in the series, click the data point twice (not a double-click); to insert labels on all data points for all series, click outside the chart to select the entire chart.

3. Right-click the selection and choose Format Data Series (or Point) or Chart Options choice on the shortcut menu. Then click the Data Labels tab in the *dialog box*.
4. Select the Data Labels option you want to use, such as Show Value, Show Percent, or Show Label. (Depending on the chart type, some options might not be available.) Choose the None option if you want to remove existing data labels. Click OK.

NOTE If you want to format the font or number of the data labels, right-click a label and choose Format Data Labels.

Chart: Data Source Change

In some cases, you might want to change the source for the data for the chart. Maybe you copied the *form* or *report* and want to use the same chart type and setup but not the same *data source*. Or perhaps you need to change your *criteria* when using *Chart Wizard*.

CAUTION If you change the name of your table, your charts, forms, queries, and reports no longer work for data used from the table. Try to develop a good naming convention so you wont have to change table and field names midway through your database design.

Steps

1. From a Report or Query *Design View*, right-click the chart *object* (you are not in Microsoft Graph) and choose Properties if the *Property* sheet is not visible.
2. In the Row Source property, use the drop-down arrow to choose an existing *table* or *query* or click the build (...) button to enter the *SQL* Statement: Query *Builder*.
3. Choose fields from the *field* lists, add criteria and expressions, and change the Total choices (Sum, Avg, Count, and so on) as desired.

4. Click the SQL window's close button and choose Yes to save the changes you made.

NOTE The SQL query builder window is the same as a normal query window. You can use the same procedures mentioned in the Queries and Filters and Calculations parts of this book.

Chart: Edit

In order to add labels, change colors, or change chart types, you need to be in Microsoft Graph, the applet that comes with Microsoft Office. The *Chart Wizard* automatically uses Microsoft Graph but you can also double-click a chart to enter this applet.

Steps

1. In *Design View* of a *report* or *form*, double-click the chart to open Microsoft Graph.
2. Select the part of the chart you want to modify. For data series, you click once to select an entire data series. You click a second time to select an individual point in the series. To select the entire chart, click outside the chart.
3. Right-click the selected object to bring up the shortcut menu. Make choices on the dialog boxes specific to the object. Choose OK when finished with each dialog box.
4. Repeat Steps 2 and 3 for each object you want to change.
5. When finished with your changes, click the Close (X) button in Microsoft Graph's upper right corner.

6. Back in Design View of the report or form, click the Save button to save the changes to your chart.

Chart: Grid Display

Use *gridlines* to help viewers compare markers and read values in a chart. If you use the Chart Wizard to create a chart, Access enables you to add gridlines as you are creating the chart.

You can add gridlines that originate from either the category or value axis, or both.

Steps

1. In *Design View* of a *report* or *form*, double-click the chart to open Microsoft Graph.

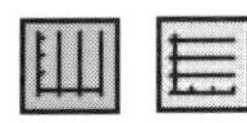

2. Click the Category Axis Gridlines or Value Axis Gridlines buttons on the toolbar to turn gridlines on or off.

Chart: Labels Enter

You can add a *label* attached to a specific portion of a chart (See also "Chart: Titles Add" and "Chart: Data Labels") or add a label and move it anywhere you want.

Steps

1. In Design View of a report or form, double-click the chart to open Microsoft Graph.
2. Type new text and press Enter.

You can move the label by selecting it and then dragging an edge of the title with the left mouse button to the desired location. If you select an existing label and then type, you replace the existing text. To delete a label, select it and press Delete. To edit a label, click once to select it and then position the mouse I-beam in the text and add or delete text.

Chart: Legend Display

A legend explains the markers or symbols used in a chart. When you use the *Chart Wizard* to create a chart, Access asks if you want to create a legend by default, based on the labels of the values you added to the Series box. You can edit the chart to add or remove the legend. You also can customize a legend with border, pattern, and font selections.

Steps

1. In Design View of a report or form, double-click the chart to open Microsoft Graph.

2. Click the Legend button on the toolbar to turn the legend on or off.

You can move the legend by selecting it and then dragging the legend to the desired location. To resize the legend, select it and then drag one of the black handles surrounding the legend.

TIP To format the legend, right-click the legend and choose Format Legend from the shortcut menu. Make your desired selections from the Format Legend *dialog box* and then click OK.

Chart: Titles Add

You can add titles to help explain the data in your chart. Normally, you should include a main chart title, as well as titles for the category and value axes. If you use the *Chart Wizard* to create a chart, Access enables you to add chart titles as you are creating the chart. You also can choose to add chart titles later, or modify existing chart titles.

Steps

1. In *Design View* of a *report* or *form*, double-click the chart to open Microsoft Graph.
2. Choose Chart, Chart Options; then click the Titles tab in the Chart Options *dialog box.*
3. Select the *text box* for the title you want to add (such as Chart Title), and type the title; then click OK.

You can move the title by selecting it and then dragging an edge of the title to the desired location. To delete a title, select it and press Delete.

TIP To format a chart title, right-click the title and choose Format Title from the shortcut menu. Make your desired selections from the Format Title dialog box and then click OK.

Chart: Trendlines

You can add a trendline to a chart to show the direction of the charted data and to make predictions. Regression analysis is used to create the trendline from the chart data. You can choose from five types of regression lines or calculate a line that displays moving averages.

Steps

1. In *Design View* of a *report* or *form*, double-click the chart to open Microsoft Graph.
2. Choose Chart, Add Trendline; then select the Type tab in the Add Trendline *dialog box*.
3. Select the data series for which you want to create a trendline in the Based On Series list.
4. Select from the six Trend/Regression types: Linear, Logarithmic, Polynomial, Power, Exponential, and Moving Average. For more information on these types, click the question mark in the title bar of the dialog box, then click the option for which you want more information.
5. Select the Options tab if you want to set any additional options for the trendline, such as the Trendline Name or Forecast options. Click OK.

Chart: Type Change

You can change an Access chart type to represent another type of data. You can change to any of the chart types that Access offers—bar charts, line charts, pie charts, or special custom charts like floating bar charts.

NOTE While it is fun to play with all the different chart types that come with Access, try to pick something that your audience will understand and that is appropriate to understanding the data.

When to Change Chart Types

You should use an appropriate chart type for the data you want to chart. The following list illustrates some common chart types and explains their purpose. For more detailed information on all the chart types, and examples of their use, search on "example chart types" in Microsoft Graph help.

- **Column chart**. Illustrates individual values at a specific point in time or summarizes changes in a text value. The column chart emphasizes variation over time.
- **Bar chart**. Same as a column chart, but displays bars horizontally rather than vertically. This emphasizes values and there is less focus on time.
- **Line chart**. Illustrates changes in a large number of values over equal time intervals.
- **Pie chart**. Shows the *relationship* of each item to the sum of the items.
- **XY (Scatter) chart**. Plots two groups of numbers as one series of XY coordinates; commonly used in scientific applications.
- **Area chart**. Shows how volume changes over time and emphasizes the amount of change.

Steps

1. In *Design View* of a *report* or *form*, double-click the chart to open Microsoft Graph.
2. Right-click in a blank area of the chart, and choose Chart Type from the shortcut menu.
3. In the Chart Type *dialog box*, click the Standard Types or Custom Types tab.
4. Select the chart type you want; then click OK. Resize the chart, if necessary.

NOTE In some cases, data can be more effective when presented in a Totals *query* or report. (See also "Calculations: Sum of Values" in the Calculations part of this book.) Don't overload your charts with too many data points. Combine data into logical units to make your charts more effective.

TIP You can change the chart type for just one of the of the series. Right-click the bar or line for the series and choose Chart Type. The other data series are graphed in the old type, while the selected series is graphed with the new type.

Controls: ActiveX Add

ActiveX controls provide additional functionality for your forms. They provide additional input options or show feedback. The Calendar *control* is an option you can select during setup. If you have the Developer Edition of Microsoft Office, you have access to additional ActiveX controls. You can also buy additional controls from third-party vendors and perhaps download controls from the Web. Before you can complete this task, you must register the ActiveX control. (See also "Controls: ActiveX Register.")

NOTE In versions prior to Access 97, ActiveX controls were referred to as OLE (Object Linking and Embedding) controls or custom controls.

Steps

1. Open a *form* in *Design View*.
2. Click the More Controls button on the *Toolbox* and select the control from the list.
3. Drag the mouse to draw the location where you want the control to be placed on your form.
4. After the control appears on your form, right-click the *object* and set its specific properties through the controlname Object choice on the shortcut menu.
5. To program other properties and events, right-click the object and choose the item in the *Property* sheet.

NOTE For additional help on specific ActiveX controls, reference them in help. For Developer Edition tools, the help will be integrated with Access Contents and *Index* help (not necessarily the *Office Assistant*). For other controls, you will need to read the help that comes with the controls.

Controls: ActiveX Register

Before you can use an ActiveX control, you need to register it. Some controls are registered automatically when you install them, others need to be registered. The Calendar control comes with Microsoft Access. If you don't have it installed, this option is a choice under the Microsoft Access options during the setup procedure. If your control is not registered, or if you want to unregister the control, use the following procedure.

Steps

1. Choose Tools, *ActiveX Controls*
2. To unregister a control, move to the name in the Available Controls list and choose the Unregister button.
3. To add a control, click the Register button and search for the file (extension is OCX) and choose the Open *command button.*

Controls: Add

A *control* is any *object* such as a *text box*, line, *subform*, or *label* added to a *form* or *report*. You can add controls in many different ways. This section summarizes how to add controls. On reports, the controls you normally add include text boxes, labels, lines, rectangles, page-breaks, and perhaps check boxes. On forms you can use all the controls in the *Toolbox*. For more details, see the following tasks for descriptions on how to add specific controls.

Steps

1. To add text boxes, *check boxes*, or *Bound* Object Frames that are appropriate to the *field* type, use a wizard to build the form or click the Field List button in Form *Design View* and drag the field name onto a form from the Field *List box.*

2. To add *combo boxes*, *option groups*, list boxes, command buttons, subforms, or *subreports*, click the Control Wizards button on the Toolbox in Form Design View, click the specific button in the Toolbox, click the form where you want to place the control, and follow the *dialog boxes* of the wizard.

3. To add a *toggle button, option button*, or check box outside of an option *group*, select that button on the Toolbox first, and drag the field name from the Field List box to the form.
4. To draw a line, rectangle, or tab control, click that button in the Toolbox and then drag the mouse pointer in the form or report.
5. To add a label, click the Label button in the Toolbox, click in the form or report, and then type the text for the label.

TIP To lock a control in the Toolbox so that you can create several of those controls, double-click the control tool before you create the control on the design surface. That tool stays selected until you select another.

Controls: Align

When you move *controls* (see "Controls: Move) it is sometimes difficult to get the controls to line up. In these cases, align the controls with menu options.

Steps

1. In the *Design View* of a *form* or *report,* select two or more controls (drag a selection box or hold down Shift and click each control).
2. Choose Format, Align.
3. Choose one of the menu items: Left, Right, Top, or Bottom.

The To *Grid* item on the Align menu aligns the controls to the nearest grid dot. To have controls line up to the grid as you place them on the form or report, choose Format, Snap to Grid. (See also "Controls: Add.") To see the grid, choose View, Grid.

TIP If you often align controls, you can create your own toolbar or add the align tools to the *Toolbox* or other toolbar. Right-click the Toolbox and choose Customize. Click the Commands tab of

continues

continued

the Customize *dialog box* and choose Form/Report Design in the Categories list. Scroll down the Commands list and drag the Align Left, Align Right, Align Top, and Align Bottom to your toolbar.

Controls: Bound Control Create

Controls are devices that display data. When a control displays data from a *data source*, it is called a *bound* control.

Steps

1. Open a *form* or a *report* in *Design View.*
2. Click the *Field* List button on the toolbar to display the Field List.
3. Select the field(s) that your control is bound to.
4. Drag the selected field(s) to the form or report and position the upper-left corner of the icon where the upper-left corner of the control (not its associated *label*) will be positioned, then release the mouse button.

Access creates the appropriate control for that field and sets *properties* of the control based on the underlying field properties from the *table* and default display control properties.

If the bound control isn't the one you want, click the control and press Delete.

Controls: Calculation Create

You can create controls on your forms and reports that perform calculations. After you create a control, you type in the *expression* for the calculation. (See "Calculated Fields: Forms and Reports—Create by Typing" and other tasks in the Calculations part for details on the types of calculations you can create.)

Steps

1. In Design View of a form or report, click the *Text Box* button in the *Toolbox* and click where you want the calculation to appear.

2. Type equals (=) and then type the expression to calculate. Include *field* names in square brackets. For example, **=[Unit Price]*[Amount]** for an extended price. If the control is in a header or footer section of a report, use summary functions such as `Sum()` or `Avg()` and include the field names in brackets within the parentheses.
3. To edit the formula, right-click the control, choose Properties. In the Control Source *property*, change the expression. If the formula is too large to see, press Shift+F2 to zoom on the Control Source property.

Controls: Change Control Type

Access offers you an easy way to change an existing control on a *form* or a *report*. The Change To command can convert one control to another control. When doing so, the appropriate property settings are preserved. When a property exists, it is copied; when a property doesn't exist, it is ignored. If a property is left blank in the original control, Access sets it using the default control style.

The Change To command is used most often to change one type of control to another of the same type (for example, a *bound* control to another type of bound control). Only appropriate choices are available in the Change To submenu when you select a particular type of control.

Steps

1. Open the form or report in *Design View*.
2. Select the control you want to change.
3. Select new control type from the available choices on the Format, Change To submenu.

Controls: Check Box Create

A check box allows for speedy input of yes/no type fields. A check mark in the box indicates yes; a blank indicates no. When you're inputting, you can also move to the *field* with the keyboard and press Spacebar to turn the box on or off.

Steps

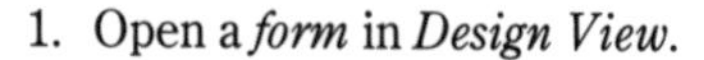

1. Open a *form* in *Design View.*

2. Display the Field List by clicking the Field List button on the toolbar.
3. Drag a field with a yes/no *data type* to the form. The default control for the field is a check box.

Controls: Colors

When you're designing an input form, consider using colors. The effective use of color can make inputting less boring and draw attention to important parts of the form. If you have a color printer, you can also print the form in color.

Steps

1. Open the form or *report* in Design View and select the *control* or the background of the detail or a header or footer section.

2. For text controls, click the Font/Fore Color button to change the text to the color on the button, or use the button's drop-down arrow to choose another color.

3. For text controls, rectangles, and the background of each section, click the Fill/Back Color button to change the background to the color on the button, or use the button's drop-down arrow to choose another color.
4. For lines, text controls, and rectangles, click the Line/ Border Color button to change the line or the outline of the control to the color on the button, or use the button's drop-down arrow to choose another color.

If you want to see a grayed button when the value is *Null*, change the Triple State *property* to Yes. (See "Data: Blanks, Nulls, and Zero-Length Strings" in the Table and Database Design part of this book.)

NOTE To change the formatting of the control programmatically, look at the format properties on the Property sheet. The code for the property name (`BackColor`) is without a space. To change the back color to red, the code would be `controlname.BackColor = 255`. To find the values for the colors, first change the color using the build button... for that property on the Property sheet. Then copy the number and paste it into your code.

Controls: Combo Box Create

A *combo box* enables the user to type or choose from a list of predetermined options. A combo box is especially useful if you have a code you need to place in a *form* and the code corresponds to a value. Instead of having to remember the codes, a user can select from more meaningful data. Using a combo box can also help avoid data entry errors.

The source for the drop-down list in a combo box can be a *table* or *query*, values you type during design, or a list of *field* names from a table or query. If you drag a field from the Field List whose *data type* is already a Lookup Field, Access will automatically create a combo box for you from the properties of the field in Table Design (see "Lookup Column: Create with Wizard" in the Table and Database Design part of this book). As an alternative to a combo box, you can also use a *list box*. (See "*Controls*: List Box Create.")

Steps

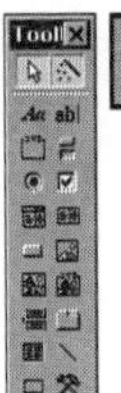

1. From the *Design View* of a form, click the *Toolbox* if necessary and make sure the *Control* Wizards button is selected.
2. Click the Combo Box button on the toolbar and click in the form where you want the combo box to appear. The Combo Box Wizard opens.
3. To type your own values of what will appear in the combo box, choose I Will Type the Values I Want, choose Next, and type the number of columns and values in each column you want. If you type more than one column, choose which column will be the source for the data to store in the field underlying the combo box, which field you want to store the value in, and the *label* for the combo box on the next screens.

4. To use an existing table or query, on the first screen of the Combo Box Wizard, choose the I Want the Combo Box option. Choose the table or query, the fields you want to see when you choose the drop-down arrow, the column width of the fields, and whether you want to hide the *key* column. As in Step 3, also choose which column becomes the value to store, which field you want to store the value in, and the label for the combo box on the next screens of the wizard.
5. If you want to use the combo box to move the form to a specific *record*, you usually place the box in the form header. On the first step of the Combo Box Wizard, choose the Find a Record (third choice), choose the fields you want, the column widths, and the label for your combo box on the next screens of the wizard.

After you finish the wizard, the combo box appears on your form. To see or modify the properties, right-click the combo box and choose Properties. The important *properties* and the property tab they appear on are as follows:

- *Control Source (Data tab)*. This property is the field in your table where you're storing data.
- *Row Source (Data tab)*. The name of the table or query used to lookup values. You can click the build button (...) to access the query *builder* and choose the fields and sort order of items that appear in the drop-down list. If you typed the list, the values appear separated by semi-colons with text enclosed in quotes.
- *Column Count (Format tab)*. The number of columns from the row source used for the list.
- *Column Widths (Format tab)*. The width displayed for each column in the list; 0 will not display a column.
- *Bound Column (Data tab)*. The column from the row source that will be placed in the field on the form.
- *List Width (Format tab)*. The width of the entire drop-down list.

- *Limit to List.* This *property* determines whether you want to limit values to the table/query/list for your combo box or enable the user to type other values as well.

NOTE When you use a table or query for the source of the combo box list, you often want to store the value of the *primary key* in a field on your form. The primary *key field* needs to be one of the fields you choose during the wizard setup. However, you can set the Column Width property to 0. Then, after you move off this field in Form View, the second field of the Row Source is visible.

Controls: Combo Box Not in List

To limit the user to values in the *combo box*, choose Yes on the Limit To List property. If the user types a value that is not in the list, you can have Access give the standard error message or create a procedure to run. For more help on procedures, see the Special Features and Programming part of this book.

Steps

1. In *Design View* of the *form*, right-click the combo box and choose Properties.
2. Move to the On Not In List property (on the *Event* tab), click the build button (...) on the right and double-click *Code* Builder. You will enter the *VBA* code window in a procedure with your `*Controlname*_NotInList`.
3. Type your code. Notice that the procedure has two variables, `NewData` and `Response`. `NewData` contains whatever you typed in the combo box. `Response` is for your return value whether you want the default error message to be returned or skipped. Use `Response = acDataErrContinue` if you want to skip the message or `Response = acDataErrDisplay` if you want the default error message.

4. Click the *Compile* Loaded Modules button, close the code window, and test your procedure.

NOTE For an example of the `NotInList` code, see the `CategoryID` *field* on the `EnterorEditProducts` form in the Solutions *database*. The example databases are in the Office or Access directory in the Samples folder (for example, C:\Office\Samples).

Controls: Command Button Create

Command buttons are common in forms and enable you to go to another *form*, preview a *report*, perform *record* navigation tasks, and more. Command buttons are the primary method for moving a user through a series of options. Command buttons can be part of a form with other controls or the form can consist only of command buttons. This kind of form is called a switchboard form.

Steps

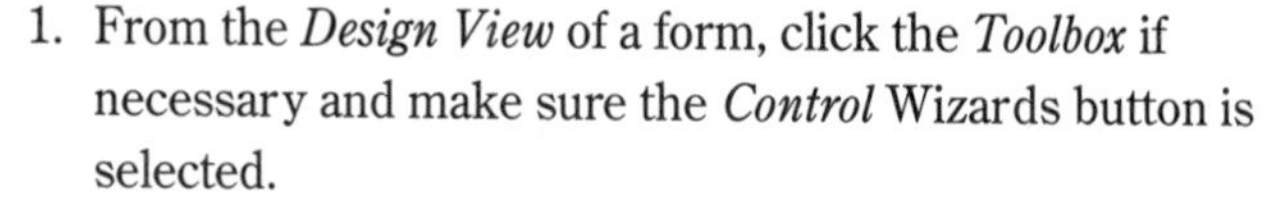

1. From the *Design View* of a form, click the *Toolbox* if necessary and make sure the *Control* Wizards button is selected.

2. Click the Command Button tool on the toolbar and click in the form where you want the button to appear. The Command Button Wizard opens.
3. Choose the category and action to perform from the first step of the wizard. Choose Next.
4. Type the text you want to appear on the button or choose a picture. If you want to see more pictures, check the Show All Pictures *check box*. Choose Next.
5. Type a name for your button on the last step of the wizard. A good convention is to start the name with **cmd** and then give the button a meaningful name such as **cmdPreviewEmployees**.

If you want to view or edit the *code* created by the wizard, right-click the button in Form Design View and choose Build *Event*. The code procedure's name is the *`buttonname`*`_click`.

Controls: Copy

If you are creating a series of the same type of controls, you can copy the *controls* and move them on your *form*. (See also "Controls: Move).") Copying controls works especially well for lines and *command buttons* to create uniformly sized objects.

Steps

1. From the *Design View* of a form or *report*, select the control to copy.
2. Choose Edit, Duplicate.
3. Move the new control to the desired position.

NOTE You can also select the control and click the Copy button. Move to the new location (including a different form or report) and choose the Paste button.

Controls: Data Source

If you create a *control* and later need to change the *field* that it refers to, you can change the *Data Source property*. This might be necessary if you copied the *form* or *report* (see also "Database Object: Copy" in the File Management part of this book) and changed the *Record* Source property to a different *table* or *query*. You might also need to change the Data Source property if you copied the control. (See also "Controls: Copy.")

Steps

1. In Design View of a form or report, double-click a control.
2. Move to the Control Source property (on the Data tab) and click the drop-down arrow to choose a different field.
3. If the control is a calculated *expression*, type an equal sign (=) and then type the expression or click the build button (...) and use the Expression *Builder*.

For more help on the expression builder, see "Expression: Using the Builder" in the Calculations part of this book.

Controls: Defaults Change

Each *control* has its own default *properties*. For example, when you select a *text box* control and click in the design area, the *label* associated with the control normally appears to the left of the text box. You can change the label properties of the text box as well as other default properties on controls you add.

Steps

1. In the *Design View* of a *form* or *report*, click the *Toolbox* button on the toolbar if the Toolbox is not showing.
2. Click the button in the Toolbox and then click the Properties button on the toolbar.
3. Change the properties for all controls of this type in the Properties sheet.

The default is set for all controls of this type for this form or report only.

NOTE To set defaults for all forms or reports in the *database*, create a template. Create a form or report with all the settings for the default controls and background colors. Save the form. Then choose Tools, Options, click the Forms/Reports tab. In the Form Template or Report Template text box, type the name of the form or report. If you want to use the templates for other databases, copy them into each database you need to use the defaults. For more information on templates, see "Forms and Reports: Default Template."

Controls: Delete

When you no longer need a control on a form or report, you can delete it. Deleting the control does not delete the underlying data in the *table*. However, if the *field* is required or used in table *validation* rules, you won't be able to save the *record*.

Steps

1. In Design View of a form or report, select one or more controls. Press Delete. Any labels attached to the data control are also deleted.

2. To delete only the attached *label*, select the label and press Delete. You cannot delete a control with an attached label and leave the label.

Controls: Display or Hide

In some instances, you might need to hide a *control* on a *form* or *report*. You might need to use the value for calculations or programming.

Steps

1. In *Design View* of a report or form, right-click the control and choose Properties.
2. Move to the Visible *Property* (on the Format tab). Choose No to hide the control or Yes to display the control.

NOTE To hide a control programmatically, type **Controlname.Visible = False**. To display the control, type **Controlname.Visible = True**.

Controls: Font Size and Face

Font attributes such as typeface and size provide legibility for your forms and reports as well as make the document attractive. To change the text attributes of any control (label, *text box*, *combo box*, *list box*, and so on), you can use the buttons on the Formatting (Form/Report) toolbar. You can also use the properties of the control.

Steps

1. In the Design View of a form or report, select the control(s) you want to format.

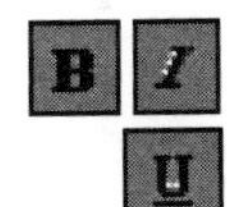

2. Click the Bold, Italic, or Underline buttons to apply that formatting.
3. Click the Font button's down arrow and choose a different typeface.

4. Click the Font Size button's down arrow and choose a different font size.

TIP If the font is too big for the control, use Format, Size, To Fit to change the control size to fit the text.

NOTE To change the formatting of the control programmatically, look at the format properties on the *Property* sheet. The *code* for the property is without a space. To change the font size, you would type the code ***controlname*.FontSize = 14**.

Controls: Labels Create

Labels are automatically created with controls such as text boxes, combo boxes, and so forth. The label itself is a control with its own control properties. They direct the user where to input text or what the data means. There are some instances where you want to add additional labels to a *form* or *report*. You can add a title to the form or report header and also replace a *label* that you deleted.

Steps

1. In *Design View* of a form or report, click the Label button on the *Toolbox*.
2. Click in the design area where you want the label to go.
3. Type the text for the label.

To edit the label, click once to select the *control* and click a second time to enter edit mode. You can also change the *Caption* property on the Property sheet.

NOTE The default is for a label to be created with data controls. However, you can turn off this feature by clicking the *Text Box* control in the Toolbox, clicking the Properties button, and changing the Auto Label property (on the Format Tab) to No. Please note that the items on the Format tab of the Default Text Box are not alphabetically listed. You have to scroll down to find the Auto Label property.

Controls: List Box Create

Creating a *list box* is similar to creating a *combo box* (See "Controls: Combo Box Create."), especially for important properties such as Bound Column, Row Source, and Column Widths. A list box allows you only to choose from an item in the list and does not allow you to type new values. However, when you click in a list box, you can type the first letter to move to an existing item.

NOTE If you don't have adequate room on a form, use a combo box instead of a list box.

Steps

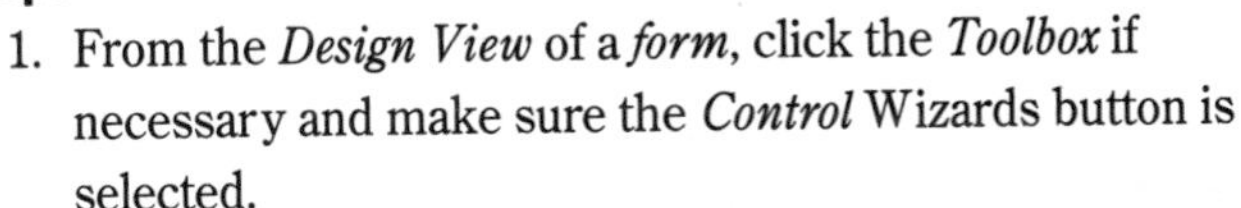

1. From the *Design View* of a *form*, click the *Toolbox* if necessary and make sure the *Control* Wizards button is selected.

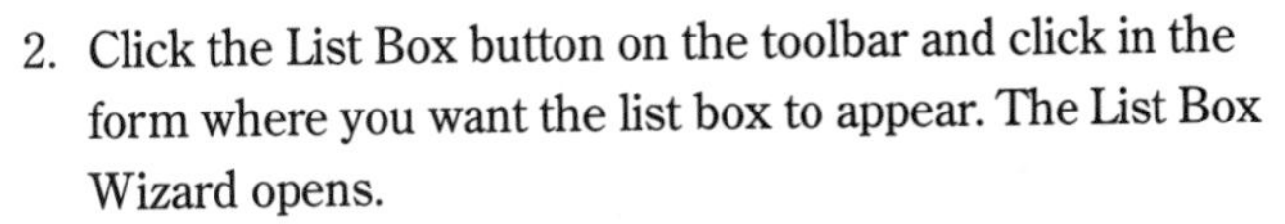

2. Click the List Box button on the toolbar and click in the form where you want the list box to appear. The List Box Wizard opens.
3. To type your values that will appear in the list box, choose I Will Type the Values I Want, choose Next, type the number of columns and values in each column you want. If you type more than one column, choose which column will be the source for the value for the underlying *field*, which field you want to store the value in, and the *label* for the list box on the next screens.
4. To use an existing *table* or *query*, on the first screen of the wizard choose the I Want The List Box To Look Up The Values In A Table Or Query. Choose the table or query, the fields you want to see in the list, and the column width of the fields and whether you want to hide the *key* column. As in Step 3, also choose the column source underlying field, which field you want store the value in, and the label for the list box on the next screens.

5. If you want to use the list box to move the form to a specific *record*, you usually place the box in the form header. On the first step of the List Box Wizard, choose the Find a Record (third choice), choose the fields you want, the column widths, and the label for your list box on the next screens.

After you finish the wizard, the list box appears on your form. To see or modify the properties, right-click the list box and choose Properties.

NOTE If you use a list box (or combo box) to locate a record (see preceding Step 5), Access creates a procedure for the After Update *property*. See the Event Tab in List Box *dialog box*.

TIP You can convert a list box to a combo box or *text box*. Choose Format, Change To and Combo Box or Text Box.

Controls: Move

You drag controls to move them to a desired location. However, getting the controls to line up is easier to accomplish if you use the Format, Align menu. (See "Controls: Align.")

Steps

1. In *Design View* of a *form* or *report*, select one or more controls.
2. Position the mouse pointer hand on the border of one of the controls and drag to move the selected *control*(s) and attached labels.
3. To move only the control or attached *label*, position the mouse pointer finger on the upper left corner of the control (the larger box) and drag.

Controls: Option Button Create

Generally, it's a good idea to use standard Windows conventions for your forms' interface. For this reason, a *check box* means a yes/no option and an *option button* means only one option out of a *group* of options can be selected. (See "Controls: Check Box Create" and "Controls: Option Group Create.") However, you can create an option button as a yes/no alternative where a filled circle means yes and a blank circle means no. Some programs call these radio buttons.

Steps

1. In *Design View* of a *form*, make sure the *Toolbox* and *Field* List are visible.

2. Click the Option Button tool on the Toolbox and then drag the name of the *yes/no field* from the Field List to the form design area.
3. If you want to add another option button to an option group, click the Option Button tool and move into the option group (it will become selected) and click. If necessary, change the Option Value on the Properties Sheet Data tab and the *caption* (Properties Sheet Format tab) of the *label* attached to the option.

Controls: Option Group Create

An *option group* enables you to click one of a series of possible answers. The option group itself contains the reference to the field in its *Control* Source *property*. Each *option button* within the group refers to a potential value for the option group field. The values for the option buttons must be numeric (with no decimals) so the option group feature can only be used for numeric fields that can accept Byte, *Integer*, or Long Integer field sizes. (See also "Field: Size" in the Table and Database Design part of this book.)

Because screen space constrains you to about four options in a group, a *combo box* can be a better alternative if you have more options. (See "Controls: Combo Box Create.")

Steps

1. In Form Design View, click the Option Group button on the toolbar and click in the form where you want the option group to appear. The Option Group Wizard opens.

2. On the first steps of the wizard, type the *label* names for each option within the group. Also, choose if you want one of the options to be the default choice for new records and the values that each option represents.
3. On the next step, choose which field stores the value of the option. The other choice, Save the Value for Later Use, could be used in programming. Choose Next.
4. Decide whether you want option buttons, *toggle buttons*, or *check boxes* within your option group and what style the group will have; then, choose Next.
5. On the final screen of the wizard, give the option group a *caption*. Type the name and choose Finish.

To add option buttons, toggle buttons, or check boxes into the option group after it is created, click one of those buttons in the *Toolbox* and drag into the option group until it is highlighted. Edit the caption of the label and change the Option Value property of the new option.

NOTE If you are using the option group for programming rather than to fill in a field, you would add *code* to the After Update property (on Event tab). A common way to handle options would be to use the `Select Case`, `End Case` statements. Between these two statements, use Case *number* on one line followed by programming statements on the next lines. *Number* would be the value for each option within the group.

Controls: Properties Change

Controls are edited in the Design View for forms and reports. Some aspects of a control can be altered, for example, through manipulating the control's shape on the design surface or resizing the control. Most aspects of controls are edited in the *Property* sheet for that control.

To view a control's Property sheet, select the control and click the Properties button on the toolbar.

You can click either the All, Format, Data, *Event*, or Other page to see a subset of the properties for that control.

Steps

1. In *Design View* of a *form* or *report*, click a control or section, and click the *Properties* button on the toolbar to open the Properties sheet.
2. Click the Property you want to set; or navigate to it using the Up or Down arrow keys, or the Page Up or Page Down keys.
3. Enter or edit the value of the property.
4. If the property has a down arrow displayed, you can select the value from the drop-down list; or if the property displays a build button (...), you can click that button and alter the *expression* in the Expression *Builder.*
5. Press the Enter *key* or click outside of the row to establish your changes.

For more help on the expression builder, see "Expression: Using the Builder" in the Calculations part of this book.

TIP If you need to open up a larger window for that property, press the Shift+F2 key to open a Zoom box. To get help for a particular property, press the F1 key while that property is current.

Controls: Select

Before you move, delete, change font attributes, align, or change properties of a *control*, you need to select the control first. Depending on your needs, there are numerous ways to select controls.

When you select a control, small, black sizing handles appear around the border of the control. When the mouse pointer is on a sizing handle, the pointer turns to a double-headed arrow, enabling you to size the control. (See also "Controls: Size.") The upper left corner of a selected control displays a larger box that enables you to move the control independent of the attached *label.* (See also "Controls: Move.") In each of the following steps, you are in Design View of a form or report.

Steps

1. To select one control, click it. If you want to select the control by its name, choose it from the list on the *Select Objects* button on the Formatting (Form/Report) toolbar.
2. To select multiple adjacent controls, drag the mouse to draw an outline around the controls (do not start dragging on top of a control). All the controls within the outline and any control that touches the outline are selected. This is sometimes referred to as lassoing controls.
3. To select multiple controls, click the mouse on the first control, hold down Shift, and click the other controls.
4. To select all controls in a vertical or horizontal column or row, move the mouse pointer into the horizontal or vertical ruler and click or drag in the ruler.

CAUTION When trying to select controls, you might accidentally move or size one or more controls. Immediately click the Undo Current Field/Record button to return the controls to the previous position.

To unselect controls, click in the design background, not on a control.

NOTE You can change the effect of lassoing controls. Choose Tools, Options, Forms/Reports tab. In the Selection Behavior section, choose Partially Enclosed to lasso as mentioned in the preceding Step 2 or Fully Enclosed to require that the entire control be within the outline to be selected.

Controls: Size

For some controls, especially labels with larger fonts, you will need to resize the *control*. This is also true for most other controls with underlying *field* values. When you use a Form or *Report* wizard (see also "Forms: Create with Form Wizard" and "Reports: Create with Report Wizard") or AutoForm or

AutoReport (see also "Forms: Create with AutoForm" and "Reports: Create with AutoReport") to create a form or report, *text box* controls are generally wide enough to display the widest value. When you drag fields from the Field List to add them in Design View, the control might not be wide enough to display the field's text.

Steps

1. In *Design View* of a *form* or *report,* select the control or select multiple controls if you want to size them at once.
2. If the control is a *label,* choose Format, Size, To Fit (this does not work with data controls).
3. For all controls, move to the center sizing handle on any edge. Drag the double-headed black arrow.
4. To size all selected controls the same, choose Format, Size and make one of the following choices: To Tallest, To Shortest, To Widest, or To Narrowest.

Controls: Space

Spacing on a form or *report* is often an important issue if you want to make the document legible or if you need to fit more items into an area. You can move the controls (see also "Controls: Move") or choose one of the Format menu options.

Steps

1. In Design View of a form or report, select multiple controls in a row or column.
2. For a column of controls choose Format, Vertical Spacing or for a row of controls choose Format, Horizontal Spacing.
3. Choose one of the following: Make Equal, Increase Spacing, Decrease Spacing.

Controls: Text Box Create

Text box and *label* controls (see also "Controls: Labels Create") are the most common controls on your forms and reports.

Text boxes are used to display the underlying fields in the *table* or *query*. In *Form View*, you also use text boxes to edit or type new values. You can also use them to show the results of calculations. (See also "Controls: Calculation Create.")

Steps

1. In *Design View* of a *form*, make sure the *Toolbox* and *Field* List are visible.
2. Drag the field name from the Field List into the design area.

The *Control* Source *property* of the control shows the name of the field. You can use the drop-down arrow to change the field.

NOTE If you have a large text or *memo* field, you can change the size of the control. (See also "Controls: Size.") Then change the Scroll Bars property (on the Format tab) to Vertical. This will enable you to scroll to see more text when you are in Form View and in the control.

Controls: Toggle Button Create

A *toggle button* is an alternative to a *check box,* enabling you to input Yes/No responses on a form. (See also "Controls: Check Box Create.") When the value is Yes or True, the button appears pressed. When the value is No or False, the button appears raised. You can also use toggle buttons as part of an *option group.* (See also "Controls: Option Group Create.")

Steps

1. In Design View of a form, make sure the *Toolbox* and *Field* List are visible.
2. Click the Toggle Button tool on the Toolbox and then drag the name of the *yes/no field* from the Field List to the form design area.
3. If you want to add another toggle button to an option group, click the Toggle Button tool and move into the option group (it will become selected) and click. If necessary, change the Option Value on the Properties Sheet.

4. Click in the middle of the toggle button and type text to appear on top of the button.

Unless you complete Step 4, it is difficult to tell when a toggle button is pressed. If you want a picture on the toggle button instead of text, choose the Picture *property* on the Property sheet's Format tab and click the build (...) button to choose the picture. If you want to see a grayed button when the value is *Null*, change the Triple State property to Yes. (See "Data: Blanks, Nulls, and Zero-Length Strings" in the Table and Database Design part of this book.)

Controls: Unbound Control Create

A *control* that is connected to a *data source* is called a *bound control*; one with no data source is called an *unbound* control; and one attached to an *expression* is called a *calculated* control. How you create a control, or add it to a form or a *report*, depends on the type of control it is.

Steps

1. Open a *form* or a *report* in *Design View*.
2. Click the button in the *Toolbox* for that unbound control.

   Typical unbound controls are text labels, pictures, lines, and so on.
3. Click and drag the control onto the form or report.
4. If you used the Image or Unbound *Object* Frame buttons, complete the *dialog boxes* to insert the file or create the object.

Data: Default Value

One way to simplify data entry is to have Access automatically enter values that you use often in certain fields. For example, if most of your clients were from the same state, have Access set the *default value*. You can set the default value during *table* design. (See also "*Field*: Default Value" in the Table and *Database* Design part of this book.) However, you might have multiple forms for one table and decide to enter different default values for each form.

> **CAUTION** Make sure the default value does not click with the Validation Rule property (Data tab).

Steps

1. Open the *form* in *Design View* and double-click the *control* to display the *Property* sheet.
2. Move to the Default Value property on the Data tab and type the value you want for all new records.

When you enter values in a new *record* you can always replace the default value with an actual value.

Data: Validate

If you want to make sure the correct data is entered on a form, you can use data *validation* procedures. One alternative is to use a *combo box* or *list box* to make sure only one of the valid choices is entered. (See also "Controls: Combo Box Create" and "Controls: List Box Create.") You can also set data validation properties originally during *table* design. (See also "Validate Data: *Field* Validation" in the Table and *Database* Design part of this book.) If you do this before you create the form, the validation properties are automatically carried on to the *control*.

Examples of validation rules include >**100** and **between 0 and 50** for number fields, or >**Date()** (greater than today's date). (See the *Criteria* tasks in the Queries and Filters part and *Expression* tasks in the Calculations part of this book.)

Steps

1. In Form Design View, double-click the control to open the Property sheet.
2. Move to the Validation Rule property (on the Data tab) and enter an expression.
3. If you want your own error message to appear if this rule is violated, type the message in the Validation Text property.

NOTE If you want to create more complicated data validation rules, see also "Validate Data: *Record* Validation" in the Table and Database Design part of this book. You can also create a procedure that you would apply to the Before Update property (on the Event tab) of the control.

Date and Time: Insert on Report

When you want to know when a *report* or form was printed, you can insert the date and or time using menu choices. As an alternative, you can also create a *text box* on a report or a form and insert and format a date *expression.* (See also "Calculations: Date" in the Calculations part of this book.)

Steps

1. Open the *report* or *form* in *Design View.*
2. Choose Insert, Date and Time. The Date and Time *dialog box* appears.
3. Choose Include Date and one of the date format options. If desired, choose Include Time and one of the time format options; choose OK.
4. Drag the *control* to where you want it on the report or form.

Format: AutoFormat

If you like a particular background and format settings for a form or report, you can use the *AutoFormat* feature. When you initially create the form or report with a wizard you can also choose an existing AutoFormat. (See also "Forms: Create with Form Wizard.") An alternative to AutoFormats are Templates, used when you create a new form or report in Design View. (See also "Forms and Reports: Default Template.")

Steps

1. Open a form or report in Design View and click the AutoFormat button. The AutoFormat dialog box opens.
2. Choose from the list of Form (or Report) AutoFormats and preview the format.

3. If desired, choose Options and choose whether you want to apply the fonts of the example, the colors of the controls, or the border surrounding the controls. Choose OK when finished.

NOTE You can also use the Customize button on the AutoFormat dialog box to save your current form as a new AutoFormat.

TIP You can also change the background of the form (including graphics that are not included in AutoFormat) by changing the Picture *property* (on Format tab) of the form. Click the build button (...) to select the file you want to insert.

Format: Copy

To format all of your forms the same way, consider using the *AutoFormat* feature. (See also "Format: AutoFormat.") However, when you just want to copy the style (font, font size, and colors) from one *control* to another, use the Format Painter button.

Steps

1. Open a *report* or *form* in *Design View* and click the control whose attributes you want to copy.

2. Click the Format Painter button once to copy only to one control or double-click for multiple controls.
3. Click the control(s) for which you want to change attributes.
4. If you double-clicked the Format Painter button, click it again to turn off the feature.

Format: Numbers and Dates

Generally, when you format numbers in a *table* or *query*, the format should be sufficient for your form or report. However, there are instances when the format is not appropriate. This happens especially when you create calculated controls.

Steps

1. Open the form or report in Design View and double-click a numeric or date *control* to open the *Property* sheet.
2. Move to the Format property (on the Format tab).
3. Use the drop-down arrow to choose from the list of format options or type a custom format.

NOTE To see custom format options, click the *Office Assistant* button on the toolbar, type Format Property, and click Format Property.

Format: Special Effects

When you create a form with the Form Wizard, Access will prompt you for a style that includes special effects for the *controls*—for example, raised, sunken, or normal. If you want to change these effects or create them during Form Design, you can use the Special Effect button on the Formatting toolbar.

Special effects for controls include raised, sunken, flat (border outline), shadowed, etched (carved outline), or chiseled (carved line on bottom of control).

Steps

1. Open a *form* in *Design View* and select the control or controls you want to change.

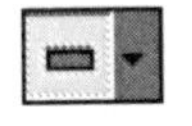

2. Click the Special Effect button to choose the current effect or use the drop-down arrow and choose one of the six effects.

3. If you want to put a simple border around the control and remove the special effect, use the Line/Border Width button.

Format: Text

When you are inputting text, you can have your entry converted to all uppercase or all lowercase.

Steps

1. Open the form or report in Design View and double-click a text control to open the *Property* sheet.
2. Move to the Format property (on the Format tab).
3. Type a > (greater than sign) to format the entry as all upper case or a < (less than sign) to format the text as all lower case.

While inputting, when you press Enter or Tab to leave the *field*, the text will format as you indicated.

Forms and Reports: Data Properties

While you are designing forms, you might want to use some of the data properties available for the form or controls. You can make a form or control read-only, for input only, or determine how you want to control simultaneous users.

Steps

1. To change a *form property* in Form *Design View*, double-click the Form and *Report* Selector at the top left of the form to open the Property sheet.
2. To change a control property, double-click the control to bring up the Property sheet.
3. Click the Data tab of the property sheet.
4. Once the form or control is open, make changes to any of the properties shown in the bulleted list by following these steps.

   - *Record Source.* Underlying *query* or *table* for the form or report. (See also "Forms and Reports: Data Source.")
   - *Filter.* Indicates which records will show. Access remembers the filter when you save a form after using one of the filter buttons or Records, Filter choices in *Form View*. Filters are not available when the Allow Filters property is set to No. This property is also available on reports and is active if the Filter On property is set to Yes.

- *Order By.* Type the name of the *field* to sort the records. This property is filled in when you choose the Sort Ascending or Sort Descending button in Form View. This property is also available on reports and is active if the Order By On property is set to Yes.
- *Allow Edits.* If this is set to No, the data on the form cannot be edited. To get the same effect just on a control, set the individual Locked control property to Yes.
- *Allow Deletions.* If this is set to No, you cannot delete a *record.*
- *Allow Additions.* If this is set to No, you cannot add a record.
- *Data Entry.* When this property is set to Yes, the form automatically opens to a new, blank record.
- *Recordset Type.* When this property is set to Snapshot, data on the form cannot be edited. *Dynaset* means that most forms can be edited. For more information, press F1 for help.
- *Record Locks.* Select No Locks to allow any user to change a record. If the same record is changed by two users at the same time, the second user to save the record is prompted to decide which record to keep. Select Edit Records to not allow a second user to edit the record while it is being edited by the first user. Select All Records to prevent anyone from editing the underlying table while the Form is open. This property is also available for Reports with the No Locks and All Records options.
- *Enabled.* When this control property is set to No, the control cannot have the *focus* and it appears dimmed.

Forms and Reports: Data Source

After you copy a form or report, you can change the attached *query* or *table,* which is the source for your data. In some cases, you need to change the *data source* to add additional fields to the underlying query or sort.

Steps

1. Open the *form* or *report* in *Design View* and double-click the Form and Report Selector (the square above the vertical ruler and to the left of the horizontal ruler). The *Property* sheet for the form or report appears.
2. Move to the Record Source property (on the Data tab). Click the drop-down arrow to choose another table or query.
3. If you need to add fields or sort your data, click the build button (...). You will enter a *SQL* query *builder* that is the same as a normal query window. Drag the fields you need from the *Field* List; use the Close (X) button to get back to the Property sheet.

NOTE To use the SQL query builder, use the same techniques as shown in "Query: Create with Design View" in the Queries and Filters part of this book.

Forms and Reports: Default Template

If you like the colors, location of labels relative to data controls, and other form or report properties, you can save the form or report as a default template. Then when you create a form or report in Design View (not through a wizard), those properties are the defaults for the new form or report. Existing forms and reports are not affected. If you have multiple forms or reports you would like to use as templates, consider using the *AutoFormat* feature. (See also "Format: AutoFormat.")

Steps

1. Create a form or report. Change the default properties of any control on the *Toolbox*. Display the *sections* you want and change any section properties including size and colors.

2. Save the form or report and choose Tools, Options, and click the Forms/Reports tab.
3. Type the name of the form or report in the Form Template or Report Template *text box* and choose OK.
4. If you want to export this form or report to another *database*, choose File, Save As/Export, choose the To An External File or Database option, and choose the database in the file *dialog box*.

NOTE If you want to use a template from another database, you can also use File, Get External Data, Import to copy the template. Otherwise, Access will revert to the Normal template even if you have another template listed. Options remain in effect for all databases, not just the current database.

Forms and Reports: Design View Options

You can turn on or off different Design View options to help you create forms and reports. These options help you add, size, and align controls. The following list describes these options in more detail:

- *Properties Sheet*. Click the Properties button on the Design toolbar to turn the *Property* sheet on or off. To set properties, see also "Controls: Properties Change" and "Forms and Reports: Detail Properties." You can also double-click a control, section, or Form and Report Selector to open the Property sheet for that control.

- *Field List*. Click the *Field* List button on the Design toolbar to turn the Field List on or off. You can drag a field name to create a control for that field. (See also "Controls: Add.")
- *Ruler*. Turn on or off the horizontal ruler (at the top of the Design window) and the vertical ruler (at the left of the window) by choosing View, Ruler. You can use the ruler to estimate the position of controls on forms and

reports and to select controls in a row or column . (See also "Controls: Select.")

- *Grid.* Turn the *grid* on or off by choosing View, Grid. Even without the grid visible, you can still move the controls and they will stop at dots on the grid if the Format, Snap to Grid choice is selected. If you want to temporarily ignore the grid when you are moving a control, hold down Ctrl while you drag the mouse. To line up your selected controls, choose Format, Align, To Grid. To size controls to the nearest grid points, choose Format, Size, To Grid. To change the spacing between the dots, double-click the Form and Report Selector to open the Property sheet for the form or report and change the Grid X and Grid Y values. The values indicate the number of dots per unit of measurement (such as inches).

- *Toolbox.* The *Toolbox* enables you to place different kinds of controls on your form or report. Click the Toolbox button on the Design toolbar to turn the Toolbox on or off.

Steps

1. To select your *Design View* options, open a form or report in Design View.
2. Turn the appropriate option on or off. For descriptions of these particular options, see the preceding list.

Forms and Reports: Detail Properties

The detail section of a *report* and *form* is where the data controls from each *record* normally go. While headers and footers summarize data and show labels for the report or form as a whole, the values in the detail section change for every record. Six of the detail properties are described as follows:

- *Keep Together.* Move to the Keep Together property. Choose Yes to try to keep all records in the detail section together on one page when printing. This will not work if the detail section is larger than a page.

- *Visible.* Move to the Visible property and choose No to show just the summaries on a report and not the individual values for records.
- *Can Grow* and *Can Shrink.* Change the Can Grow property to Yes if you want the section to be able to expand to accommodate long labels (the control's Can Grow property should also be set to Can Grow). Set the Can Shrink property to Yes if you want the detail section to remove extra space if there are blank or short values for a record.

- *Back Color.* To change the Back Color property, you can click the detail section and then click the Fill/Back Color button on the Formatting (Form/Report) toolbar and choose a color.
- *Height.* To change the Height property, you can move to the bottom of the detail section until the mouse pointer becomes a double-headed arrow and drag the mouse up or down.

Steps

1. To select your detail properties, open a form or report in Design View.
2. Double-click the gray bar labeled Detail. The Detail Property sheet opens.
3. Click the Format tab of the Property sheet.
4. Change the appropriate option as shown in the preceding list.

NOTE To find information on other properties besides those described in this section, move to the property in the Property sheet and press F1.

Forms and Reports: Name

When you create a form or report using a wizard, Access will ask you the name of the form or report as the last step. (See also "Forms: Creating with Form Wizard" and "Reports:

Creating with Report Wizard.") When you create a form or report using any other method, you need to give the form or report a name after you create it.

The names appear in the *Database window*. A standard convention is to include a lowercase three-character frm or rpt abbreviation before the report name, to not include spaces, and to capitalize the first letter of each word. However, Access allows you to include spaces and type up to 64 characters for a name.

Steps

1. To give a *form* or *report* a name for the first time, click the Save button after completing the design and enter the name.
2. To give the form or report a new name while in Design View, choose File, Save As/Export. In the New Name *text box* enter the name.
3. To rename a form or report, right-click the name in the Database window, choose Rename, and type the new name.

Forms: Create Hypertext Links

A hypertext link enables you to go to another document on your hard drive or network drive or to a Web site. You can enter hypertext links within fields for each *record.* (See also "Hyperlinks: Enter" in the Database Essentials part of this book.) However, you can also create a form that has hyperlinks to the documents you want. This form can act as an alternative to a *switchboard* with *command buttons.* (See also "Controls: Command Button Create.")

Steps

1. In the Database window, click the Forms tab and choose the New button. Do not choose a source *table* or *query* and choose OK.

2. Click the Insert *Hyperlink* button on the Form Design toolbar. The Insert Hyperlink *dialog box* opens.

3. In the Named Location in File (Optional), choose Browse and select the *object* from the Select Location dialog box and choose OK twice.
4. If you want to change the name on the form, double-click the Hyperlink in Design View and type a new name in the *Caption* property.

NOTE If you want to go to a different database, type the *path* and file name in the Link to File or URL *text box* in the Insert Hyperlink dialog box. You can even use this form to go to different documents in different applications (Word and Excel, for example).

Forms: Create with AutoForm

The quickest way to create a form is to use one of the AutoForm options. Use this procedure if you probably won't be changing the order of fields and you plan on using most of the fields from a *table* or *query*. To add a background and choose the order of fields, use Form Wizard instead. (See also "Forms: Create with Form Wizard.") For the most control, create a form in Design View. (See also "Forms: Create with Design View.")

Steps

New Object: Form

1. In the *Database window,* highlight the name of the table or query you want to use for your form.
2. On the New *Object* button, select AutoForm if it does not show. Access creates a columnar form by default.

   If you want other AutoForm options, select Form on the New Object button and in the New Form *dialog box,* double-click AutoForm: Tabular or AutoForm: Datasheet.

Forms: Create with Design View

Forms are one of the primary methods used to work with data, navigate, and perform actions in a *database*. You create, specify the contents of, and modify forms in the *Design View*. You work with forms and enter data into them in *Form* View. This construct separates the construction of your form from its use.

Steps

1. Click the Forms tab in the *Database window*, then choose the New button.
2. Choose the *table* or *query* to base your form on from the drop-down list. If you are creating a *switchboard* or *dialog box*, you can leave the *text box* blank.
3. Double-click Design View in the New Form dialog box. Access opens the blank form in the Design View.
4. Add labels, text boxes, and other controls.

5. Click the Save button on the Form Design toolbar or choose File, Save. Enter the name of the form in the Save As dialog box, then choose OK.

(See also "Controls: Add" and other "Controls" tasks to place controls on your form.)

Forms are used to:

- Display and enter data into a database using a data entry form.
- Select options via a form. The form you create has the attributes of a dialog box (text boxes, combo boxes, option buttons, and command buttons such as OK and Cancel).
- Provide a method for launching or opening other elements of a database, such as forms and reports, through a form that looks like a switchboard.

All of the preceding forms are created in the Design View, and some can be created with the Form Wizard. In Design View, you can add graphic elements such as lines, boxes, text labels, and *bound* controls. Bound controls display data from underlying *record* sources like tables, queries, or calculations; or they contain the results of calculations based on data in your database.

When you work with forms in Design View, you add controls to the design surface of your form by clicking that control in the *Toolbox* and clicking and dragging it onto the form. You can add and delete *sections* from forms to control what appears on the form and where it appears.

Forms: Create with Form Wizard

Access contains a Form Wizard that can create many different kinds of forms based upon your input. Even if you intend to create a custom form, the Form Wizard can be a good starting place from which you can make modifications. As a quicker alternative to the Form Wizard, you can create a form automatically with AutoForm. (See also "Forms: Create with AutoForm.") You can also have more control over creating a form by going into Design View. (See "Forms: Create with Design View.")

Steps

1. Click the Forms tab in the *Database window*, then choose New. Select Form Wizard in the New Form *dialog box*. Choose the *table* or *query* from the drop-down list that will be the *data source*. Choose OK.
2. In the first step of the wizard, select the fields you want to see on your form from the Available Fields *list box* by double-clicking to place them in the Selected Fields list.

   For any related tables: Select that table from the Tables/Queries list box, then add the fields of interest to the Selected Fields list box; then choose Next.
3. If you are building a form based on a *relationship*, in Step 2 of the wizard you can specify the parent table used to control the view of your data (choose the parent table in the How Do You Want To View Your Data list box).

   If you have more than one data source, select also whether the *child* table appears in a Form with *Subform*(s) or is a Linked Form Linked Through a Button to a New Window; then choose Next.

4. Select the layout and style desired on the next two steps of the wizard. When you select a choice, a preview is shown in the window.
5. Enter a name for the form in the Form *text box*, or a name for the subform derived from the related or *linked tables* as appropriate and then choose Finish on the next screen.

Forms: Create with New Form Dialog Box

The New Form *dialog box* is your *key* to creating forms. There you can create forms from scratch, or use one of the different form wizards to create forms based on your input.

Steps

1. Choose New on the Forms tab of the *Database window.*
2. Select a *table* or a *query* to base your form on or leave blank to create a dialog box or switchboard.
3. Select one of the choices in the New Form dialog box (as detailed in the following list).

Among the choices you have in the New Form dialog box are the following:

- *Design View.* This selection opens a blank form that you can build from scratch. (See also "Forms: Create with Design View.")
- *Form Wizard.* This wizard runs you through several steps that enable you to select the tables, *relationships,* controlling table, form style, and other features you want your form to have. (See also "Forms: Create with Wizard.")
- *AutoForm Columnar.* This columnar report is one where fields are stacked vertically with text labels on the left and *text boxes* on the right. Each *record* appears on a single page. (See also "Forms: Create with AutoForm.")

NOTE Some databases refer to tabular layouts as columnar layouts.

- *AutoForm Tabular.* This wizard creates forms in which you see several records on every page.
- *AutoForm Datasheet.* This wizard creates a spreadsheet-like display for your form where records display in rows, and fields in columns.
- *Chart Wizard.* The Chart Wizard creates a form with an attached chart. This is an optional setup option when you install Access or Office. (See also "Chart: Create.")
- *PivotTable Wizard.* A *pivot table* is an interactive table where data is summarized by *field*. Access uses the Microsoft Excel PivotTable Wizard to create these types of forms. (See also, "Pivot Table: Create" in the Calculations part of this book.)

When you run an auto wizard, the wizard runs with default choices and without your intervention, creating a form. In all cases, you will need to save your form to disk using the File, Save command or the Save button on the toolbar.

Forms: Dialog Box Properties

You can create a form for user input and present the form as a *dialog box*. In this case, normally the form has no *Record* Source *property*, the *text boxes* are not *bound*, and *command buttons* are used for user confirmation. For a dialog box, you set the properties mentioned in "Forms and Reports: Data Properties" as follows: Allow Deletions and Allow Deletions set to No and RecordSet Type choose Snapshot.

Steps

1. Open the form in Design View.
2. Double-click the Form Selector (the square above the vertical ruler and to the left of the horizontal ruler). The Property sheet for the form opens. Change the properties mentioned in the following Form Properties section.

3. Click each control and change the properties mentioned in the following Control Properties section.
4. When finished, save, close, and test the form.

Form Properties

You need to change the following form properties to make your dialog box function property. These properties show how the entire form will look or act.

- *Caption (Format tab)*. Type the title for the dialog box that appears in the title bar.
- *Scroll Bars (Format tab)*. Shows horizontal or vertical scroll bars for the form. Set to Neither.
- *Record Selectors (Format tab)*. Enables the user to select the current record (for deletion). Set to No.
- *Navigator Buttons (Format tab)*. At the bottom of the form enable the user to go to the first, last, next, and previous records. Set to No.
- *Pop Up (Other tab)*. Normally set to No. This keeps the form on the top even when working on other forms. Set to Yes.
- *Modal (Other tab)*. Normally set to No. This keeps the *focus* on the dialog box. A user cannot do anything else in Access until the dialog box closes. Set to Yes.
- *Border Style (Format tab)*. Normally set to Sizable to be able to change the size of the window. Set to Dialog, which keeps the forms title bar but removes the maximize, restore, and minimize options from the window and the Control menu.
- *Shortcut menu (Other tab)*. Normally set to Yes. This enables the user to use the right-mouse click to copy, paste and do other shortcuts. Set to No.
- *Auto Center (Format tab)*. Set to Yes to have the dialog box appear in the middle of the screen.

Control Properties

The following properties are for controls that will be on your dialog box. These help the user find information or determine how the control reacts to user input.

- *Default (Other tab)*. Set the Default property of the OK command button to Yes. Only one command button can have the Default property in the form. This button has the default focus. When the user presses Enter, the procedure behind this button runs.
- *Cancel (Other tab)*. Set the Cancel property of the Cancel command button to Yes. Only one command button can have the Cancel property in the form. When the user presses Esc, the *code* behind the Cancel button runs.
- *Caption (Format tab)*. The text on the button. This does not appear when the Picture property is set.
- *Picture (Format tab)*. Places a picture rather than text on the button. Click in this property and choose the build button (...) to select from a list of icons.
- *Status Bar Text (Other tab)*. Place text in this property to provide the user with help in the *Status Bar* when the control has the focus.
- *ControlTip Text (Other tab)*. Place text in this property to provide the user with help when the user points the mouse to a control.

Forms: Multiple Records on One Form

If you want to see more than one form in the *Form View*, you can set the Default View *property* to see one line for each *record* or to see multiple records for small forms.

Steps

1. Open a form in Design View and double-click the Form Selector (the square above the vertical ruler and to the left of the horizontal ruler) to open the Property sheet.

2. Move to the Default View property (on the Format tab). Change the property to Datasheet to see one record on each line or Continuous Forms to enable you to scroll through multiple records with the vertical scroll bar. Set the Default View to Single Form to only see one record at a time.

SQL

3. If you only want the *Datasheet View* possible in Form View, change the Views Allowed property to Datasheet. To see just a form, change the property to Form. To have both options, choose Both. When Both is set, you can use the View button in Form View to switch to either view.

Forms: Navigation

You should design your form so it is easy for a user to move around and input data. If you are inputting from a paper form, design the Access form to match the paper form with the fields in the same order if possible. When you press Tab or Enter, Access moves to the fields determined by the *Tab Order.* (See also "Forms: Tab Order.") In addition to clicking the appropriate *field*, you can also use the following procedures to move around on a form when you are in *Form View.*

Steps

1. To move to the next field, press Tab or Enter. If your field is the last on the form, you generally move to the first field on the next *record* (see the following note).
2. To move to the previous field, press Shift+Tab.
3. If you are in field mode (you've tabbed into a field and the entire field is highlighted), press Ctrl+Home to get to the first field on the first record or Ctrl+End to get to the last field on the last record.
4. If you are in edit mode (you've clicked into a field and the cursor is a blinking line), press Ctrl+Home to get to the beginning of the field or Ctrl+End to get to the end of the field.
5. To switch back and forth between field and edit mode, press F2.

NOTE You can change how certain keystrokes operate in Access. Choose Tools, Options, and click the Keyboard tab. You can set the Enter *key* to move to the next field (the default), move to the next record, or not do anything. You can set the left or right arrow key to move to the next character or next field (default) and specify if you want the field to be selected or go to the beginning or end of a field when you enter into the field. If you choose Cursor Stops at First or Last field, Tab and Enter will continuously cycle through the same record rather than moving to a previous or next record.

To change the cycling through a form to just include the current record and not previous or next records, you can also change the form's Cycle *property (on the Other tab)*. For a *text box*, you can change the control's Enter Key Behavior property *(on the Other tab)* to add a new line or move to the next field.

Forms: Sorting

You can sort your forms so that the records appear in any order you want. If you have no sort specified, the records appear in the order you entered them.

Steps

1. Double-click your form in the *Database window*. The form is in *Form View*.
2. Move to the *field* to sort on and click the Sort Ascending or Sort Descending button.

When you exit the form, the sort order is saved. To remove the sort order, open the form in Design View, double-click the Form/Report Selector (the square above the vertical ruler and to the left of the horizontal ruler) and delete the value in the Order By *property* for the form.

NOTE If you want to sort on more than one field, click the Design View option on the View button and double-click the Form/Report Selector button on the top left of the window. Go to the Record Source property (on the Data tab). Click the build button (...) and add the fields for the form. Place the sort fields first and choose Ascending or Descending for the Sort row.

Forms: Tab Order

The order in which you move through fields on a form is called the *tab order*. By default, the tab order is for fields going from left to right across the screen, and top to bottom. You can change the tab order to suit your purpose, even leaving fields out of the tab order to aid in speeding up data entry when a *field* has data entered into it infrequently.

NOTE When you add a field to the form, that field automatically has the last tab order. So after you redesign a form, you will probably have to reset the tab order.

Steps

1. Open the *form* in *Design View* and choose View, Tab Order. To choose the default tab order (left to right and top to bottom), choose the Auto Order button.
2. For a custom tab order, click the control selector; then drag the selector into the position in the order you want and choose OK.
3. To test the tab order, switch to the *Form View* and tab to each of the controls.

Header/Footer: Form and Report

The header and footer of a form or *report* only occur once; the header occurs at the top of the first page and the footer occurs at the bottom of the last page. In *Form View*, the text and graphics on a form header and footer remain constant as you move from *record* to record. In both reports and forms, the header occurs at the top of the first printed page and the footer occurs at the bottom of the last printed page. (See also "Header/Footer: Page.")

Steps

1. Open the form or report in Design View.
2. If the header and footer are not shown, choose View, Form (or Report) Header/Footer.

3. Click the *Label* button on the *Toolbox* and click in the header or footer to add text. Then type the text for the label.

4. Click the Line button on the Toolbox, hold down Shift, and drag the mouse in the header or footer to add a straight line.

If you don't want to see the footer, but you want to keep the footer, delete any controls in the footer and drag the lower edge so the footer section has no height. You can also reverse this procedure to see the footer but not the header.

To remove both the header and footer, choose View, Form (or Report), Header/Footer again and confirm that you want to remove the *sections*.

Header/Footer: Page

The page header and footer only have to do with printing. In a form, you will not see the page header and footer in *Form View*, but will only see them in print preview or when you print the form. Unlike the form or report header and footer (see also "Header/Footer: Form and Report") the page header and footer appear on every page. Use the page header especially for column headings in reports.

Steps

1. Open the *form* or *report* in *Design View*.
2. If the header and footer are not shown, choose View, Page Header/Footer.
3. Use the Label control to add text.

NOTE In a report, you can specify how the page header and report header print relative to each other. Go to the Page Header *property* (on the Report Properties Format tab) and choose one of the options: All Pages, Not With Report Header, Not With Report Footer, or Not With Report Header and Footer. The same options are available for the Page Footer property.

Lines: Change Width

To change the line width, you first need to create a line or go to an existing line. (See also "Lines: Create.") You might need to change the line width to make the line more noticeable.

Steps

1. Open the *form* or *report* in *Design View.*
2. Click a line or rectangle to select it.
3. Choose the drop-down arrow on the Line/Border Width button on the Formatting toolbar and choose one of the widths.

You can also change the border around a control by using the same procedure.

NOTE If the line does not appear, make sure the Line/Border Color button is not set to Transparent or to the same color as the background.

Lines: Create

Lines add organization to your form or report. You can use them to add a visual break between column headings and the detail section of your report or between each *record.*

Steps

1. Open the form or report in Design View.
2. Click the Line button to draw a line or the Rectangle button to draw a rectangle.
3. To make the line straight, hold down Shift as you drag the line horizontally or vertically. To draw a rectangle, drag from the upper left corner to the bottom right corner of the area.

 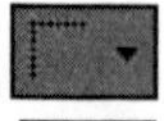 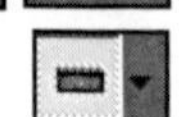

To change the color of the line or rectangle, choose an option on the Line/Border Color button. To change the width of the line or rectangle, choose an option on the Line/Border Width button. To change the effect (raised, sunken, and so on), choose an option on the Special Effects button.

Reports: Create with AutoReport

The quickest way to create a report is to use the AutoReport feature. There are two AutoReport options when you use the New button on the Reports tab, AutoReport: Tabular and AutoReport: Columnar. A tabular report presents your records in rows while a columnar report presents the fields in each *record* going down the page, similar to a label. Tabular reports are much more common than columnar reports.

Steps

1. Select the Reports tab in the *Database window* and choose the New *command button.*
2. On the New Report *dialog box* choose the name of the *table* or *query* to base the report on in the drop-down *combo box.*
3. Double-click AutoReport: Tabular or AutoReport: Columnar. Access will create a report for you, placing all the fields, and show you the report in Print Preview.

4. Click the Design View button to modify the report design or choose File, Save to save the report.

Object: AutoReport

NOTE If you want to create a columnar report, you can also select the table or query in the Database window and then click the AutoReport option on the New *Object* drop-down button.

Reports: Create with Design View

In rare cases, you might create a report from scratch and place all the controls on the report yourself. However, since the task of lining up the controls can be tedious, you will be better off using AutoReport and removing the controls you don't need. An alternative is to use the Report Wizard. If you want to create a report with few controls or if your report only contains subreports, use Design View. (See also "Controls: Add," "Controls: Align," "Reports: Create with AutoReport," "Reports: Create with Report Wizard," "*Subform/Subreport:* Create.")

Steps

1. Click the Reports tab in the *Database window*, then choose the New button. Select *Design View* in the New Report *dialog box*.
2. If you are going to base your report on a *table* or *query*, choose one in the New Report dialog box. If you are only using this *report* as a container to hold multiple subreports, you can leave the table or query box blank.
3. Double-click the Design View option. Access opens the blank form in the Design View.
4. Add labels, *text boxes* and other controls.

5. Click the Save button on the Report Design toolbar or choose File, Save and enter the name of the form in the Save As dialog box, then choose OK.

Reports: Create with Report Wizard

The Report Wizard gives you the most flexibility in creating reports. You will be prompted for the fields you want from one or more tables or queries, how you want to *group* and sort your data, if you want to add summaries, and the layout and style for your report. While you can accomplish these features in Design View, the job is often tedious. However, if you have a simple report to create, consider using AutoReport. (See also "Reports: Create with AutoReport.")

The steps and options of the wizard change depending on which options you select.

Steps

1. Click the Reports tab in the *Database window*, then choose New. Choose the *table* or *query* for your *data source* from the drop-down list and then double-click Report Wizard.
2. In the first step of the wizard, double-click the fields you want to see on your report in the Available Fields *list box*. For any related tables, select those tables from the

Tables/Queries list box, and add the additional fields, then choose Next.

If you get an error message such as `Subscript out of Range`, you chose fields from two unrelated tables. Double-click the incorrect fields in the Selected Fields list box to remove them.

3. Depending on the fields you chose, the next two steps of the wizard will ask you how to group your data. If the fields you chose come from different tables, Access will ask you how you want to view your data. Specify the table used to group your data and choose Next.

   On the next step, select the *field*(s) used to group your data, and position them in a priority order. If you want to change the group interval (first letter for text, months or years for dates, or range for numbers) choose the Grouping Options button, make your choices, and choose OK. Choose Next.

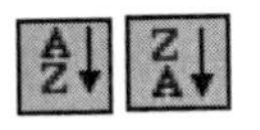

4. Select the sort field(s) of your data with the top sort field being the primary sort *key*; click the Sort button to specify ascending or descending sorts.

   If you chose any grouping options in Step 3, the Summary Options button might be available. Choose that button to find the sum, average, minimum, or maximum of numeric fields, show a summary or detailed records, and if you want to calculate percents. Choose OK to return to the sort step. From the sort step, choose the Next button.

5. Select a layout and *orientation* for your report, then choose Next. Select a presentation style for your report, then choose Next.

6. Enter a title for the report, and click either Preview the Report or Modify the Report's Design in the last step of the Report Wizard; then choose Finish.

Access creates the new report and saves it to disk. If you selected Preview, Access opens the report in the Preview mode; otherwise, it appears in the Report Design window.

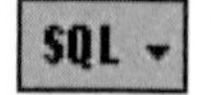

To switch between views of your report, select the appropriate command from the View menu, or from the View button's drop-down menu in the Report Design toolbar.

Reports: Grouping

When you want to see subtotals for numeric values, and you want to see the records that make up the subtotals as well, you need to use the grouping feature of reports. In a *query*, you can see the records or the subtotals only, but not both. (See also "Grouping in Queries" in the Calculations part of this book.) When you *group* records, all of one value group together, then there is a break (usually a group footer with subtotals) and then the next value group together. You can also have a group header with text introducing the group. In addition to doing subtotals, you can also group for lists of data, such as an employee phone list where all the A's are grouped together, all the B's, and so forth.

You can create a grouped report through the Report Wizard. (See also "Reports: Create with Wizard.") When you create a report with the wizard, Access creates the group headers and footers for you as well with calculated expressions for your labels and summaries. If you need to add grouping to a report, follow the procedures in these steps.

Steps

1. Open the *report* in *Design View* and click the Sorting and Grouping button if the Sorting and Grouping window is not visible.
2. In the *Field/Expression* box, choose a field from the drop-down list or type an expression.
3. In the Sort Order box, choose Ascending or Descending for the order in which the group will appear.
4. If you want a group header or footer section to appear for this group, choose Yes for either in the lower half, Group Properties section of the Sorting and Grouping window. If you do not choose Yes for either the header or footer,

you do not get grouping. As soon as you choose a header or footer, Access puts a grouping icon to the left of the field name.

5. Depending on the field *data type* you are grouping, the options in Group On will change. If the field is a date, choose a time unit such as Year or Month, and then type how many of those units you want to group together in the Group Interval box. For example, if you want to group on five-year intervals, choose Year in Group On and type **5** in Group Interval.

   If your field is a text or numeric value, you can choose Each Value in the Group On box. Then for every change in the value, you get a group header or footer. You can also choose prefix characters in the Group On box and then type the number of characters in the Group Interval box. If you are typing an alphabetical list, choose prefix characters and set the Group Interval to 1. If the first three characters of an employee ID determine the department, type a Group Interval of 3.

6. Set the Keep Together property to No to not worry about where the page breaks. Set it to With First Detail to keep the group header with the first *record.* If you have a small group that you want all to fit on one page, choose Whole Group.

When you finish setting the group properties, save your report and preview to test your settings. To turn off grouping, change both the Group Header and Group Footer options to No.

NOTE You can type an *expression* in the Sorting and Grouping window instead of a field name. For examples, see the Summary of Sales by Quarter and Employee Sales by Country in the sample Northwind *database*.

Reports: Modify

To modify a *report*, you must switch to the Report *Design View.* In Design View, you can add and remove *sections* or controls, format the report or any *object* contained therein, adjust properties, and so on. To change the grouping or sorting on a report, see also "Reports: Grouping."

Steps

1. In the *Database window*, click the report name in the Reports tab you want to modify and choose the Design button to open the report in Report Design View.
2. Remove (press Delete) or add controls (using the *Toolbox* or *Field* List); change properties in the appropriate Property sheet; remove or add sections using commands on the View menu; and format objects using the Formatting toolbar.
3. When done modifying your report, select File, Save.

   To save the resulting report as a different object, select File, Save As.

Access saves your report to disk. If you create a new report, that report's name appears in the Reports tab of the Database window.

Reports: Sorting

Your reports are based on tables or queries. If your *report* is based on a *query* and you change how the query is sorted, the report might sort in the new order determined by the query. For this reason, you can use Report *Design View* to sort records independent of the underlying query's sort. Reports also enable you to *group* records. (See also "Reports: Grouping.")

Steps

1. Open the report in Design View and click the Sorting and Grouping button if the Sorting and Grouping window is not visible.
2. In the *Field/Expression* box, choose a field from the drop-down list.
3. In the Sort Order box, choose Ascending or Descending for the order the group will appear.
4. Repeat Steps 2 and 3 for additional sort levels.

To change the sort order if you have more than one sort, move the mouse pointer until it becomes a black right arrow to the left of the field name. Click to select the row and then use the white arrow mouse pointer to drag the row to a new position.

Sections: Add and Remove

The *sections* of a form or a report enable you to set up a page for display, or to provide a particular kind of layout. Through proper use of sections, you can provide information that appears on every page at the top or bottom, at the beginning or end of a form or report, repeats for each *record*, repeats for each *group* of records, and so on.

Forms contain the following sections: Form headers and footers, Page headers and footers, and a Detail Section.

You can also create sections in *subforms* that appear inside forms: headers, detail sections, and footers.

Reports can contain all of the same sections as forms do (although they are called Report headers, and so on), but a report can also contain bands for grouped records. When a record set is grouped by a *field*, each value in that group becomes a group of records. Each group will appear in its own detail section, and can be preceded by a Group header and followed by a Group footer. (See also "Reports: Grouping.")

Steps

1. Click the *form* or *report* name in the *Database window*, then choose the Design button.
2. Choose View, Page Header/Footer or View, Form (or Report) Header/Footer to add those items to view for a form.
3. Choose those commands again to remove the check mark and eliminate them from your form or report.

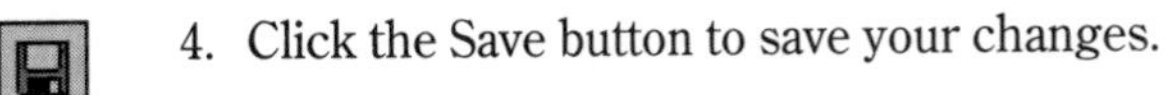

4. Click the Save button to save your changes.

You can set properties for sections that make them hidden, or set their height to 0 if you don't want them to appear.

Subform/Subreport: Create

A *subreport* is a report that is embedded inside another report. The main report can be *bound* or *unbound* to a *table, query,* or a *SQL* statement. A *subform* is a *form* that is embedded inside another form. Usually, the main part of the form can have multiple records that are related to the records in the subform.

Unbound *reports* serve as container devices into which subreports can be placed when the *subreports* are unrelated to one another and derive their data from different sources. You use a bound main report when you want to use subreports that use the main report's *data source*. An example of an unbound main report would include three unrelated subreports summing up revenue by each employee, revenue by month, and revenue by division.

Steps

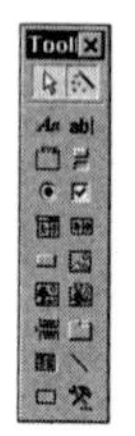

1. Open the main report or form in *Design View*; and click the Control Wizards button in the *Toolbox*, if necessary.
2. Click the Subform/Subreport tool in the toolbox. Make sure that the table relationships are correct before proceeding.
3. Click the location of the subreport or subform.
4. Follow the directions in the Subform Wizard for the data source (table/query or existing form or report), fields, relationships, and subform/subreport name.

When you finish, a subreport or subform control is added to your report. The wizard also creates a separate report or form that is displayed in the *Database window*.

NOTE The link between the main form/report and the subform/report is through two (Data tab) properties on the subform/report control. The Link Child Fields and Link Master Fields properties should be related fields between the two data sources. If you want the subform/report to expand to include all data when printed, make sure that the Can Grow (Format tab) property is set to Yes.

In most cases, you also want the subform to appear as a datasheet inside of the form. To change this property, go to the subform in Design View (you can double-click the subform control within the main form) and check that the Default View property (on the Data tab) is set to Datasheet. You can also set this property to Single Form, although this is quite a bit less common for a subform.

Toolbox: Display and Use

You see the *Toolbox* normally when you are in the *Form* or *Report Design View.* The toolbox contains buttons that let you create and manage controls.

Steps

1. Click the Toolbox button on the toolbar to bring it into view.
2. To use a tool in the Toolbox, click the button for that tool. To use a tool repeatedly, double-click the tool first. That tool stays locked until you either click another tool or press the Esc *key.*

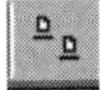

Each tool has its own default properties. To see or modify what they are, click the tool and choose the Properties button on the toolbar.

Producing Output

Access provides several methods of producing output for your data. After you preview your data and adjust the page setup options as necessary, you can send the data directly to a printer. You can print a *table*, *query*, *form*, or *report*, or portions thereof. You can create a special type of report, mailing labels, and you can merge your data to Microsoft Word.

In addition, you can fax or e-mail your data from Access, or publish your Access forms or reports on the Web.

Mail Labels: Create in Report

A mailing *label* is a special type of report formatted to repeat across or down a page. You have control over the contents of your mailing label through the placement of *bound* controls displaying your *field* data, text labels, graphics, and so on. You can also control the size of the labels and their repetition pattern.

Through the use of queries, you can specify which records will have labels printed for them. The Label Wizard makes it particularly easy to create mailing labels.

Steps

1. Click the Reports tab in the *Database window*; then choose New. Click Label Wizard in the New Report *dialog box*. Select the table or query that will supply the data for the labels in the Select Table or Query drop-down *list box*; then choose OK.
2. Select the standard Avery label you want, or choose Customize and specify the label size and type; then choose Next.

To create a custom size label, choose Customize and enter the size and page setup specification.

3. Select the font, size, and color of your text, then choose Next.
4. Create a prototype label by double-clicking any desired fields from the Available Fields list box to the Prototype Label *text box*. Type any text you want to appear on the label (spaces, commas, and so on), then press Enter to start a new line. To delete a field, select it and press Delete. When your prototype label is complete, choose Next.
5. Select the fields you want to sort your records, with the top field being the primary sort *key*.
6. Name your label report in the last step of the wizard, then preview it and save it to disk.

If you select the Modify the Label Design *option button*, then your label opens up in Report *Design View*.

TIP You can sort by any field in your underlying table or query, even those that do not appear on your prototype label.

Mail Merge to Word

If one of your tables or queries contains client data, you might want to send a letter to everyone in the list. If you have Microsoft Word installed, you can personalize each letter.

TIP Create a query to be the source of your mail merges. You can then modify the criteria every time you send a letter (when an address changes, you have a new client, or your printer mangled the first copy). See "Query: Create with Design View" in the Queries and Filters part of the book.

Steps

1. Select the *query* (or *table*) in the *Database window* and choose Merge It with MS Word from the Office Links button's drop-down list.

2. In the first step of the wizard, you can link to an existing document or create a new Word document. If you choose link to an existing document, Access will ask you for the document's location.
3. After you make your choices for the Word document, you will enter Microsoft Word, and the Mail Merge toolbar appears. Move to the location where you want an Access *field*, click the Insert *Merge Field* button, and choose the Access field. Type spaces, commas, and any additional text in your letter.

4. Save the letter and click the Merge to New Document (to preview all letters) or Merge to Printer buttons on the Mail Merge toolbar.
5. When finished, close the Word application.

NOTE If you Merge to New Document, Word creates a temporary document titled `FormLetters1` with the results of the merge. You do not need to save this document when you exit Word. You should, however, save your document with the merge field codes.

Mail or Sending Data

You can send Access tables, queries, or reports through electronic mail instead of printing and mailing through the post office. To send Access data through electronic mail, you need to use either Microsoft Exchange (or another mail system compatible with MAPI—Messaging Application Program Interface) or Lotus cc:Mail (or another mail system compatible with VIM—Vendor Independent Messaging). For additional information, search on "electronic mail" in Microsoft Access Help.

NOTE To perform this procedure, you must have already installed electronic mail software.

Steps

1. Select the *object* you want to send: a *table, query, form*, or *report* in the *Database window*, or select any portion of a datasheet in *Datasheet View.*
2. Choose File, Send.
3. In the Send *dialog box*, select the format of the data that will be attached to your message; then choose OK. Access opens a mail form with your data attached.
4. Fill in your message form, and send your message.

NOTE Depending on your Access object (table, query, form, or report), Access allows data to be sent as *HTML*, ActiveX (.ASP), Excel (.XLS), IIS (.HTX or .IDC), MS-DOS text (.TXT), or Rich Text Format (.RTF) files. ■

Page Break: Insert in Report

If you want your page to break in the middle of a section, you can insert a page break *control* on the report. For example, if you have two subreports, you might want to insert a page break between them.

NOTE You can also use this same procedure to insert a page break in Form Design View if you print your forms. n

Steps

1. Open the report in *Design View.*
2. Click the Page Break button on the *Toolbox.*
3. Click the location on the report design to set the page break. The page break control appears as a small dotted line in your document.

To remove the page break, select the page break control and press Delete.

NOTE You can also set page breaks with the properties of the *sections* on your report. Open the report in Design View and double-click the gray bars indicating the detail section or a *group* header or footer. In the *Property* sheet, move to the Force New Page property (on the Format tab) and choose to create a page break Before Section, After Section, Before & After, or None to let pages break at the end of a full page.

To try to avoid a page break within sections, change the Keep Together property to Yes. To try to keep all sections (header, footer, and detail) relating to one group together on a page, click the Sorting and Grouping button and change the Keep Together Grouping property to Yes. Access will try to place page breaks to keep a group together. However, if the group is larger than one page, it won't be able to. In this case, choose With First Detail to at least keep the group header with the first *record*.

Page Numbers: Insert in Report

For long reports, you will want Access to place page numbers on your *report*. This is especially true if you are handing out the report to various people and everyone needs to refer to specific pages.

Steps

1. Open the report in *Design View* and choose Insert, Page Numbers.
2. In the Format section, click Page N to add the word `Page` followed by a page number. If you want to include the total number of pages, click Page N of M.
3. In the Position section indicate if you want to put the page number in the header or footer, and in the Alignment section indicate if you want the page numbers left, centered, or right aligned. You can also choose inside or outside pages (for facing page bound documents).
4. If you want to include the page number on the first page, check Show Number on First Page. When finished with your selections, choose OK.

Access places a *text box* with the appropriate *expression* on your report. The `[Page]` *code* indicates the page number. `[Pages]` indicates total number of pages. Additional text is enclosed in quotes such as `"Page"`. The *Control* Source *property* of the text box shows this expression (and you can press Shift+F2 to see a long expression). To remove the page numbers, click the text box and press Delete.

Page Setup: Print Data Only

If you have a pre-printed *form*, you can design an Access form to print in the fill-in areas. When you print, you can choose to have Access print only the data.

Steps

1. Open the form in *Design View*.
2. Choose File, Page Setup, and click the Margins tab in the Page Setup *dialog box*.
3. Check the Print Data Only *check box* and choose OK.

Now when you print all the records or one *record* (see "Print Forms" and "Print One Record from Form"), Access will only print the data and not the labels for the fields.

Page Setup: Setting Margins

By default, Access prints with one-inch margins at the top and bottom, and left and right sides of the document. You can use the Page Setup dialog box to change these margins, if necessary. If your document is small, for example, you can increase the margins. If the document is slightly bigger than the page, you might want to decrease the margins.

Steps

1. From Design View in a *table*, *query*, form, or *report*, choose File, Page Setup; then click the Margins tab.
2. In the Top, Left, Bottom, and Right *text boxes*, specify the margins you want in inches. Then choose OK.

Access saves the page setup information with the design of the *object*. You might also need to change the size of columns in a table or query to fit everything on a page. (See also "Width of

Column" in the Database Essentials part of this book.) In a form or report, you might need to drag the right edge of the work area in Design View to change the printed width area.

Page Setup: Setting the Orientation

If the document you want to print is wider than it is tall, you can switch to a landscape orientation when you print. Choose Landscape orientation to print the document across the long edge of the page. Use Portrait orientation (the default) to print across the short edge of the page.

Steps

1. Choose File, Page Setup; then click the Page tab.
2. In the Orientation area, select Portrait or Landscape.
3. If you need to change the size of the paper (to Legal, for example) select the new size from the Size drop-down list.
4. If you need to select another paper tray, select it from the Source drop-down list. When finished adjusting settings, choose OK.

Print Forms

Although reports are the primary *object* for printing, you can also print information on forms. You can print one *record* (see "Print One Record From Form") or the entire *data source*. Depending on your starting location, you can print the Form or *Datasheet View*.

Steps

1. From the *Database window*, right-click a *form* name and choose Print to print the form or Print Preview to go to preview first.

2. From Print Preview or *Form View*, click the Print button to print the form.
3. From Datasheet view of the form, click the Print button to print the datasheet.

Print Labels Using Dot Matrix Printers

Some people print labels to dot matrix printers using tractor-feed stock. The best way to do this is to create a printer file that contains the page setup appropriate for this task. If the paper is a predefined *label* stock, an easier alternative is to use the mailing labels feature. (See "Mail Labels: Create in Report.")

Steps

1. Click the Start button on the Taskbar, then choose Settings, Printers.
2. Right-click the printer you will use, then select the Properties command from the shortcut menu.
3. Click the Paper tab, and in the Paper Size section click the Custom icon.
4. Enter the size of your label in the User Defined Size *dialog box*. Double-click OK.

   The width measurement extends from the left edge of the leftmost label to the right edge of the rightmost label. The length is measured from the top of the first label to the top of the second.

A label layout is a report layout that has no header or footer, only a detail part. If you are creating a label from scratch, then choose File, Page Setup to open the Page Setup dialog box to set the following:

- Set the Page tab to the Use Specific Printer; the printer Source to User-Defined Size; and the source for label stock to Tractor, Cassette, AutoSelect tray, or whatever is appropriate.
- Set the Columns tab to Same as Detail in the Column Size section.
- For a layout with more than one label across, on the Columns tab, enter the following: the number of labels across in the Number of Columns *text box*, the amount of

space between the bottom of one label and the top of another in the Row Spacing text box, the space between the right edge of one label and the left edge of the next in the Column Spacing text box, and specify whether the Column Layout is Down, Then Across or Across, Then Down.

Print One Record from Form

Sometimes you only want to get the details from one form's *record*. Perhaps you want to find missing information on a client or use the *form* for directions to a meeting. If you want to print only one record, use the record selector at the left edge of the form.

NOTE If the record selector is not available, you need to set the Form's Record Selectors *property* to Yes. To set this property, double click the Form/Report Selector in the upper-left corner of the form to open the Form property sheet, go to Record Selectors (on the Format tab) and choose Yes.

Steps

1. Open the form in *Form View.*
2. Click the record selector on the left side of the form.
3. Choose File, Print, Selected Record(s) and choose OK.

Print One Record from Form: Create Command Button

If you often print one record, consider adding a button on the form intead of using the procedure mentioned in "Print one Record from Form."

Steps

1. Open the form in *Design View.* Make sure the Control Wizards button is selected.

2. Click the *Command Button* tool in the *Toolbox* and then click where you want the button to appear on the form.

3. In the Categories list choose Record Operations, and in the Actions list choose Print Record.
4. Follow the instructions on the next two steps on the Command Button Wizard *dialog box* to identify the button; then choose Finish.

Now when you are in Form View, you can click the command button you added to print just the current record.

Print Preview

The Print Preview mode provides a view of your datasheet, *form*, *query*, or *report* as it would print to your current printer. It is always a good idea to preview your printed output before printing to find if the report contains the wrong information or is not the desired format. Especially for large reports, you'll want to use Print Preview first to avoid killing a tree.

Steps

1. Open a *table*, query, form, or report in either Design, Form, or Datasheet View.

2. Click the Print Preview button on the toolbar.
3. Use the toolbar buttons to switch your preview view, and click the page to switch between multiple or zoomed view and single page 100 percent view.

If you preview a form from Design or *Form View*, your preview is in Form View. If you preview a form from the *Datasheet View*, then your preview is in Datasheet View. If you preview a form selected in the *Database window*, then the Default View *property* controls the view you see in Preview mode. To change the default view of the form, double-click the Form/Report Selector in Design View and choose an option in the Default View property.

The following table shows you how to perform various tasks in the Print Preview view.

Print Preview Tasks

To Do This	Press This
To open the Print dialog box	P or Ctrl+P
To open the Page Setup dialog box	S
To zoom in or out on a part of the page	Z
To cancel Print Preview or Layout Preview	C or Esc
To move to the page number box; then type the page number and press Enter	F5
To view the next page (when Fit To Window is selected)	Page Down or down arrow
To view the previous page (when Fit To Window is selected)	Page Up or up arrow
To scroll down in small increments	Down arrow
To scroll down one full screen	Page Down
To move to the bottom of the page	Ctrl+down arrow
To scroll up in small increments	Up arrow
To scroll up one full screen	Page Up
To move to the top of the page	Ctrl+up arrow
To scroll to the right in small increments	Right arrow
To move to the right edge of the page	End or Ctrl+Right arrow
To move to the lower-right corner of the page	Ctrl+End
To scroll to the left in small increments	Left arrow
To move to the left edge of the page arrow	Home or Ctrl+left
To move to the upper-left corner of the page	Ctrl+Home

The Layout Preview command on the View menu enables you to see some representative data (See also "Print Preview: Layout.") From the preview window, you can merge data with

Word, publish to a Word document, or analyze data with Excel. These three options are available as toolbar buttons.

Print Preview: Layout

Access 97 offers you two different types of previews: Print Preview and Layout Preview. In the former instance, you see everything that will print to your printer, each page and all of the data contained therein. For long print jobs, it can take a while for your computer to process this information. If you want to view a small *group* of your records in preview, you can see an example layout in the Layout Preview mode. In this mode, you see just enough data to get a feeling for all of the *sections* of a *report*.

Steps

1. With your report in *Design View*, click the View button on the toolbar.
2. Select the Layout Preview command.

> **CAUTION** Layout Preview can be misleading because you don't get a view of all of your data. If you are using a *query* that contains *parameters*, for example, Layout Preview will not detect this and show you a truly representative data set. For reports that don't take a long time to process, you are better off using the Print Preview view to see your reports.

Print Reports

Reports are the best way to get data outputted to a printer. Although you can print tables, queries, and forms, none of the other objects offer the formatting and printing options that reports do. For example, only in reports can you get grouped data with subtotals and the detail data as well. (See "Reports: Grouping" in the Forms and Reports part in this book.) You can also print reports from various locations.

Steps

1. If you are in the *Database window*, right-click the report name and choose Print.
2. To select specific pages, choose the number of copies, make your choices on the Print *dialog box*, and choose OK.

NOTE To print a report without specifying print options, in Report *Design View* or Print Preview, you can click the Print button on the toolbar.

If you want to interrupt printing and you are fast, click the Cancel button that appears in the Printing dialog box. You also might be able to double-click the Printer icon in the taskbar and cancel the print job by choosing Document, Cancel Printing in the Printer window.

Print Selected Pages

You can print multiple pages of a *report* or *form*. On a form or columnar report, if you want to print different records, add a page break at the bottom of *Design View.* (See "Page Break: Insert on Report.") Then the page numbers correspond to the *record* numbers. An alternative is to go to each record you want to print in *Form View* and print that record. (See "Print One Record From Form.")

Steps

1. Open a form or report in Design View.
2. Choose File, Print.
3. In the Pages area, type the first page in From and the last page in To; choose OK.

Print Table or Query

Instead of printing a report, you can print the *Datasheet View* of a *table* or *query* for quick results. Although you have little control over the formatting (see "Datasheet: Appearance Change" in the Table and Database Design part of this book), all you might need is the *grid* produced from Datasheet View.

Steps

1. Open the table or query in Datasheet View.
2. Click the Print button.

TIP You can also print from the *Database window*. Right-click a table or query and choose Print.

NOTE Access automatically adds a header with the table or query name centered, the date right justified, and the page number centered in a footer. If you don't want to print the header and footer, choose File, Page Setup; click the Margins tab; and uncheck the Print Headings *check box*. Then follow the steps to print your table or query. You cannot edit the header and footer on a table or query.

Printing: Multiple Copies

Before you begin printing your document, you can specify how many copies you want to print. If you want to print multiple copies of a multi-page document, be sure to preview before you print.

You also can choose whether or not to collate the documents as they are printed. Normally, you will want to choose the Collate option, which prints all pages of a document before it prints the document again.

(See "Print Preview" before you complete this task.)

Steps

1. Choose File, Print.
2. Type the number of copies you want to print in the Number of Copies *text box*.
3. Be sure that the Collate *check box* is selected; or, if you don't want your printouts to collate, deselect the Collate check box. Click OK to begin printing.

Programming Events: Print

You can *control* printing to a fine degree by adding programming to the print events for a report. You add programming to print or not print certain *sections* or controls on your report, depending on choices you make on *dialog boxes* or the underlying values of the data.

One of the report print events is On No Data. If the report doesn't have any data to print, there is no sense printing a blank report. The following steps show you how to display a dialog box and cancel the printing (or previewing) of a report.

Steps

1. Open the report in *Design View* and double-click the *Form*/Report Selector to open up the *Property* sheet.
2. Scroll down to the On No Data property (on the Event tab), click the build (...) button, and double-click Code Builder in the Choose Builder dialog box. The insertion point is between a `Sub` and `End Sub` statement.
3. Type **MsgBox "No data for report. Report will not print."** and press Enter. This will display a message for the user. You can type any text you want within the quotes.
4. Type **Cancel** = **True**. If you look at the first line of your code, you will see `(Cancel as Integer)`. The procedure is looking for a *variable* called Cancel; this statement is telling Access to not print the report.
5. Close the window and try testing the procedure. This works best if you have a *query* underlying the report and you go to the query and add some criteria that wouldn't return any records.

The other print event associated with the report is On Page which will trigger before the page is printed but after the Format events for report sections. The Report and *Group* Header and Footer and Detail sections also have print events. To see help on the events, open a Property sheet, click the Events tab, select one of these sections, and move to one of the properties (On Format, On Print, or On Retreat). Then press F1.

NOTE For an example of the On Format property in the sample Northwind database, open the Sales by Year report and look at the On Format property for the Detail section. The programming includes

```
If Forms![Sales by Year Dialog]!ShowDetails =
➥False Then Cancel = True
```

When you open this report in Print Preview or attempt to print it, a form (Sales by Year Dialog) opens with a check box named ShowDetails. If the user unchecks the ShowDetails box, the detail section will not print.

Web Page: Publish

Some people will begin their foray into *database* publishing to the Web by visiting the new Web Publishing Wizard. This wizard guides you through the process of Web page and site creation. You start the Web Publishing Wizard by selecting the Save As *HTML* command from the File menu. The Web Publishing Wizard can output datasheets, forms, and reports as static or dynamic Web documents using template files. It can create a home page that has links to your other documents. You can use the Web Publishing Wizard to copy the files and folder created to your Web server.

TIP Microsoft Office contains a Web Fast Find Search page that you can use to search for files on an intranet. You can locate files by keywords. Consider including this page in any site you create with the Web Publishing Wizard. Consult your administrator to get a copy, or learn about the location of this page on your intranet.

Steps

1. Choose File, Save As HTML with a datasheet, *form*, or *report* open; click the I Want to Use a Web Publication Profile check box; and select that publication if you have already created a Web page or set of pages in the format you want using the wizard (if you don't have any Web pages already created, this option will be grayed out). Choose Next.

2. Click either Select or Select All in the check box to select the *table*(s), *query*(s), form(s), and report(s) you want to publish. Choose Next.
3. Select the HTML template document you want to use, then choose Next. You can select the type of document you want to create: Static HTML, Dynamic HTX/IDC, or Dynamic ASP.
4. On the next one or two screens (depending on your choice in Step 3), enter the location of the folder (and server if prompted) that you want to save your files to.
5. Click the Yes, I Want to Create a Home Page check box if you want that feature; name that page (Default is the default); then choose Next.
6. On the final page of the wizard, select the Yes, I Want to Save the Answers to the Wizard check box if you want to create a Web publication profile; enter the name in Profile Name; then choose Finish.

Access creates the pages you specified from each *object*. It also creates, if specified, the publication profile.

Special Features and Programming

If you develop your *database* into an application for others to use, there are many features you can use to help users navigate through your database and to keep them where you want them to be. You can manage the toolbars and menus that come with Access as well as create your own.

On forms and reports, each time a user performs an action, an *event* occurs. You can program responses to these events. The programming of Access is divided into two pieces: macros and *Visual Basic for Applications (VBA)*. The response to an event can be either a *macro* or VBA procedure (also called *code*). You can also create VBA code for general use throughout Access.

When you have large databases and multiple users, you might also be concerned with optimizing your database as well as startup, multiuser, keyboard, and other options.

Events: Creating Event Response

Events are user actions such as clicking the mouse, pressing a *key*, or opening a *form*. Events can also be triggered by a Visual Basic statement or by the program itself. Events are associated with forms and reports, *sections* on forms and reports, and *controls* on forms. You can respond to an event by creating a *VBA* procedure or choosing a macro.

Steps

1. Open the form or *report* in *Design View* and double-click the Form/Report Selector, a section, or a control (on a form) to open the properties sheet.

2. Move to an Event *Property* (on the Event tab).
3. Type or choose the name of a macro from the drop-down list or click the build button (...) to bring up the Choose *Builder dialog box.*
4. Double-click Macro Builder to enter in macro statements or *Code* Builder to enter VBA statements.
5. When finished building the macro or code, click the Close (X) button. If you are building a macro, give the macro a name and choose OK.

For more help on building a macro, see also “Macros: Create in Design Window.” For more help on building code, see also “Programming: Create a Procedure.”

Hyperlink Appearance

The default appearance of *hyperlinks* is blue underlined text for links that have not been accessed. The default is purple for links that have been accessed (also called followed hyperlinks) since you opened the *database.* This is a general standard for Internet programs. However, you can change the appearance if you like.

Steps

1. Choose Tools, Options and click the Hyperlinks/*HTML* tab.
2. Choose a color from the Hyperlink Color and Followed Hyperlink Color drop-down lists and check whether you want to Underline Hyperlinks.
3. If you want the hyperlink address shown in the status bar, check Show Hyperlink Address in Status Bar. Choose OK when finished.

Locking Records

You have some options on what you want to happen when two people try to edit the same *record* at the same time. The

Record Locks options deal with multiple users. You can set Record Locks globally for all databases, or for a specific *form* or *report*. There are three possible choices:

- *No Locks*. There is no locking. The second user to save a record gets a prompt notifying that the record was changed by another user. The second user can choose which changes to keep.
- *All Records*. The *table* is not accessible for editing for anyone else (and any related tables that the form uses).
- *Edited Record*. Not available for reports; where the current record (and possibly some surrounding records) is not available for editing.

Steps

1. To set *record locking* for all databases, choose Tools, Options; click the Advanced tab.
2. Choose one of the following: No Locks, All Records, Edited Records; choose OK when finished.

NOTE To set record locking for a form, open the form in *Design View*, click the Properties button, and choose No Locks, All Records, or Edited Records from the Record Locks *property* (on the Data tab). On a report, choose No Locks or All Records on the Property Sheet Other tab.

Macros: Create in Design Window

A *macro* is a series of stored actions that you can use for automating often-used procedures. You can attach macros to *command buttons*, menu choices, or other events for a form or report. When you use the Menu *Builder* in versions prior to Access 97, you automatically create a series of macros. (See also "Menu: Create Custom.")

For most macros, you can also create a *VBA* procedure. VBA procedures give you more control than macros, especially the ability to control errors. (See also "Programming: Create a Procedure.")

Steps

1. Click the Macros tab in the *Database window* and choose the New command button. The Macro Design Window opens.
2. In the Action column, type or choose an action from the drop-down list.
3. If desired, type a comment on the same row in the Comment column.

4. In the lower half of the screen, type or choose any Action *Arguments* for the specific action you chose in Step 2. For some arguments, you have the choice of a Build button to help you create the argument.

5. Repeat steps 2–4 for each action you want in the macro. Click the Save button to save the macro and give it a name, then choose OK.

To attach a macro to an *event*, type the macro name in the Event *property*. (See also "Events: Creating Event Response.")

NOTE There is a special macro that will run when you open your database. Name your macro AutoExec. If you don't want this macro to run when you open the database, hold down the Shift key as you open the file.

Macros: Create with Database Window

You can also create macros by using drag-and-drop from the Database window. This is especially useful if you want to open multiple forms or print multiple reports. After you drag-and-drop objects into the *Macro* Design window, you can modify the macro actions to suit your needs. Before you begin, first close all windows except the Database window.

Steps

1. Click the Macros tab in the Database window and choose the New *command button*. The Macro Design window opens.

2. Choose Window, Tile Vertically to move the Database window and Macro Design window side-by-side.
3. Click the *object* tab button (such as Reports) and drag the object names into each line of the Macro Design window.
4. If desired, change the *arguments* for each object.

5. Click the Save button to save the macro and give it a name and choose OK.

After you create a macro, you can attach it to a button or menu item. (See also "*Controls*: Command Button Create" in the Forms and *Reports* part of this book.)

NOTE The defaults for each object you drop in the Macro Design window are as follows:

- *Table* and *query* in *Datasheet View* and Edit mode
- *Form* in *Form View* and Normal mode
- Report in Print View (prints reports)
- A macro will run, and a *module* will open for editing.

Macros: Groups

If you use a separate *macro* name for every macro you create, your macro list can become long and unwieldy. You might have problems finding and managing your macros. An alternative is to keep related macros together by creating macro groups and name the macros within each *group*. First, create the actions for a macro. (See "Macros: Create with Database Window.")

Steps

1. Select a macro in the Database window and choose Design.

2. If the Macro Name column is not visible, click the Macro Names button on the toolbar.
3. Type the name of the macro in the Macro Name column in the first row of the macro.

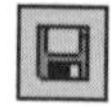

4. Click the Save button to save the macro group and give it a name (if you haven't already), and choose OK.

To choose the macro within a group in an *event* procedure (or the RunMacro action within another macro), choose or type the macro group name, a period, and then the macro name.

NOTE If you always want the Macro Name column to appear by default, choose Tools, Options; click the View tab; and choose Names Column.

Macros: Keyboard Shortcuts

If you want to create your own keyboard shortcuts that will operate throughout your *database*, you can use the *Macro* Name column and type characters representing keyboard combinations. Be careful, however, not to include keyboard combinations you often use such as Ctrl+C for Copy or Alt plus any of the underlined letters of each of the menus. First, complete the procedures in the previous "Macros: Groups" section before proceeding with this task.

NOTE As an alternative to creating *global* keyboard shortcuts, you can create keyboard shortcuts for each *form*. In the *Caption property* of a button or of a *label* attached to another control, type an ampersand (**&**) before the letter you want to be the shortcut. Then pressing Alt+*the letter* is the same as clicking the option.

Steps

1. Select a macro group in the Database window and choose Design (or create a new macro and the actions to be called with shortcut keys).
2. Type the keyboard representation in the Macro Name column in the first row of the macro (to the left of where the macro actions start). Use a caret (^) to represent Ctrl and plus (+) to represent Shift. Include function keys and edit keys in curly braces such as **{F1}** or **{Delete}**. **^p** would mean Ctrl+P.

3. Repeat Step 2 to add more keys.

4. Choose File, Save As/Export to save the macro group, type **AutoKeys** in the New Name text box, and choose OK. Close the macro group.

Macros: Save as VBA Module

There has been some speculation whether Microsoft will continue to have macros in future versions of Access (see *Special Edition Using Microsoft Access 97* by Roger Jennings). According to Jennings, macros are only used for backward compatibility and probably will not be included in the next version of Access. Therefore, he recommends that you work entirely in *VBA*. To ease the transition, you can create a *macro* and then save it as a VBA *module*.

Steps

1. In the *Database window*, select a macro. You can also have the macro open in *Design View*.
2. Choose File, Save As/Export.
3. In the File Save As *dialog box*, click Save as Visual Basic Module and choose OK.
4. In the Convert Macro dialog box, choose whether you want to add error handling and add comments, and choose Convert.

Your converted macro is now listed on the Modules tab of the Database window. To rename the module, right-click and choose Rename from the shortcut menu. If what you converted was a macro *group*, each macro is a separate procedure in the module.

Macros: Set Conditions

While you are working with macros, there are cases when you want to run one action if one condition exists and another action if another condition exists. For example, you can create a *dialog box* that prompts the user before a *report* is generated or create alphabetical *filter* buttons on a *form*.

Steps

1. In the Database window, click the Macro tab and choose New.

2. If the Conditions column is not visible, click the Conditions button on the toolbar.

3. Type an *expression* in the Conditions column in the first row of the *macro*. Remember to include *field* names in square brackets. If you want to include more complex conditions, you can click the Build button.
4. Create the macro action and its *arguments* on the same line as the condition. The action will run if the condition evaluates to `True`. If you want more than one action to run, include three periods (...) in the next row(s) in the Conditions column and choose the action(s).
5. On the next row (without ...), include any action you want to run if the condition evaluates to `False`.

6. Click the Save button to save the macro, give it a name (if you haven't already), and choose OK.

NOTE If you always want the Conditions column to appear by default, choose Tools, Options; click the View tab; and choose Conditions Column.

Menu: Create Custom

A menu bar contains the words that appear under the title bar of your application. The default menu bar starts with File and ends with Help. Each menu drops down from one of the words on the menu bar (the File menu and Help menu). When you create an application for someone else to use, you can limit menu options and toolbars to make the job easier for the user or to help the user avoid getting in trouble. You can attach menu bars and toolbars to forms and reports and have a menu appear at startup as well.

NOTE In Access 95 and Access 2, you could use the Menu *Builder* to create menu bars. In a *form* or *report*, go to the Menu Bar *property* and click the Build button.

Steps

1. Choose View, Toolbars, Customize; click the Toolbars tab; and choose the New *command button*.
2. Type the name of the menu bar in the New Toolbar *dialog box* and choose OK. If necessary, drag the title bar of the Customize dialog box to see the new menu/ toolbar.
3. On the Customize dialog box, the *focus* should be on your new toolbar name. Choose the Properties command button and change the Type to Menu Bar. To have your menu bar be a shortcut menu, choose Popup. When finished choose Close.
4. Click the Commands tab of the Customize dialog box. To put one of Access' menus on your menu, choose Built-in Menu in the Categories list and drag one of the menus from the Commands list onto your menu. To create your own menu, choose New Menu from the Categories list and drag New Menu from the Commands list onto your menu.
5. To change the menu name (or item on the menu), right-click the name and type the new menu name or menu item name in the shortcut menu's Name box. To add a hotkey, type an ampersand (**&**) before the letter. For menu items, you can also change the button image that appears next to the menu item or choose just to have the text appear.
6. To add or delete items from one of your menus on the menu bar, click the menu to first open it. Drag items off. To add items, drag them from the Commands list in the Customize dialog box. When finished, choose Close in the Customize dialog box.

To have this menu appear as the default menu for your application, see "Menu: Startup." To add this menu to a form or report, see "Menus and Toolbars: Add to Form/Report."

NOTE If you are creating a shortcut menu, you need to check the Shortcut Menus item in the Toolbars list of the Customize dialog box to display the shortcut menu bar with your menu name (and others) in order to add or remove items.

Menu: Startup

If you want your *database* application to start with a menu other than the default Access menu, you can choose a menu you've already created. The first step is to create the menu. (See "Menu: Create Custom.")

Steps

1. Choose Tools, Startup.
2. In the Menu Bar drop-down list, pick your menu.
3. If you do not want Access' menu bars visible (when you open any *object* or go to *Design View*), uncheck Allow Full Menus.
4. You can also choose another menu for the shortcut menu in the Shortcut Menu Bar *list box* and uncheck Allow Default Shortcut Menus.
5. When finished with all choices, choose OK.

NOTE If you uncheck Allow Full Menus in Step 3, the next time you open your database, Access' menus will not be available. If you need access to the default menus (such as going back to the Startup *dialog box*), hold down Shift as you open your database to override the Startup options.

Menus and Toolbars: Add to Form/Report

When you design an application for other users, generally you have a startup switchboard *form* (see "Controls: Command

Button Create" in the Forms and Reports part of this book) to add buttons that will make your switchboard. In addition to the buttons on the form itself, you can add a menu and toolbar that are different from the Access default choices. You can add a menu and toolbar to any form or *report* through properties. To accomplish this procedure, you must first create a menu or a toolbar. (See "Menu: Create Custom" and "Toolbar: Create Custom.")

Steps

1. Open the form or report in *Design view* and double-click the Form/Report selector to open the *Property* sheet.
2. Move to the Menu Bar, Shortcut Menu, or Toolbar property (on the Other tab) and type or choose the name of your menu or toolbar from the drop-down list.

NOTE To see or change which menus or toolbars are available for form or report menu bars, shortcut bars, or toolbars, choose View, Toolbars, Customize; select your toolbar or menu on the Toolbars tab; and click the Properties command button. Choose one of the items on the Type *combo box*. Use Popup for shortcut menus.

Optimization: General Suggestions

Because Access writes all of its data and design to a single file, as data and objects are deleted and created, free space and fragmented data structures are created. This is similar to what happens with your computer's file system. Over time, the *database* file grows larger than it needs to be and performance can suffer. To optimize performance, you can compact the database. Doing so creates a new file where all of the data is stored efficiently and in sequence.

Steps

1. Save any design changes for any open object (form, report, and so on) you have been working on.

2. To compact a database, choose Tools, Database Utilities, Compact Database.

NOTE To compact the current database, see the topic "Database: Compact" in the File Management part of this book.

Additional Ways to Optimize Your Database

Compacting the database is just one of many ways you can improve the performance of your database (See also other Optimize tasks in this section). Some additional options for optimizing the performance of a database include:

- *Running in Exclusive mode.* You can run the database in Exclusive mode by setting that *check box* in the Open *dialog box* when you open the database.
- *Installing to a hard drive.* You can install the database file to a local hard drive instead of a network *server.*
- *Assigning more memory.* You can assign more memory to Access, or close other programs or unnecessary system utilities like wallpaper, to free up additional RAM. (You can add additional RAM to your computer, but do not set up a RAM disk because Access creates its own.)
- *Defragmenting the hard drive.* You can defragment your hard drive using the Disk Defragmentor. Choose the Windows 95 Start button, Programs, Accessories, System Tools, Disk Defragmentor.
- *Upgrading.* You could improve your processor by upgrading your computer.

Optimization: Performance Analyzer

The performance of your *database* might be limited by the design of the database itself. If you have tables with redundant data, you can have poorly constructed indexes, inappropriate *data types*, or the wrong *join* definition for relationships. Run the Performance Analyzer to see suggestions on optimizing database objects, and then perform the suggestions as desired.

> **CAUTION** The Performance Analyzer can take a significant amount of time to run. Experiment with it first on a small database. Also, make sure you back up your database before you run the Performance Analyzer. (See "Backup Data" in the File Management part of this book)

Steps

1. Choose Tools, Analyze, Performance.
2. Click an *object* tab or the All tab in the *Database window* and select the objects you want to analyze (or click the Select All button). Choose OK.
3. The results appear in the Analysis Results *list box*. Icons appear for recommendations, suggestions, ideas, and whether something was fixed. Move to each item on the list and look at the lower half of the screen (Analysis Notes) for a description of the item and additional tips for fixing the problem.
4. For recommendations and suggestions, you can click the Optimize button to make the change. Choose Close when finished.

Optimization: Split Database

You can split a *database* into two files: one that contains the tables, and another that contains all of the other *objects* in the database that act on the base tables (*queries*, *forms*, *reports*, *macros*, and *modules*). This is useful when you want to put the *table* object(s) on a network server and the other object(s) on the user's machine. This is also useful when you want to provide a means for users to access data while maintaining their own forms and reports or database interface.

You can use the Database Splitter Wizard to perform the function of splitting an existing database into its tables and other component objects.

Steps

1. Choose Tools, Add-Ins, Database Splitter.
2. Choose the Split Database command button.
3. Enter the name for the tables database in the File Name *text box* on the Create Backend Database *dialog box*, then click the Split command button.

Access creates a new database based on your current data and structure. In the original database, Access attaches the tables to the backend database created.

Optimization: Table Analyzer

You can analyze your *database table* structure using the Table Analyzer Wizard. This wizard checks for redundant data, and can create smaller related tables and a *query* with relationships between the former tables to improve performance.

> **CAUTION** Because Access makes significant changes throughout your database when you use the Table Analyzer, you should back up your database first. (See "Backup Data" in the File Management part of this book.)

Steps

1. To run the Table Analyzer Wizard, choose Tools, Analyze, Table. On the first two steps of the wizard, Access can show you some examples of duplicating information and how to deal with updating information. Choose Next twice if these screens appear.
2. Choose the table in the list you want to analyze. Also, uncheck Show Introductory Pages if you don't want to see the pages mentioned in Step 1. Choose Next.
3. Tell the wizard to suggest fields to go into the tables and choose Next.

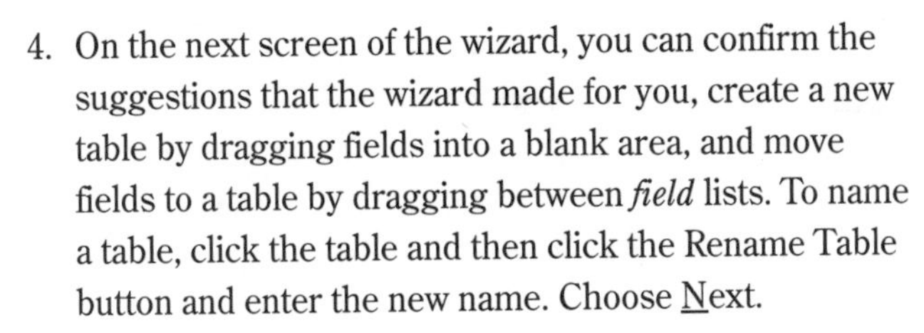

4. On the next screen of the wizard, you can confirm the suggestions that the wizard made for you, create a new table by dragging fields into a blank area, and move fields to a table by dragging between *field* lists. To name a table, click the table and then click the Rename Table button and enter the new name. Choose Next.

5. Select any ***primary keys*** you want by clicking the field and then clicking the Set Unique Key button. You can also create an *AutoNumber* primary ***key field*** by clicking the Add Generated Unique Key button. Choose Next.
6. The wizard might find close duplications in the values for tables. In the Correction column, choose Leave As Is to ignore the corrections. Choose Next; on the last step of the wizard, tell Access to create a query that will be used in place of your original table in forms and reports. Choose Finish.

Access creates the tables and query in your *Database window* and renames your original table with an _OLD extension.

TIP If you are finding and sorting records, creating an *index* specifically composed for this purpose can improve performance considerably. (See the tasks relating to Index in the Table and Database Design part of this book.)

Programming: Create a Procedure

Procedures are the basic programming units of *VBA*. They are alternatives to creating macros and offer much greater flexibility, including the ability to trap and handle errors. (See also "Macros: Create with Database Window.")

There are two types of procedures: sub procedures and function procedures. The major difference between the two is that a function procedure can return a value where a sub procedure cannot. To create a function procedure, see also "Programming: Create Function." Many of the other following tasks in this part help you create procedures.

TIP This book covers only some of the fundamentals of Visual Basic. For more details, you can choose from several Que titles. These titles include *Special Edition Using Microsoft Access 97,* which is the companion piece to this Quick Reference; *Access 97 Expert Solutions;* and *Access 97 Power Programming.*

Steps

1. From the Database window, click the Modules tab and then click the New button to create a new module. Make sure that the `Option Explicit` statement appears at the top of the module.
2. Type **Sub** followed by the procedure name.
3. If there are any *arguments* that are required to run the procedure, include those in parentheses as well as the keyword `As` and the *data type* for each argument. Press Enter. Access will automatically add `End Sub` at the end of the procedure.
4. Type any statements between the `Sub` and `End Sub`. As you type, Access' AutoComplete feature might show a drop-down list. You can click one of the entries in the drop-down list or press Ctrl+Enter to enter the selected item.
5. To add comments to your procedure, type an apostrophe (') and then the *comment*. The apostrophe can begin a line or can be added after any statement.

6. When finished writing the procedure, choose the Save button and give the module a name.

NOTE This task shows how to create a new *module* and new procedure within the module. If you want to add a procedure to an existing module, select the module and click the Design button. Move to the end of the module (press Ctrl+End) and type the Sub statement mentioned in Step 2.

The following is an example of a `Sub` procedure:

```
Sub ShowTableNames() 'Names of tables in current database
```

```
Dim x As Integer, tdef As TableDef

'CurrentDb is the Current Database

For Each tdef In CurrentDb.TableDefs

    Debug.Print tdef.name

Next tdef

End Sub
```

Programming: Create Function

You might need a *function* that Access does not supply as one of the built-in functions. You can try creating one from Excel or you can create one of your own. (See also "Programming: Function Create from Excel.")

Steps

1. Open an existing *module* in *Design View*, or click the New button on the Modules tab to create a new module.
2. In a blank area outside of any procedures, type **Function Functionname(**, any *arguments* you need to run your function, and a closed parenthesis**)**, and press Enter. If you have arguments, include the keyword **Type** after the name and the *data type*. Replace *Functionname* with the name of your function. For example, type **Function FahrenheitToCelsius (Fdegree as Single)**. Access will automatically add `End Function` at the end of the procedure.
3. If necessary, type any lines for declaring variables additional to the arguments or any other statements required for processing the function. In the line that will return the value, type the function name again, an equal sign, and the formula that calculates the function. For example, type **FahrenheitToCelsius = 5/9*(Fdegree - 32)**.

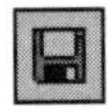

4. Click the Save button to save the module, and then test the procedure.

You can use this function within another procedure or as part of a calculated *field* in a *query, form*, or *report*. (See "Calculated Fields: Queries—Create by Typing" and "Calculated Fields: Forms and Reports—Create by Typing" in the Calculations part of this book.)

NOTE To see a list or use a built-in function from Access, click the Build button when you are creating a formula or *expression* in Design View of a query, form, or report. Choose Expression *Builder* and double-click Functions in the folder area. To see Access functions, click the Built-In Functions folder. To see functions you've created, click your *database* name folder.

CAUTION Be aware that there are two similar but distinctive Build Buttons in Access. There is the toolbar Build button, denoted by a wand over an ellipses (...); and there is the Properties tab build button, denoted by simply an ellipses (...).

Programming: Create Function from Excel

Access has a significant number of built-in functions, but Excel has even more. If you are familiar with an Excel *function* that you want to use in Access, follow these steps. Excel has to be loaded for this procedure to work. For steps on creating a function in Access, see also "Programming: Create Function."

Steps

1. Go into Excel and look up the *syntax* for the function including any required *arguments* within the parentheses. For example, the `Round` function requires a value and number of decimal places.
2. Return to Access and open an existing *module* in *Design View* or click the New button on the Modules tab to create a new module.

3. Make sure Excel is registered by choosing Tools, References and checking Microsoft Excel in the Available References *list box*. Choose OK.
4. In the function statement, include the new function name (it can be the same name as the Excel function) and any arguments required. For example, type **Function ExRound (Number as Single, Places as Byte)**. Access will automatically add `End Function` at the end of the procedure.
5. On the line that returns the value, type **Functionname = Excel.Application.ExcelFunctionname** and include the names of the arguments you added in Step 3. Replace *Functionname* with the name you want to use in Access, and *ExcelFunctionname* with the name of Excel's function. For example, type **ExRound = Excel.Application.Round (Number,Places)**.

6. Save the module and test the procedure.

The first time you run this function, it will take a few moments to run as Excel is opened and the function is retrieved. You can use this function in *VBA* procedures, queries, forms, reports and the *Debug window*.

SPECIAL FEATURES & PROGRAMMING

Programming: Create Messages

Often you will want to create messages that tell users what is going on in your program or ask users for input. You add the `Msgbox` statement as part of your procedure. You first need to create a procedure or function. (See "Programming: Create a Procedure" or "Programming: Create Function.")

Steps

1. Open the *module* with the procedure in *Design view* and click the Procedure *list box* (the arrow on the right side below the VBA module window title bar) to choose your procedure.
2. In the upper portion of your procedure, declare a return value for the message box. For example, type **Dim**

RetValue as Integer. You do not have to use the return value in your procedure, but if you do, Access will save the value associated with the button that the user chooses so you can use it later in the procedure.

3. Move to the location in your *code* to insert the message box and type **RetValue=MsgBox("Prompt",Buttons, "Title")** where *Prompt* is whatever you want the *dialog box* to say, and *Title* is the title of the dialog box. *Buttons* is a Visual Basic constant(s) identifying the buttons and icons on the dialog box. Some examples include `vbYes`, `vbYesNo`, `vbOKOnly`, `vbQuestion`, and `vbExclamation`. You can include a button and an icon by using an *expression* such as `vbYes + vbQuestion` where the `Buttons` argument is needed.
4. If you want to use the `RetValue` later in your procedure, test it with some statement like `If RetValue = vbYes Then`.

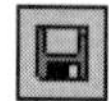

5. When finished with your procedure, click the Save and test it.

NOTE For more choices for the `Buttons` argument, look up `MsgBox` function in the online help.

You can also create message boxes by choosing the `MsgBox` action in a *macro* and filling in the action *arguments* in the lower half of the screen.

Programming: Debug with Breakpoint

If you've tried debugging your program (see "Programming: Debugging") and there are no visible errors, and you know there is still something wrong with your program, you might need to step through your program one line at a time until an error occurs. When you want to see the changing values associated with your variables, you can set a watch expression. As you move through your procedure, the watch expression changes. A breakpoint enables you to stop the procedure at a specific statement and then step through the rest of the program to look for errors.

Steps

1. Open the procedure in *Design View* and click the mouse in the first line of questionable *code*. The cursor cannot be on a blank line, a line with only a comment, or on lines declaring variables.

2. Click the Toggle BreakPoint button.

3. If you want to see the value of variables or expressions during the procedure, select the *variable* or *expression* and click the Quick Watch button.

4. Run the procedure by performing the *event* that triggers the procedure or clicking the *Debug Window* button and typing the procedure name. Include values for *arguments* in parentheses if the procedure requires arguments, and type a ? before function names. After you press Enter, Access will run until it reaches the location where you set the breakpoint, then display the code window and Debug window. Any variables or expressions you chose will appear on the Watch tab of the Debug window.

5. Click the Step In button to go to the next line of your code. If the line of code calls another procedure, click Step Over if you don't want to step through the sub procedure. Continue this step, viewing the Debug window for any watches you set until you find your error.

6. If you want to run your code to the end without going step-by-step, click the Go/Continue button. If you want to stop running your code, click the End button.

Programming: Debugging

When you create a procedure (see also "Programming: Create a Procedure" or "Programming: Create a Function"), there are a few things you can do to find errors with your program.

NOTE To help you avoid misspelling *variable* names, choose Tools, Options; click the Modules tab; and check Require Variable Declaration. To view this statement or add it manually, choose General on the *Object* drop-down list (on the left) and Declarations on the Procedure drop-down list (on the right). Type **Option Explicit** in this section if it doesn't appear.

Steps

1. As you type statements and press Enter, *syntax* errors appear in red with an error message.

2. If there are no apparent errors in your procedure, click the *Compile* Loaded Modules button to see if you have any compile errors. If you have any errors, Access will highlight the line or variable containing the error

3. If you have no apparent syntax or compile errors, try running the procedure by clicking the *Debug Window* button or performing the *event* that calls the procedure.

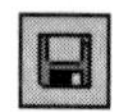

4. Fix the error in your program, and click the Save button to save your changes.

If there are no syntax, compile, or runtime errors, and you know the program is wrong, you have a *logic error*. You might need to add a breakpoint and a watch *expression* and then step through the program. (See also "Programming: Debug with Breakpoint.")

NOTE In the preceding Step 3, the procedure you test can be in different locations. If the procedure is on a *module*, click the Debug Window button to open the Debug window, type the procedure name, and press Enter. If the procedure is a function procedure that returns a value, type a question mark and the function name. If either the sub procedure or function procedure require *arguments*, enclose values in parentheses after the name in the Debug window. If there is a runtime error, Access might describe the error well enough for you to debug the program.

TIP You can also press Ctrl+G to open the Debug window.

Programming: Find Procedures

If you want to view or edit Visual Basic procedures, there are a number of ways you can find the procedure.

Steps

1. In Design View of a module, click the *Object* Browser button on the toolbar.
2. In the top drop-down list, find the name of the current *database* file. In the second drop-down list, type the name of the procedure (or text within the procedure) and then click the Search button.
3. In the Search Results area of the Object Browser window, double-click the procedure.

NOTE You can also go to procedures in other ways depending on where the procedure is. If you are in the *Design View* of a *module* and the current procedure calls another procedure, click the name of the procedure and press Shift+F2 to move to the referenced procedure.

In Design View of a *form* or *report*, open the *Property* sheet and go to the *event* procedure. Click the Build button.

If in Design View of a module with the current procedure, click the Object drop-down list and choose the object associated with the procedure (if it is a form module, for example). Then click the Procedure drop-down list and choose the procedure name or event.

Programming: Printing

To document your work or show examples, you will want to print your Visual Basic programming statements.

Steps

1. Open a module in Design View. If you are in Design View of a form or report, click the *Code* button.

2. Click the Print button to print all procedures within the module.

3. If you want to print multiple modules at one time as well as see other properties including owner, date created (and *controls* for forms and reports), choose Tools, Analyze, Documentor and choose the objects you want. Then click OK. The document will show in Print Preview. To print, click the Print button.

> **CAUTION** If you use the Documentor, there will be many pages for each form or report. If you want to print just the code, choose the Options button on the Documentor *dialog box* and uncheck everything in the include area except Code. In the Include for Sections and Controls area, choose Nothing.

Programming: Variables Setting

At the beginning of each procedure, you need to identify the variables that you will be using. *Variables* are useful if you will be referring over and over to the same value or *object*. When you declare variables, it is a good idea to also declare the *data type* instead of letting Access use the default `Variant` type to help determine programming errors.

Steps

1. Open up the *module* in *Design view*.
2. To identify *global* variables which you will use in more than one procedure, choose General from the Object drop-down list and Declarations from the Procedure drop-down list. To identify local variables which you will only use in the procedure, choose the object (such as a *command button*), if necessary, from the Object drop-down list and choose the procedure name or *event* from the Procedure drop-down list.
3. Type **Dim**, a space, and the *variable* name.
4. Type **As**, a space, and then a data type such as **String** (for text), **Integer**, **Single**, **Double**, **Boolean** (for Yes/No), **Control**, **Form**, or other data type. If you leave off

As and the data type, Access assumes a `Variant` type which can be any data type.

5. Repeat Steps 3 and 4 for all variables. Finish the procedure, save the module, and test it.

NOTE For more help on data types, search for Data Type Summary on the Help Find tab.

Programming: View Button Wizard Results

You can have Access create a button and the programming behind it. (See also "Controls: Command Button Create" in the Forms and Reports part of this book.) To see what the programming is and modify it, you need to look at the Visual Basic *code*.

Steps

1. Open the *form* in *Design View*, right-click the command button, and choose Build Event on the shortcut menu.
2. Access opens into a *VBA* code window. The name of the command button appears in the *Object* drop-down list at the top left, and the `Click` procedure appears in the Procedure drop-down list on the right. To go to a different object and procedure, choose from these lists.
3. The procedure starts with `Sub` and then the procedure name. The procedure name includes the command button's name, an underscore, and the word `Click`. The procedure ends with `End Sub`.
4. Near the top of the procedure, Access declares any variables it needs (with `Dim` statements) and then uses these variables later. A common *variable* is `strDocName` which holds the name of a document (usually a form or *report*) that you are opening. You can edit the statement `strDocName = "NameofDocument"` and type any document of the same type in the quotes. Another common variable is `strLinkCriteria` which holds the criteria for choosing which records to display. You can edit the statement defining the criteria as well.

5. When finished viewing or modifying the procedure, click the Close (X) button and save the form.

NOTE Access also has a simple error handler in the procedure which starts with the statement `On Error GoTo` and then has the label `Err`, underscore, and then the procedure name. Near the `End Sub` statement is the `Err` label which shows statements that will run if Access encounters an error. For buttons created with the wizard on the Toolbox, Access will simply show a message box with the error description and then exit the procedure. You can modify these statements.

Programming: View Options

While you are working in *VBA*, you can set viewing options to make programming easier. These options include the size and color of fonts for the *code* window, and whether you want to see multiple procedures at one time.

Steps

1. Choose Tools, Options, and click the *Modules* tab.
2. To change the text that appears in the code window, choose one of the types of text from the Text Area drop-down list (such as Keyword Text) and change the options for the color. You can also change the font and size of the font for all text in the code window.
3. To have Access indent the same for each line after you press tab, check AutoIndent and choose the Tab Width. Also in the coding area, include whether you want Access to check *syntax*, require you to declare variables, *compile* modules automatically, and help complete statements with Auto List Members and Auto Quick Info. Check Auto Data Tips to show value of variables as ScreenTips in Break mode.
4. If you want to see one procedure after the other (instead of one procedure per screen), check Full Module View and Procedure Separator to add a line between procedures.

5. Select additional choices in the Windows Settings area to allow drag-and-drop editing, keep the *Debug window* on top, and show icons representing breakpoints and bookmarks in the code window. When finished making all selections, choose OK.

NOTE For more help on any option, click the Help (?) button at the top right of the Options *dialog box* and click the option.

Startup Options

You can specify a number of options that are set when a *database* starts. For example, you can open a particular *form*, display and customize toolbars, and allow or disable shortcut menus. The Startup dialog box now covers almost anything you would do with the AutoExec *macro*. (See also "Macros: Create in Design Window.") If you are going to create a run-time version of Access with the Developer's Tools, fill out the options on this dialog box.

Steps

1. Choose Tools, Startup with a database open.
2. Type the text you want to appear in the title bar in Application Title, and choose the icon you want in the title bar by clicking the Application Icon button.
3. Choose the Menu Bar and Shortcut Menu Bar you want at startup. Choose the check boxes determining which Access default menus and toolbars should appear.
4. From the Display Form drop-down list, choose the form you want to appear at startup and choose whether you want the *Database window* and *status bar* to be visible or hidden.
5. Click the Advanced button and choose whether you want to see the *code* after an error is made and allow the following keys to be available: F11 (Database window), Ctrl+G (*Debug window*), Ctrl+F11 (toggle between menu from step 3 and built-in menu), and Ctrl+Break (stop procedures). Choose OK when finished setting all options.

NOTE If you don't want to have these startup options run, hold down Shift when you open the database file.

Toolbar: Create Custom

When you design a *form* or *report*, you can display a toolbar different than the default toolbar for that *object*. You can also set a non-default toolbar to appear for your entire application. The first step is to create the toolbar.

Steps

1. Choose View, Toolbars, Customize; click the Toolbars tab; and choose the New *command button*.
2. Type the name of the toolbar in the New Toolbar *dialog box* and choose OK. If necessary, drag the title bar of Customize dialog box to see the new small toolbar.
3. Click the Commands tab of the Customize dialog box. Choose one of the names in the Categories list and drag one of the items from the Commands list onto your toolbar. To add a *macro* to a button, choose All Macros from the Categories list and drag a macro from the Commands list.
4. To add a Visual Basic function procedure to a button, drag any item from the Commands list. Right-click the button on the new toolbar and choose Properties. Type a name for the button in the *Caption* box, and type text for a ToolTip if desired. In the On Action box, type **=functionname()** where *functionname* is the name of your function (you cannot use a sub procedure).
5. To change the image of the button, right-click the button, choose Change Button Image, and pick a picture.
6. Repeat Steps 3–5 for all the buttons on your toolbar, and choose the Close button on the Customize dialog box when finished.

To delete a button on your customized toolbar, drag it off the toolbar while the Customize dialog box is visible. To view or hide the toolbar, see also "Toolbars: Display."

TIP While customizing a toolbar you can also right-click the button and choose Edit Button Image (and draw your own image) or Copy Button Image from another button and then return to the button and choose Paste Button Image. Another alternative is to type text in the Name box and choose Text Only.

NOTE There are some toolbar properties you can change. On the Customize dialog box, choose the Properties command button and decide if you want to allow customizing, moving, resizing, and show/hide for your toolbar.

Toolbars: Display

Generally you should let Access display the toolbars that are the default for each part of the program (the *Table* Design toolbar in Table *Design View*, *Form* Design and Form/*Report* Formatting toolbars in Form Design View, and so forth). If you display too many toolbars, it is difficult to tell which buttons you need and you have much less space as your work area. However, you might want to display the Web toolbar or custom toolbars you've created.

Steps

1. Choose View, Toolbars, Customize and click the Toolbars tab on the Customize *dialog box.*
2. Place a check mark by each toolbar you want to see.
3. If a toolbar appears when it should not, select the toolbar name and choose the Reset button.
4. If you want to see large buttons on the toolbars, show ScreenTips (names of tools), or include shortcut keys with the ScreenTips, click the Options tab and make your choices. Choose Close when finished.

NOTE You can also use the *macro* action Show Toolbar to display or hide a toolbar or type in a *VBA* procedure **DoCmd.ShowToolbar "*Toolbarname*", *ShowConstant***. Type the

continues

continued

name of the toolbar in quotes in place of *Toolbarname*. Type one of the following Access constants in place of *ShowConstant*: **acToolbarNo**, **acToolbarYes**, or **acToolbarWhereApprop**. The default is `acToolbarYes` if you leave off this option.

Glossary

Terms

This glossary contains the terms that appear italicized throughout this book. Look them up as you go along or scan for any terms that you might not be familiar with.

A

action query A query that updates a table (such as deleting records, updating records, creating a new table, or appending records to an existing table).

Active Web Shared by all Microsoft Office 97 programs, this feature is used to author and browse documents on an intranet or on the Web.

ActiveX Controls Additional dialog objects that you insert on a form to help data input or viewing. These include the calendar control and spinner control and are supplied from files with an OCX extension.

add-in A wizard (such as the Report Wizard) or a builder (such as the Expression Builder) that helps users perform a potentially complex operation.

aggregate functions Functions you use to summarize data on a query, report, or form. These include Sum(), Avg(), Min(), Max(), and Count().

alias When you use a self-join, a temporary name assigned to a table to help differentiate one table joined to itself.

arguments Inputs used to calculate functions and procedures. Arguments are enclosed in parentheses. Arguments passed to procedures are also called parameters.

AutoFormat An Access feature that applies a set of predefined formatting choices to reports and forms.

AutoNumber An Access data type that automatically increments by one for every new record. This data type replaced Counter in Access 1.x and 2.0. AutoNumber fields are usually mostly for primary keys.

B

bound On a form or report, data is bound to a control when the data is linked to an underlying query or table. Thus, for every record, the value in the control changes.

Briefcase replication A Windows 95 and Windows NT 4.0 feature implemented in Access that creates more than one copy of a database (on a network and laptop, for example) where changes in any copy can be updated to other copies.

builder A help feature that provides assistance in creating expressions for formulas and properties. The Expression Builder is an example.

C

caption The text that appears in the title bar of a window. The caption property of a field in table design becomes the label associated with a text box or other control. The label itself has a caption property that is the text that appears on the form.

cascade delete When referential integrity is set in a relationship, the property that causes records on the many side of a relationship to delete when the related record is deleted.

cascade update When referential integrity is set in a relationship, the property that causes the related key on the many side of a relationship to change to the new value on the related record.

Chart Wizard An Access feature that automates the creation of a chart.

check box On a form or dialog box, a small square that the user can click to turn on or off. A check box is usually associated with a Yes/No field.

child Data or an element that is related to another object but lower in hierarchical level than the related (parent) object. An Access subform is related to an Access form. The Link Child Fields property indicates the field that links the Child to the master (Parent) form (which is related to the Link Master Fields property field).

code The text you enter in a program to create your application. In Access, you enter code in modules.

combo box On a form or dialog box, a combination of a text box and a list box where the user can type a value or choose one from a list.

command button On a form or dialog box, a rectangular object that a user can click that confirms the choices, cancels the choices, or causes another action. The most common command buttons are OK and Cancel.

compile To translate text programming into something the machine can read. In Access, when you click the Compile Loaded Modules button, you will check for some errors in your programming.

concatenation Combining text, numbers, or dates within a text box. In Access, you use the ampersand (&) symbol to join the contents of multiple cells.

controls Data-entry objects commonly used in Access forms, such as text boxes, combo boxes, and check boxes.

criteria The basis for selection in a query, established by entering it on a line in the Query Design grid.

D

data type A description on a field that determines what kind of information you can enter in the field. Field data types include Text, Memo, and Number.

data source Where an object gets its information. The data source for a form or report is called the record source. The data source for a text box or other control is called the control source.

database A set of related tables, queries, forms, reports, macros, and modules. In Access, the database is a single file indicated by a MDB extension.

Database window The primary window visible in Access where you can view or design all objects such as tables, queries, and other objects. To view the Database window, press F11.

Datasheet View A row and column view of a table, query, or form where you can generally input data.

Debug window A window that enables you to test code statements and expressions as well as check on the values of variables within your procedures.

Design View The view of table, query, form, and macro objects that enables you to create or change the object.

dialog box A form within the Windows application or created in Access that accepts input from the user. Also called a dialog, this form is usually modal, which means it stays in front of other objects until it is closed.

dynaset Short for dynamic set of data. A dynaset is the datasheet (row and column) view of a query that you can edit.

E

embedded object A document (the source) stored inside of another document (the container). For example, a Word document could be stored in an OLE field of the Access database. The information is actually stored in the container rather than pointing to a linked document somewhere else on a disk.

empty A VBA variable that has been declared but has not yet received a value. Empty is not the same as null or a zero-length string.

encryption The process of rendering a file unreadable without the use of a key to decrypt the file.

event An action taken by a user such as a mouse click or keystroke that is recognized by one of Access' event properties such as On Click or On DblClick. Events can also be triggered by the program such as when a form opens or the Timer Interval is reached.

expression A combination of field or variable names and arithmetic or other operators used to perform a calculation, manipulate characters, or test data. For example, =Date(), [Price]*[Quantity], and =[FirstName] & " " & [LastName] are expressions.

F

field The information in one column of a list or database. Also, a single item of information in a record.

filter To show only certain records from a table. A filter in Access can also include sorting information. A filter is not stored in the Database window while a query is.

flow control Programming expressions that direct the execution of a procedure. If, Then, Else, End If is a flow control statement.

focus The capability of a control, form, or dialog box to receive keyboard or mouse input. Only one object, such as a text box, can have the focus at a time.

foreign key A field (or fields) on the many side of a one-to-many relationship between tables that relates to the primary key of the other table. Foreign keys do not need to be unique within the table.

form An organized and formatted document that facilitates data entry.

Form View The view of a form where users can input data. This is opposed to Design View where you can create and modify the form.

front-end The visible, user entry part of an application. Access can act as a front-end with the forms, reports, and queries attached to a back-end database on another system such as SQL Server.

function A predefined formula that performs a specific operation in Access. Sum() is the most used function in both Access and Excel.

G

global When dealing with procedures and variables, those that any other part of Access can use. VBA uses the reserved word Public to refer to global variables.

grid On a form, a set of non-printing lines that aides the user in aligning objects such as text boxes and other controls. In Design View, Access shows the grid as a series of dots.

gridlines On a datasheet, the lines that indicate the rows and columns. On a chart, the lines that start at and are perpendicular to the category and value axes.

group In an Access report, one or more records that are combined together and identified with a group header and summarized with a group footer.

H

HTML (Hypertext Markup Language) The underlying code of Web pages.

hyperlink A link in an Access field that enables you to quickly jump to Internet or intranet sites, or to other Access or Office documents.

I

index In an Access table, the property that will speed up searches and sorts. One or more fields can be part of an index.

inner join In an Access query, the link between two related tables, that only returns related fields that are common in both tables.

input mask An input aid that adds characters such as dashes for social security numbers or parentheses for phone numbers. An input mask can also force the user to input text or numeric characters.

integer A number with no decimal places. Access integer data types include integers that can be numbers +/- 32,000 or long integers that can be +/- 2 billion.

J

join Connect two tables together in a query on a common field. The field is usually a primary key in one table and a foreign key in the second table.

K

key or key field A field that identifies a record. Tables are indexed and sorted on key fields. Within a sort, the fields that determine sort order.

L

label Text on a form or report that appears for every record. A label can be a title on the top of the form or attached to a control such as a text box identifying the contents of the control. Last Name: is an example of a label.

linked table Within a database a table whose data originates in another file. The file could be another Access file or a file from a different database application.

list box On a form or dialog box, a rectangular area that enables the user to choose one from a choice of many values. When the list of values is larger than the space provided, Access and Windows provide a scroll bar to see more of the values.

lookup column A combo box within a field of a table. By choosing Lookup Wizard in the Data Type column in Table Design View, you create a lookup column for the field.

M

macro A stored list of commands that are automatically executed by Access.

mail merge The process of combining a list (usually of addresses) into another document (usually a letter or envelope).

master In Access, the main form or report. The subform becomes the child form. In the subform's properties, the Link Master Fields property is a field from the main form that links to the subform's field mentioned in the Link Child Fields property.

memo An Access data type that can hold a great deal of text (up to 64,000 characters).

merge field Used to identify which category of data source information will be printed in its location.

modal A form (or dialog box) that keeps the focus until it is closed.

modeless A form (or dialog box) that can be minimized or can lose the focus to another form or dialog box. A pop-up modeless form remains on top of other forms yet allows you to input in the other forms.

module A collection of stored procedures. Modules are named on the Modules tab in the Database window. However, forms and reports also have modules associated with them. Form and report modules are also called class modules.

N

null A field with no value. This is not the same as a 0 or a zero-length string. Use Is Null in the criteria grid of a query to find fields without an entry.

O

object On one level in Access, the specific tables, queries, forms, and any other items listed in the Database window. On another level, anything that can be manipulated in Access including controls, procedures, and the database itself.

Office Assistant An on-screen, interactive program that provides tips and Help information, and also interprets what Help you might need based on your current actions.

operator A mathematical symbol (such as +) or logical keyword (such as AND) that is a part of an expressions.

optimization The process of improving the application's performance.

option button On a form or dialog box, a small circle that the user can click to turn on. Also called a radio button. A check box is usually associated with an option group but can also represent a Yes/No value.

option group On a form or dialog box, a group of controls where only one of them can be selected at once. Usually the controls inside an option group are option buttons but they can also be toggle buttons or check boxes.

outer join In an Access query, the link between two related tables, that returns all the records from one table and records from related fields that are common in both tables.

P

parameters In an Access query, prompts for user input. In an Access procedure, variables that are supplied to the procedure from outside the procedure.

permissions In Access security, authority given to perform operations (such as read or modify) on a database object.

pivot table A feature that enables you to summarize and analyze data in lists and tables. Pivot tables are called such because you can quickly rearrange the position of pivot table fields to give you a different view of the table.

PivotTable Wizard An Access and Excel feature that automates the creation of a pivot table.

primary key The field (or fields) that uniquely identify a record in a table. You cannot have duplicate primary keys within a table.

property An attribute or characteristic of an object. Properties can define the appearance of an object (such as color) or what happens when the user performs an action on the object (such as click).

Q

query In Access, an object that chooses and sorts selected records and fields from another query or table. A query can also modify a table (see action query).

R

record The information in one row of a list or database.

record locking In a multiuser system, when one person is modifying a record, you can set the record locking properties to lock other users out of the record or to verify changes made when two users edit the same record at the same time.

referential integrity Rules between primary and foreign keys of tables. Referential integrity requires that every foreign key must have a related field in the primary table. Access accomplishes this through cascade delete and cascade update. If these properties are not set in the relationship window, Access will not allow deletions or updates of primary keys who have related records in a foreign table.

relationship Between two tables, the common field (or fields) that identify how they are connected.

replication The process of copying a database in more than one location. After the two (or more) databases are updated, changes can be propagated to both databases.

report An Access object used for printed output that details or summarizes records in a table or query.

S

sections Divisions in a form or report that each have their own properties. Sections include the form or report header and footer, page header and footer, details, and in reports group headers and footers.

self-join In a query, a table that is related to itself by two different fields. For example, an employee table can include the ID of a manager who is also in the same table.

SQL (Structured Query Language) Pronounced "sequel." A standard computer language used by many programs, including mainframes and client/server databases. The SQL used in Access is a subset of the available language. To see a SQL statement, choose SQL View on the View button while you are in Design View of a query.

string A data type used in programming that accepts text values.

subform A form that is inside a main form. Usually the subform displays in Datasheet View and many records can be related to the one in the main form.

subprocedure A procedure called from within another procedure.

subqueries A query that is used within another query. This can be where the second query was created using the first as the data source or where a SQL statement is typed in a criteria cell.

subreport A report that is inside another report.

syntax The rules for writing functions or programming statements. For example, you need to include parentheses with the Sum function and include a field name in the parentheses. If the field name includes a space, you must surround the field name with brackets.

T

tab order The order of the fields on a form accessed when you press Tab or Enter.

table The primary building block within a database where data is actually stored. You must have at least one table before you can create a query, form, or report.

text box On a form or dialog box, a rectangular area where the user can type an entry.

toggle button On a form or dialog box, a rectangular button that appears pressed or unpressed. A toggle button usually is attached to a Yes/No field or is part of an option group.

Toolbox In form and report design, a toolbar that contains buttons for adding controls such as check boxes, combo boxes and text boxes to the design.

U

unbound On a form or report, data that is not connected to a particular record in a table. The most common unbound control is a label but you can also have graphics such as a logo on your form or report as well.

union query A query that combines two tables with multiple common field names. The union query is most often used with a history table and a current table where the field names correspond to each other. The two tables remain in separate locations but the Datasheet View of the union query shows the records from one table below the other.

V

validation A rule for correct data entry within a series or range of acceptable values. If a field's Validation Rule is broken, the Validation Text appears in a message box to the user.

variable The name given to a symbol that represents a value that can be a string, number, or Access object. The value of a variable can change during program execution.

VBA (Visual Basic for Applications) The programming language provided with Access, Excel, Word, and PowerPoint.

W

wild card A symbol that can represent one or more characters. You use the * wild card to represent multiple characters in the criteria row of a query.

workgroup In Access, a group of users that are part of the same security file who share database files. The names of the users and their passwords are stored in the workgroup file (the default is SYSTEM.MDW).

Y

Yes/No field A field data type that can accept one of two responses such as Yes/No, True/False, or On/Off.

Z

zero length string Also called empty string, a zero length string indicates no data and is entered with two double quotes with no space between them (""). A zero length string generally represents that you know that there is no value for the field. This is contrasted with the null value where the value could be unknown.

Index

Symbols

A

D

G

H

M

N

Q

S

T

U

V

W

X-Y-Z

Check out Que® Books on the World Wide Web http://www.mcp.com/que

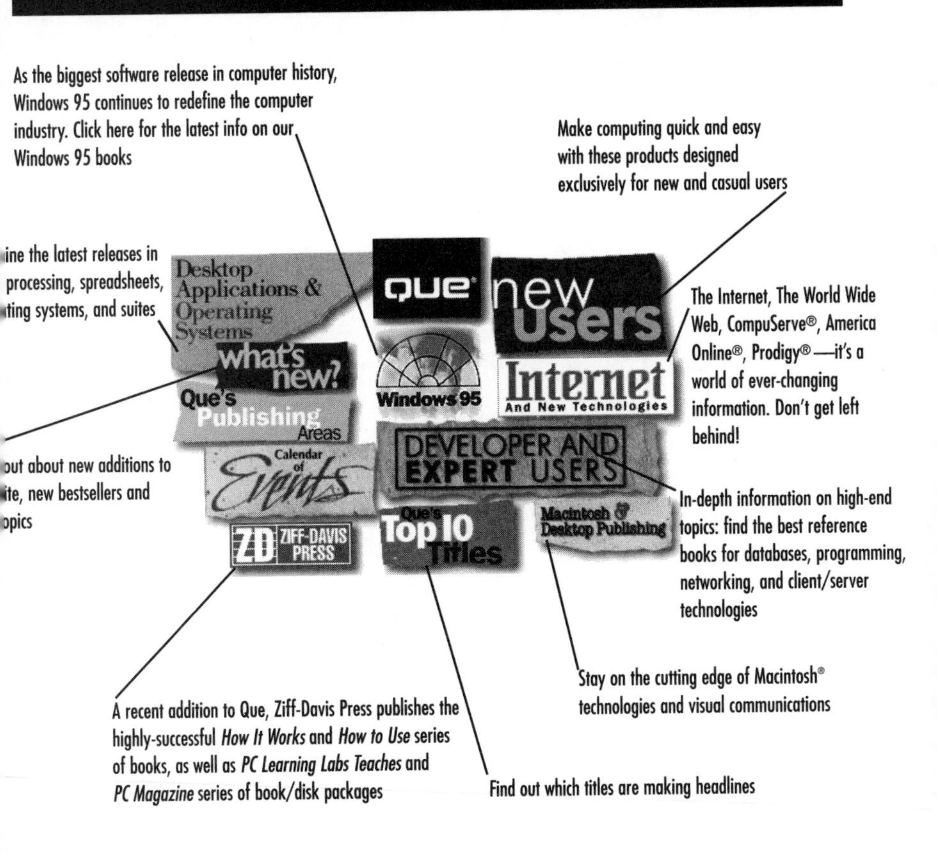

As the biggest software release in computer history, Windows 95 continues to redefine the computer industry. Click here for the latest info on our Windows 95 books
Make computing quick and easy with these products designed exclusively for new and casual users
ine the latest releases in processing, spreadsheets, ting systems, and suites
Desktop Applications & Operating Systems
que
new Users
what's new?
Windows 95
Internet And New Technologies
The Internet, The World Wide Web, CompuServe®, America Online®, Prodigy®—it's a world of ever-changing information. Don't get left behind!
Que's Publishing Areas
Calendar of Events
DEVELOPER AND EXPERT USERS
out about new additions to ite, new bestsellers and opics
In-depth information on high-end topics: find the best reference books for databases, programming, networking, and client/server technologies
Macintosh & Desktop Publishing
ZD ZIFF-DAVIS PRESS
Que's Top 10 Titles
Stay on the cutting edge of Macintosh® technologies and visual communications
A recent addition to Que, Ziff-Davis Press publishes the highly-successful How It Works and How to Use series of books, as well as PC Learning Labs Teaches and PC Magazine series of book/disk packages
Find out which titles are making headlines

6 separate publishing groups, Que develops products for many specific market segments and areas of mputer technology. Explore our Web Site and you'll find information on best-selling titles, newly published titles, upcoming products, authors, and much more.

- Stay informed on the latest industry trends and products available
- Visit our online bookstore for the latest information and editions
- Download software from Que's library of the best shareware and freeware

Copyright © 1996, Macmillan Computer Publishing-USA, A Viacom Company

Complete and Return this Card for a *FREE* Computer Book Catalog

Thank you for purchasing this book! You have purchased a superior computer book written expressly for your needs. To continue to provide the kind of up-to-date, pertinent coverage you've come to expect from us, we need to hear from you. Please take a minute to complete and return this self-addressed, postage-paid form. In return, we'll send you a free catalog of all our computer books on topics ranging from word processing to programming and the Internet.

.r. ☐ Mrs. ☐ Ms. ☐ Dr. ☐

ame (first) ☐☐☐☐☐☐☐☐☐☐☐ (M.I.) ☐ (last) ☐☐☐☐☐☐☐☐☐☐☐☐☐☐☐

ddress ☐☐☐☐☐☐☐☐☐☐☐☐☐☐☐☐☐☐☐☐☐☐☐☐☐☐☐☐☐☐☐☐☐☐

☐☐☐☐☐☐☐☐☐☐☐☐☐☐☐☐☐☐☐☐☐☐☐☐☐☐☐☐☐☐☐☐☐☐

ity ☐☐☐☐☐☐☐☐☐☐☐☐☐☐☐ State ☐☐ Zip ☐☐☐☐☐ ☐☐☐☐☐

ıone ☐☐☐ ☐☐☐ ☐☐☐☐ Fax ☐☐☐ ☐☐☐ ☐☐☐☐

ompany Name ☐☐☐☐☐☐☐☐☐☐☐☐☐☐☐☐☐☐☐☐☐☐☐☐☐☐☐☐☐☐☐☐

-mail address ☐☐☐☐☐☐☐☐☐☐☐☐☐☐☐☐☐☐☐☐☐☐☐☐☐☐☐☐☐☐☐☐

1. Please check at least (3) influencing factors for purchasing this book.

- Front or back cover information on book .... ☐
- Special approach to the content .... ☐
- Completeness of content .... ☐
- Author's reputation .... ☐
- Publisher's reputation .... ☐
- Book cover design or layout .... ☐
- Index or table of contents of book .... ☐
- Price of book .... ☐
- Special effects, graphics, illustrations .... ☐
- Other (Please specify): __________ ☐

2. How did you first learn about this book?

- Internet Site .... ☐
- Saw in Macmillan Computer Publishing catalog .... ☐
- Recommended by store personnel .... ☐
- Saw the book on bookshelf at store .... ☐
- Recommended by a friend .... ☐
- Received advertisement in the mail .... ☐
- Saw an advertisement in: __________ ☐
- Read book review in: __________ ☐
- Other (Please specify): __________ ☐

3. How many computer books have you purchased in the last six months?

This book only .... ☐ 3 to 5 books .... ☐
2 books .... ☐ More than 5 .... ☐

4. Where did you purchase this book?

- Bookstore .... ☐
- Computer Store .... ☐
- Consumer Electronics Store .... ☐
- Department Store .... ☐
- Office Club .... ☐
- Warehouse Club .... ☐
- Mail Order .... ☐
- Direct from Publisher .... ☐
- Internet site .... ☐
- Other (Please specify): .... ☐

5. How long have you been using a computer?

Less than 6 months .. ☐ 6 months to a year ..... ☐
1 to 3 years .... ☐ More than 3 years ...... ☐

6. What is your level of experience with personal computers and with the subject of this book?

	With PC's	With subject of book
New	☐	☐
Casual	☐	☐
Accomplished	☐	☐
Expert	☐	☐

Source Code — ISBN: 0-7897-1212-1

7. **Which of the following best describes your job title?**

Administrative Assistant .... ☐
Coordinator .... ☐
Manager/Supervisor .... ☐
Director .... ☐
Vice President .... ☐
President/CEO/COO .... ☐
Lawyer/Doctor/Medical Professional .... ☐
Teacher/Educator/Trainer .... ☐
Engineer/Technician .... ☐
Consultant .... ☐
Not employed/Student/Retired .... ☐
Other (Please specify): .... ☐

8. **Which of the following best describes the area of the company your job title falls under?**

Accounting .... ☐
Engineering .... ☐
Manufacturing .... ☐
Marketing .... ☐
Operations .... ☐
Sales .... ☐
Other (Please specify): .... ☐

9. **What is your age?**

Under 20 .... ☐
21-29 .... ☐
30-39 .... ☐
40-49 .... ☐
50-59 .... ☐
60-over .... ☐

10. **Are you:**

Male .... ☐
Female .... ☐

11. **Which computer publications do you read regularly? (Please list)**

____

Comments: ____

Fold here and scotch-tape to r

NO POSTAGE
NECESSARY
IF MAILED
IN THE
UNITED STATES

BUSINESS REPLY MAIL
FIRST-CLASS MAIL PERMIT NO. 9918 INDIANAPOLIS IN

POSTAGE WILL BE PAID BY THE ADDRESSEE

ATTN MARKETING
MACMILLAN COMPUTER PUBLISHING
MACMILLAN PUBLISHING USA
201 W 103RD ST
INDIANAPOLIS IN 46290-9042

Technical Support:

If you need assistance with the information in this book or with a CD/Disk accompanying the book, please access the Knowledge Base on our Web site at **http://www.superlibrary.com/general/support**. Our most Frequently Asked Questions are answered there. If you do not find the answer to your questions on our Web site, you may contact Macmillan Technical Support **(317) 581-3833** or e-mail us at **support@mcp.com**.

Microsoft Access 97 Shortcuts and Function Keys

IntelliMouse

Operation	Shortcut
Scroll datasheet a few rows at a time	Roll wheel up or down
Move to next records in Form View	Roll wheel down
Move to previous records in Form View	Roll wheel up
Pan in datasheet, form, or print	Hold down wheel and drag preview window in any direction

Global Function Keys

Key	Function
F1	Help
Shift+F1	Help pointer (Context-sensitive help)
Alt+F1	Selects Database window as active window
Alt+F2	Opens File Save As dialog
Alt+Shift+F2	Saves your open database; the equivalent of the File, Save menu choice
Ctrl+F4	Closes active window
Alt+F4	Exits Access or closes an open dialog
Ctrl+F6	Selects each open window in sequence as active window
F11	Selects Database window as active window
F12	Opens the File Save As dialog
Shift+F12	Saves your open database; the equivalent of the File, Save menu choice

Function Keys for Fields, Grids, and Text Boxes

Key	Function
F2	Toggles between displaying the caret for editing and selecting the entire field.
Shift+F2	Opens the Zoom box for entering expressions and other text.
F4	Opens a drop-down combo list or list box.
Shift+F4	Finds the next occurrence of a match of the text entered in the Find or Replace dialog, if the dialog is closed.
F5	Moves the caret to the record-number box. Enter the number of the record that you want to display and press Enter.
F6	In Table Design View, cycles between upper and lower parts of the window. In Form Design view, cycles through the header, body (detail section), and footer.
Shift+F6	In Form Design view, cycles through the footer, body (detail section), and header, moving backward.
F7	Starts the spelling checker.
F8	Turns on extend mode. Press F8 again to extend the selection to a word, the entire field, the whole record, and then all records.
Shift+F8	Reverses the F8 selection process.

A (+) sign in these tables indicates that you should hold down the first key while pressing the second key, as in Alt+A.

If your keyboard has only 10 function keys, use Alt+F1 for the F11 key and Alt+F2 for the F12 key.

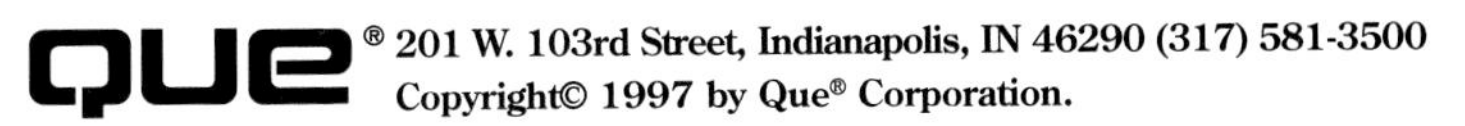
® 201 W. 103rd Street, Indianapolis, IN 46290 (317) 581-3500
Copyright© 1997 by Que® Corporation.

Microsoft Access 97 Integration Grid

If you want to move information from Access to another Microsoft application, you might find the suggestions in this grid helpful. Each numbered item represents a different option. This is not a full explanation. These are just some ideas to get you started.

Word

1. Table/Query/Form—Tools, Office Links, Publish it With MS Word—creates table in Word.
2. Table/Query—Tools, Office Links, Merge it With MS Word (letters/envelopes).
3. Report—Tools, Office Links, Publish it With MS Word—formatted Word document.
4. Table/Query Edit, Copy, Word: Paste Special Unformatted Text—creates tabbed columns.

Excel

1. Table/Query/Form—Tools, Office Links, Publish it With MS Excel— workbook in Excel.
2. Report (grouped)—Tools, Office Links, Publish it With MS Excel—outline workbook in Excel.
3. Table/Query—Edit, Copy. Excel: Edit, Paste Special, Text—copies without formatting.

Access

1. File, Get External Data, Link Tables—creates link between Access databases.
2. File, Get External Data, Import—grabs any object.
3. File, Save As/Export—saves any object to another database.

PowerPoint

1. Table/Query—Edit, Copy. PowerPoint: Edit, Paste creates table.
2. PowerPoint: Insert, Hyperlink choose any database object.

Outlook

1. Access: File, Send.
2. Outlook: File, Import and Export, Import from Schedule+ or… (table from Access).
3. Outlook: Contacts notes field, Insert, Object, Display As Icon.

General Instructions for All Products

Insert Hyperlink. Use to launch Office application and document and optionally go to specific part of document.

1. Optionally type and select text to appear as description instead of file name and path.
2. Insert Hyperlink.
3. Enter file name or URL and location within file.

Insert Object. Use to embed instructions for editing source information but stored in target file. Also, link information so when source changes, target updated.

1. Insert, Object, Create New or Create from File.